YOGA SŪTRAS OF PATAÑJALI

Yogi Madhvācārya / Michael Beloved

ISBN:
978-0-9793916-1-3

Library of Congress Control Number :

2010918321

LORD SHIVA - Master of the Yogis

EDITORIAL CREDITS:

Computer Formatting Editor: Marcia Beloved
Advisory Editor: Sir Paul Castagna
Final Editor: Author
Computer Consultant: Raymond Grant
Front-Back Cover/Shiva Art: Sir Paul Castagna
Krishna-Balaram logo: Sundarananda devi dasi
Glossary: Bhagiratha das
Indexes: Author

FINANCIAL CREDITS:

Bhagiratha das,
Curt Simon, Surya das,
Christopher Hall,
Dear Beloved,
Bharat Patel.

HARE KRISHNA HARE KRISHNA
KRISHNA KRISHNA
HARE HARE
HARE RAMA HARE RAMA
RAMA RAMA
HARE HARE

Correspondence Book Orders:

Paul Castagna
P.O. Box 152
Iron Belt, WI 54536
USA

Michael Beloved
3703 Foster Ave
Brooklyn, NY 11203
USA

Michael Beloved
13 Goodhope, Canal No.1
West Bank Demerara
GUYANA

Inquiries:
axisnexus@gmail.com

Table of Contents

Introduction

Anyone who does not have a basic knowledge of Sanskrit is at a disadvantage when studying a translation. This is because the reader is at the mercy of the translator and is liable to be exploited. Texts like the *Bhagavad-gīta* and the Yoga Sūtras were and are being translated by many writers. Each translator has a motive. If the reader is naive, he can hardly sort between the intentions of the original writer and the agenda of the translator.

I was prompted to attempt this translation by Sir Paul Castagna, but I did have some schooling in the practice of this yoga by Srila Yogeshwarananda, one of my yoga gurus. He showed me much in the astral dimensions. I must admit however that until Sir Paul brought it to my attention, I did not regard the implications of these *sūtras* for modern people. The question remains: What was my motive in the translation? I may evade that by stating that I did this without motive just after Sir Paul asked me to translate. However, it is true that even a motiveless translator develops a particular interest and loads that into his translation as he proceeds. My interest was a curiosity to see exactly what *Śrī Patañjali* expounded. I was to an extent shocked at his crude pronouncements and his total disregard for the psychosis or disordered and uncontrolled mental and emotional status of an average human being.

With all due respects to *Patañjali*, his Sanskrit text and my translation is presented first. Then a simplification entitled "An Approach to Patañjali's Yoga Sūtras" is given. And at last the text, the word-for-word meanings, the translation and a commentary is presented.

I would suggest however, that readers tackle the second part first, that is the "approach to the *sūtras*. " Then read the first part, the actual translation. Then study the third part, which is the translation and my commentary. And always remember that *Patañjali*'s ideas cannot be utilized except through the practice of yoga.

Mdv

Part 1

Yoga Sūtras:
Verses and Translation

CHAPTER 1: SAMĀDHI PĀDA

Transcendence Accomplishment

Verse 1

अथ योगानुशासनम्॥ १॥

atha yogānuśāsanam

This is the explanation of yoga and its practice.

Verse 2

योगश्चित्तवृत्तिनिरोधः॥ २॥

yogaḥcittavṛtti nirodhaḥ

The skill of yoga is demonstrated by the conscious non-operation of the vibrational modes of the mento-emotional energy.

Verse 3

तदा द्रष्टुः स्वरूपेऽवस्थानम्॥ ३॥

tadā draṣṭuḥ svarūpe avasthānam

Then the perceiver is situated in his own form.

Verse 4

वृत्तिसारूप्यमितरत्र॥ ४॥

vṛtti sārūpyam itaratra

At other times, there is conformity with the mento-emotional energy.

Verse 5

वृत्तयः पञ्चतय्यः क्लिष्टा अक्लिष्टाः॥ ५॥

vṛttayaḥ pañcatayyaḥ kliṣṭā akliṣṭāḥ

The vibrations in the mento-emotional energy are five-fold, being agonizing or non-troublesome.

Verse 6

प्रमाणविपर्ययविकल्पनिद्रास्मृतयः ॥ ६ ॥

pramāṇa viparyaya vikalpa nidrā smṛtayaḥ

They are correct perception, incorrect perception, imagination, sleep and memory.

Verse 7

प्रत्यक्षानुमानागमाः प्रमाणानि ॥ ७ ॥

pratyakṣa anumāna āgamāḥ pramāṇāni

Correct perception may be acquired directly, by correct analysis or by correct reference.

Verse 8

विपर्ययो मिथ्याज्ञानमतद्रूपप्रतिष्ठम् ॥ ८ ॥

viparyayaḥ mithyājñānam atadrūpa pratiṣṭham

Incorrect perception is based on false information and on perception of what is not the true form.

Verse 9

शब्दज्ञानानुपाती वस्तुशून्यो विकल्पः ॥ ९ ॥

śabdajñāna anupātī vastuśūnyaḥ vikalpaḥ

Verbal or written information, which is followed by concepts which are devoid of reality, is imagination.

Verse 10

अभावप्रत्ययालम्बना वृत्तिर्निद्रा ॥ १० ॥

abhāva pratyayaḥ ālambanā vṛttiḥ nidrā

Sleep is the vibrational mode which is supported by the absence of objective awareness.

Verse 11

अनुभूतविषयासम्प्रमोषः स्मृतिः ॥ ११ ॥

anubhūta viṣaya asaṁpramoṣaḥ smṛtiḥ

Memory is the retained impression of experienced objects.

Verse 12

अभ्यासवैराग्याभ्यां तन्निरोधः ॥ १२ ॥

abhyāsa vairāgyābhyāṁ tannirodhaḥ

That non-operation of the vibrational modes is achieved by effective practice in not having an interest in the very same operations.

Verse 13

तत्र स्थितौ यत्नोऽभ्यासः ॥ १३ ॥

tatra sthitau yatnaḥ abhyāsaḥ

In that case, practice is the persistent endeavor (to cultivate that lack of interest).

Verse 14

स तु दीर्घकालनैरन्तर्यसत्कारासेवितो दृढभूमिः ॥ १४ ॥

sa tu dīrghakāla nairantarya

satkāra āsevitaḥ dṛḍhabhūmiḥ

But that is attained on the firm basis of a continuous reverential sustained practice which is executed for a long time.

Verse 15

दृष्टानुश्रविकविषयवितृष्णस्य वशीकारसञ्ज्ञा वैराग्यम् ॥ १५ ॥

dṛṣṭa ānuśravika viṣaya vitṛṣṇasya

vaśīkārasaṁjñā vairāgyam

The non-interest in the operations of the mento-emotional energy is achieved by one who has perfect mastery in consciousness and who does not crave for what is perceived or what is heard of in the mundane existence.

Verse 16

तत्परं पुरुषख्यातेर्गुणवैतृष्ण्यम् ॥ १६ ॥

tatparaṁ puruṣakhyāteḥ guṇavaitṛṣṇyam

That highest non-interest occurs when there is freedom from desire for the features of material nature and thorough awareness of the spiritual person.

Verse 17

वितर्कविचारानन्दास्मितारूपानुगमात्सम्प्रज्ञातः ॥ १७ ॥

vitarka vicāra ānanda asmitārūpa

anugamāt saṁprajñātaḥ

The observational linkage of the attention to a higher concentration force occurs with analysis, reflection and introspective happiness or with focus on self-consciousness.

Verse 18

विरामप्रत्ययाभ्यासपूर्वः संस्कारशेषोऽन्यः ॥ १८ ॥

virāmapratyayaḥ abhyāsapūrvaḥ

saṁskāraśeṣaḥ anyaḥ

The other state is the complete departure from the level where the remaining impressions lie in the mento-emotional energy.

Verse 19

भवप्रत्ययो विदेहप्रकृतिलयानाम् ॥ १९ ॥

bhavapratyayaḥ videha prakṛtilayānām

Of those who are diffused into subtle material nature and those who exist in a bodiless state, their psychology has that content.

Verse 20

श्रद्धावीर्यस्मृतिसमाधिप्रज्ञापूर्वक इतरेषाम् ॥ २० ॥

śraddhā vīrya smṛti samādhiprajñā

pūrvakaḥ itareṣām

For others, confidence, stamina, introspective memory, the continuous effortless linkage of the attention to a higher concentration force, and profound insight, all being previously mastered, serve as the cause.

Verse 21

तीव्रसंवेगानामासन्नः ॥ २१ ॥

tīvrasaṁvegānām āsannaḥ

For those who practice forcefully in a very intense way, the skill of yoga will be achieved very soon.

Verse 22

मृदुमध्याधिमात्रत्वात्ततोऽपि विशेषः ॥ २२ ॥

mṛdu madhya adhimātratvāt tataḥ api viśeṣaḥ

**Then there are even more ratings,
according to intense, mediocre, or slight practice.**

Verse 23

ईश्वरप्रणिधानाद्वा ॥ २३ ॥

īśvara praṇidhānāt vā

**Or by the method of profound religious meditation
upon the Supreme Lord.**

Verse 24

क्लेशकर्मविपाकाशयैरपरामृष्टः पुरुषविशेष ईश्वरः ॥ २४ ॥

*kleśa karma vipāka āśayaiḥ aparāmṛṣṭaḥ
puruṣaviśeṣaḥ Īśvaraḥ*

**The Supreme Lord is that special person
who is not affected by troubles, actions, developments
or by subconscious motivations.**

Verse 25

तत्र निरतिशयं सर्वज्ञबीजम् ॥ २५ ॥

tatra niratiśayaṁ sarvajñabījam

There, in Him, is found the unsurpassed origin of all knowledge.

Verse 26

स पूर्वेषामपि गुरुः कालेनानवच्छेदात् ॥ २६ ॥

sa eṣaḥ pūrveṣām api guruḥ kālena anavacchedāt

**He, this particular person being unconditioned by time,
is the guru even of the ancient teachers,
the previous authorities.**

Verse 27

तस्य वाचकः प्रणवः ॥ २७ ॥

tasya vācakaḥ praṇavaḥ

Of Him, the sacred syllable *āuṁ* (*Oṁ*) is the designation.

Verse 28

तज्जपस्तदर्थभावनम्॥ २८॥

tajjapaḥ tadarthabhāvanam

That sound is repeated, murmured constantly for realizing its meaning.

Verse 29

ततः प्रत्यक्चेतनाधिगमोऽप्यन्तरायाभावश्च॥ २९॥

tataḥ pratyakcetana adhigamaḥ api

antarāya abhāvaḥ ca

As a result there is an inwardness of the sense consciousness and the disappearance of obstacles to progress.

Verse 30

व्याधिस्त्यानसंशयप्रमादालस्याविरतिभ्रान्तिदर्शनालब्धभूमिकत्वानवस्थितत्वानि

चित्तविक्षेपास्तेऽन्तरायाः॥ ३०॥

vyādhi styāna saṁśaya pramāda ālasya avirati

bhrāntidarśana alabdhabhūmikatva

anavasthitatvāni cittavikṣepaḥ te antarāyāḥ

These obstacles are disease, idleness, doubt, inattentiveness, lack of energy and proneness to sensuality, mistaken views, inability to maintain the progress attained, unsteadiness in progression, scattered mental and emotional energy.

Verse 31

दुःखदौर्मनस्याङ्गमेजयत्वश्वासप्रश्वासा विक्षेपसहभुवः॥ ३१॥

duḥkha daurmanasya aṅgamejayatva

śvāsapraśvāsāḥ vikṣepa sahabhuvaḥ

Distress, depression, nervousness and labored breathing are the symptoms of a distracted state of mind.

Verse 32

तत्प्रतिषेधार्थमेकतत्त्वाभ्यासः॥ ३२॥

tatpratiṣedhārtham ekatattva abhyāsaḥ

For the removal of the obstacles, there should be the practice of a standard method used in the pursuit of the reality.

Verse 33

मैत्रीकरुणामुदितोपेक्षाणां सुखदुःखपुण्यापुण्यविषयाणां भावनातश्चित्तप्रसादनम्॥ ३३ ॥

maitrī karuṇā muditā upekṣānāṁ

sukha duḥkha puṇya apuṇya

viṣayāṇāṁ bhāvanātaḥ cittaprasādanam

The abstract meditation resulting from the serenity of the mento-emotional energy comes about by friendliness, compassion, cheerfulness and non-responsiveness to happiness, distress, virtue and vice;

Verse 34

प्रच्छर्दनविधारणाभ्यां वा प्राणस्य॥ ३४ ॥

pracchardana vidhāraṇābhyāṁ vā prāṇasya

or by regulating the inhalation and exhalation of the vital energy;

Verse 35

विषयवती वा प्रवृत्तिरुत्पन्ना मनसः स्थितिनिबन्धिनी॥ ३५ ॥

viṣayavatī vā pravṛttiḥ utpannā

manasaḥ sthiti nibandhanī

Or fusion and steadiness of the mind is produced by the operation of the mento-emotional energy towards an object which is different to but similar to a normal thing;

Verse 36

विशोका वा ज्योतिष्मती॥ ३६ ॥

viśokāh vā jyotiṣmatī

or by sorrowless and spiritually-luminous states;

Verse 37

वीतरागविषयं वा चित्तम्॥ ३७ ॥

vītarāga viṣayaṁ vā cittam

or by fixing the mento-emotional energy on someone who is without craving;

Verse 38

स्वप्ननिद्राज्ञानालम्बनं वा ॥ ३८ ॥

svapna nidrā jñāna ālambanaṁ vā

or by taking recourse to dream or dreamless sleep.

Verse 39

यथाभिमतध्यानाद्वा ॥ ३९ ॥

yathābhimata dhyānāt vā

Or it can be achieved from the effortless linkage of the mind to a higher concentration force which was dearly desired.

Verse 40

परमाणुपरममहत्त्वान्तोऽस्य वशीकारः ॥ ४० ॥

paramāṇu paramamahattvāntaḥ asya vaśīkāraḥ

The mastery of the psyche results in control of the relationship to the smallest atom or to cosmic scale.

Verse 41

क्षीणवृत्तेरभिजातस्येव मणेर्ग्रहीतृग्रहणग्राह्येषु तत्स्थतदञ्जनता समापत्तिः ॥ ४१ ॥

kṣīṇavṛtteḥ abhijātasya iva maṇeḥ grahītṛ

grahaṇa grāhyeṣu tatstha tadañjanatā samāpattiḥ

In regards to the great reduction of the mento-emotional operations, there is fusion of the perceiver, the flow of perceptions and what is perceived, just like the absorption of a transparent jewel.

Verse 42

त▯ शब्दार्थज्ञानविकल्पैः सङ्कीर्णा सवितर्का समापत्तिः ॥ ४२ ॥

tatra śabda artha jñāna vikalpaiḥ

saṅkīrṇā savitarkā samāpattiḥ

In that case, the deliberate linkage of the mento-emotional energy to a higher concentrating force occurs when a word, its meaning and the knowledge of the object alternate within the mind, blending as it was.

Verse 43

स्मृतिपरिशुद्धौ स्वरूपशून्येवार्थमात्रनिर्भासा निर्वितर्का ॥ ४३ ॥

smṛtipariśuddhau svarūpaśūnya iva

arthamātranirbhāsā nirvitarka

**Non-analytical linkage of the attention
to a higher concentration force occurs
when the memory is completely purified
and the essential inquiring nature disappears as it were,
so the value of that higher force shines through.**

Verse 44

एतयैव सविचारा निर्विचारा च सूक्ष्मविषया व्याख्याता ॥ ४४ ॥

etayaiva savicārā nirvicāra ca

sūkṣmaviṣayā vyākhyātā

**By this, the investigative linkage and non-investigative linkage
of one's attention to a higher concentration force
consisting of subtler objects, was explained.**

Verse 45

सूक्ष्मविषयत्वं चालिङ्गपर्यवसानम् ॥ ४५ ॥

sūkṣmaviṣayatvaṁ ca aliṅga paryavasānam

**The insight into the subtle nature of gross objects
terminates when one becomes linked
to the higher concentration force which has no characteristics.**

Verse 46

ता एव सबीजः समाधिः ॥ ४६ ॥

tā eva sabījaḥ samādhiḥ

**The previous descriptions concern the effortless
and continuous linkage of the attention
to a higher concentration force,
as motivated by the mento-emotional energy.**

Verse 47

निर्विचारवैशारद्येऽध्यात्मप्रसादः ॥ ४७ ॥

nirvicāra vaiśāradye adhyātmaprasādaḥ

On gaining competence in the non-investigative linkage of one's attention to the higher concentration force, one experiences the clarity and serenity which results from the linkage of the Supreme Soul and the limited one.

Verse 48

ऋतम्भरा तत्र प्रज्ञा ॥ ४८ ॥

ṛtaṁbharā tatra prajñā

There with that competence, the yogin develops the reality-perceptive insight.

Verse 49

श्रुतानुमानप्रज्ञाभ्यामन्यविषया विशेषार्थत्वात् ॥ ४९ ॥

śruta anumāna prajñābhyām

anyaviṣayā viśeṣārthatvāt

It is different from the two methods of insight which are based on what is heard and what is reasoned out, because those are limited to a particular aspect of an object.

Verse 50

तज्जः संस्कारोऽन्यसंस्कारप्रतिबन्धी ॥ ५० ॥

tajjaḥ saṁskāraḥ anyasaṁskāra pratibandhī

That impression which is produced from the reality-perceptive insight, acts as the preventer of the other impressions.

Verse 51

तस्यापि निरोधे सर्वनिरोधान्निब�जः समाधिः ॥ ५१ ॥

tasyāpi nirodhe sarvanirodhāt nirbījaḥ samādhiḥ

The continuous effortless linkage of the attention to the higher concentration force which is not motivated by this mento-emotional energy, occurs when there is a non-operation, even of that preventative impression which caused the suppression of all other lower memories.

CHAPTER 2: SĀDHANA PĀDA

Practice Accomplishment

Verse 1

तपःस्वाध्यायेश्वरप्रणिधानानि क्रियायोगः ॥ १ ॥

tapas svādhyāya Īśvarapraṇidhānāni kriyāyogaḥ

**Austerity, study of the psyche
and profound religious meditation on the Supreme Lord
is the dynamic *kriyā* yoga practice.**

Verse 2

समाधिभावनार्थः क्लेशतनूकरणार्थश्च ॥ २ ॥

samādhi bhāvanārthaḥ kleśa tanūkaraṇārthaś ca

**It is for the purpose of producing
continuous effortless linkage of the attention
to a higher concentration force and for causing
the reduction of the mental and emotional afflictions.**

Verse 3

अविद्यास्मितारागद्वेषाभिनिवेशाः क्लेशाः ॥ ३ ॥

avidyā asmitā rāga dveṣa abhiniveśaḥ kleśāḥ

**The mental and emotional afflictions
are spiritual ignorance, misplaced identity,
emotional attachment, impulsive emotional disaffection
and a strong focus on mundane existence, which is due to an instinctive fear of death.**

Verse 4

अविद्या क्षेत्रमुत्तरेषां प्रसुप्ततनुविच्छिन्नोदाराणाम् ॥ ४ ॥

avidyā kṣetram uttareṣāṁ prasupta

tanu vicchina udārāṇām

**Spiritual ignorance is the existential environment
for the other afflictions, in their dormant, reduced,
periodic or expanded stages.**

Verse 5

अनित्याशुचिदुःखानात्मसु नित्यशुचिसुखात्मख्यातिरविद्या ॥ ५ ॥

anitya aśuci duḥka anātmasu nitya
śuci sukha ātma khyātiḥ avidyā

Spiritual ignorance is exhibited when what is temporary, impure, distressful and mundane, is identified respectively as being eternal, pure, joyful and spiritual.

Verse 6

दृग्दर्शनशक्त्योरेकात्मतेवास्मिता ॥ ६ ॥

dṛg darśanaśaktyoḥ ekātmatā iva asmitā

Mistaken identity occurs when the supernatural vision and what is seen through it, seem to be identical.

Verse 7

सुखानुशयी रागः ॥ ७ ॥

sukha anuśayī rāgaḥ

Craving results from a devoted attachment to happiness

Verse 8

दुःखानुशयी द्वेषः ॥ ८ ॥

duḥkha anuśayi dveṣaḥ

Impulsive emotional disaffection results from a devoted attachment to distress.

Verse 9

स्वरसवाही विदुषोऽपि तथारूढोऽभिनिवेशः ॥ ९ ॥

svarasavāhī viduṣaḥ 'pi tatha rūḍho 'bhiniveśaḥ

As it is, the strong focus on mundane existence,
which is due to the instinctive fear of death,
which is sustained by its own potencies,
and which operates for self-preservation,
is developed even in the wise man.

Verse 10

ते प्रतिप्रसवहेयाः सूक्ष्माः ॥ १० ॥

te pratiprasavaheyāḥ sūkṣmāḥ

These subtle motivations are to be abandoned by reverting their expression backwards.

Verse 11

ध्यानहेयास्तद्वृत्तयः ॥ ११ ॥

dhyānaheyāḥ tadvṛttayaḥ

Their vibrational modes are to be abandoned or ceased by the effortless linkage of the attention to a higher concentration force or person.

Verse 12

क्लेशमूलः कर्माशयो दृष्टादृष्टजन्मवेदनीयः ॥ १२ ॥

kleśamūlaḥ karmāśayaḥ dṛṣṭa

adṛṣṭa janma vedanīyaḥ

The psychological storage of the impressions left by performance of cultural activities which is itself the cause of the mental and emotional distress, is experienced in realized and non-realized births.

Verse 13

सति मूले तद्विपाको जात्यायुर्भोगाः ॥ १३ ॥

sati mūle tadvipākaḥ jāti āyuḥ bhogāḥ

In the case aforementioned, there exist the resulting effects which manifest as a particular species of life with certain duration of body and type of experiences gained in that form.

Verse 14

ते ह्लादपरितापफलाः पुण्यापुण्यहेतुत्वात् ॥ १४ ॥

te hlāda paritāpa phalāḥ puṇya apuṇya hetutvāt

They produce happiness and distress as results, on the basis of merits and demerits.

Verse 15

परिणामतापसंस्कारदुःखैर्गुणवृत्तिविरोधाच्च दुःखमेव सर्वं विवेकिनः ॥ १५॥

pariṇāma tāpa saṁskāra duḥkaiḥ guṇavṛtti
virodhāt ca duḥkham eva sarvaṁ vivekinaḥ

The discriminating person knows
that all conditions are distressful
because of circumstantial changes, strenuous endeavor, impulsive motivations, clashing aspects
and the vibrational modes of the mento-emotional energy.

Verse 16

हेयं दुःखमनागतम्॥ १६॥

heyaṁ duḥkham anāgatam

Distress which is not manifested is to be avoided.

Verse 17

द्रष्टृदृश्ययोः संयोगो हेयहेतुः ॥ १७॥

draṣṭṛdṛśyayoḥ saṁyogo heyahetuḥ

The cause which is to be avoided is the indiscriminate
association of the observer and what is perceived.

Verse 18

प्रकाशक्रियास्थितिशीलं भूतेन्द्रियात्मकं भोगापवर्गार्थं दृश्यम्॥ १८॥

prakāśa kriyā sthiti śīlaṁ bhūtendriyātmakaṁ
bhogāpavargārthaṁ dṛśyam

What is perceived is of the nature
of the mundane elements and the sense organs
and is formed in clear perception, action or stability.
Its purpose is to give experience or to allow liberation.

Verse 19

विशेषाविशेषलिङ्गमात्रालिङ्गानि गुणपर्वाणि॥ १९॥

viśeṣa aviśeṣa liṅgamātra aliṅgāni guṇaparvāṇi

The phases of the influences of material nature
are those which are specific, regular, indicated or not indicated.

Verse 20

द्रष्टा दृशिमात्रः शुद्धोऽपि प्रत्ययानुपश्यः ॥ २० ॥

draṣṭā dṛśimātraḥ śuddhaḥ api pratyayānupaśyaḥ

The perceiver is the pure extent of its consciousness but its conviction is patterned by what it perceives.

Verse 21

तदर्थ एव दृश्यस्यात्मा ॥ २१ ॥

tadarthaḥ eva dṛśyasya ātmā

The individual spirit, who is involved in what is seen, exists here for that purpose only.

Verse 22

कृतार्थं प्रति नष्टमप्यनष्टं तदन्यसाधारणत्वात् ॥ २२ ॥

kṛtārthaṁ prati naṣṭam api
anaṣṭaṁ tadanya sādhāraṇatvāt

It is not effective for one to whom its purpose is fulfilled, but it has a common effect on the others.

Verse 23

स्वस्वामिशक्त्योः स्वरूपोपलब्धिहेतुः संयोगः ॥ २३ ॥

sva svāmiśaktyoḥ svarūpa upalabdhi hetuḥ saṁyogaḥ

There is a reason for the conjunction of the individual self and its psychological energies. It is for obtaining the experience of its essential form.

Verse 24

तस्य हेतुरविद्या ॥ २४ ॥

tasya hetuḥ avidyā

The cause of the conjunction is spiritual ignorance.

Verse 25

तदभावात्संयोगाभावो हानं तद्दृशेः कैवल्यम्॥ २५॥

tad abhāvāt saṁyogā abhāvaḥ

hānaṁ taddṛśeḥ kaivalyam

The elimination of the conjunction which results from the elimination of that spiritual ignorance is the withdrawal that is the total separation of the perceiver from the mundane psychology.

Verse 26

विवेकख्यातिरविप्लवा हानोपायः॥ २६॥

vivekakhyātiḥ aviplavā hānopāyaḥ

The method for avoiding that spiritual ignorance is the establishment of continuous discriminative insight.

Verse 27

तस्य सप्तधा प्रान्तभूमिः प्रज्ञा॥ २७॥

tasya saptadhā prāntabhūmiḥ prajñā

Concerning the development of discriminative insight, there are seven stages.

Verse 28

योगाङ्गानुष्ठानादशुद्धिक्षये ज्ञानदीप्तिराविवेकख्यातेः॥ २८॥

yogāṅgānuṣṭhānāt aśuddhikṣaye

jñānadīptiḥ āvivekakhyāteḥ

From the consistent practice of the parts of the yoga process, on the elimination of the impurity, the radiant organ of perception becomes manifest, until there is steady discriminative insight.

Verse 29

यमनियमासनप्राणायामप्रत्याहारधारणाध्यानसमाधयोऽष्टावङ्गानि ॥ २९ ॥

yama niyama āsana prāṇāyāma pratyāhāra

dhāraṇā dhyāna samādhayaḥ aṣṭau aṅgāni

Moral restraints, recommended behaviors, body posture, breath infusion, sensual energy withdrawal, linking of the attention to higher concentration forces or persons, effortless linkage of the attention to higher concentration forces or persons, continuous effortless linkage of the attention to higher concentration forces or persons are the eight parts of the yoga system.

Verse 30

अहिंसासत्यास्तेयब्रह्मचर्यापरिग्रहा यमाः ॥ ३० ॥

ahiṁsā satya asteya

brahmacarya aparigrahāḥ yamāḥ

Non-violence, realism, non-stealing, sexual non-expressiveness which results in the perception of spirituality (brahman) and non-possessiveness are the moral restraints.

Verse 31

जातिदेशकालसमयानवच्छिन्नाः सार्वभौमा महाव्रतम् ॥ ३१ ॥

jāti deśa kāla samaya anavacchinnāḥ

sārvabhaumāḥ mahāvratam

Those moral restraints are not to be adjusted by the status, location, time or condition. They, being the great commitment, are related to all stages of yoga.

Verse 32

शौचसन्तोषतपःस्वाध्यायेश्वरप्रणिधानानि नियमाः ॥ ३२ ॥

śauca santoṣa tapaḥ svādhyāya

īśvarapraṇidhānāni niyamāḥ

Purification, contentment, austerity and profound religious meditation on the Supreme Lord are the recommended behaviors.

Verse 33

वितर्कबाधने प्रतिपक्षभावनम्॥ ३३॥

vitarkabādhane pratipakṣabhāvanam

In the case of the annoyance produced by doubts, one should conceive of what is opposite.

Verse 34

वितर्का हिंसादयः कृतकारितानुमोदिता लोभक्रोधमोहपूर्वका मृदुमध्याधिमात्रा दुःखाज्ञानानन्तफला

इति प्रतिपक्षभावनम्॥ ३४॥

vitarkaḥ hiṁsādayaḥ kṛta kārita anumoditāḥ lobha krodha moha pūrvakaḥ mṛdu madhya adhimātraḥ

duḥkha ajñāna anantaphalāḥ iti pratipakṣabhāvanam

Doubts which produce violence and related actions, which are performed, caused to be done or endorsed, and which are caused by greed, anger and delusion, even if minor, mediocre or substantial, cause endless distress and spiritual ignorance as the results. Therefore, one should consider the opposite features.

Verse 35

अहिंसाप्रतिष्ठायां तत्सन्निधौ वैरत्यागः॥ ३५॥

ahiṁsāpratiṣṭhāyāṁ tatsannidhau vairatyāgaḥ

On being firmly established in non-violence, the abandonment of hostility occurs in his presence.

Verse 36

सत्यप्रतिष्ठायां क्रियाफलाश्रयत्वम्॥ ३६॥

satyapratiṣṭhāyāṁ kriyāphalāśrayatvam

On being established in realism, his actions serve as a basis for results.

Verse 37

अस्तेयप्रतिष्ठायां सर्वरत्नोपस्थानम्॥ ३७॥

asteyapratiṣṭhāyāṁ sarvaratnopasthānam

On being firmly established in non-stealing, all precious things wait to serve a yogin.

Verse 38

ब्रह्मचर्यप्रतिष्ठायां वीर्यलाभः ॥ ३८ ॥

brahmacaryapratiṣṭhāyāṁ vīryalābhaḥ

On being firmly established in the sexual non-expressiveness which results in the perception of spirituality, vigor is gained.

Verse 39

अपरिग्रहस्थैर्ये जन्मकथन्तासम्बोधः ॥ ३९ ॥

aparigrahasthairye janmakathaṁtā saṁbodhaḥ

The reason for and the correct perception of one's birth is known when there is consistent non-possessiveness.

Verse 40

शौचात्स्वाङ्गजुगुप्सा परैरसंसर्गः ॥ ४० ॥

śaucāt svāṅgajugupsā paraiḥ asaṁsargaḥ

From purification comes a disgust for one's own body and a lack of desire to associate with others.

Verse 41

सत्त्वशुद्धिसौमनस्यैकाग्र्येन्द्रियजयात्मदर्शनयोग्यत्वानि च ॥ ४१ ॥

sattvaśuddhi saumanasya ekāgra indriyajaya

ātmadarśana yogyatvāni ca

Purification of the psyche results in benevolence, the ability to link the attention to one concentration force or person, conquest of the sensual energy, vision of the spirit and fitness for abstract meditation.

Verse 42

सन्तोषादनुत्तमसुखलाभः ॥ ४२ ॥

saṅtoṣāt anuttamaḥ sukhalābhaḥ

From contentment, the very best in happiness is obtained.

Verse 43

कायेन्द्रियसिद्धिरशुद्धिक्षयात्तपसः ॥ ४३ ॥

kāya indriya siddhiḥ aśuddhikṣayāt tapasaḥ

Austerity, resulting in the elimination of impurity produces perfection of the body and sensual energy.

Verse 44

स्वाध्यायादिष्टदेवतासम्प्रयोगः ॥ ४४ ॥

svādhyāyāt iṣṭadevatā samprayogaḥ

From study of the psyche comes intimate contact with the cherished divine being.

Verse 45

समाधिसिद्धिरीश्वरप्रणिधानात् ॥ ४५ ॥

samādhisiddhiḥ īśvarapraṇidhānāt

From the profound religious meditation upon the Supreme Lord comes the perfection of continuous effortless linkage of the attention to that Divinity.

Verse 46

स्थिरसुखमासनम् ॥ ४६ ॥

sthira sukham āsanam

The posture should be steady and comfortable.

Verse 47

प्रयत्नशैथिल्यानन्तसमापत्तिभ्याम् ॥ ४७ ॥

prayatna śaithilya ananta samāpattibhyām

It results in relaxation of effort and meeting with the infinite.

Verse 48

ततो द्वन्द्वानभिघातः ॥ ४८ ॥

tataḥ dvandvāḥ anabhighātaḥ

From then on, there are no botherations from the dualities like happiness and distress or heat and cold.

Verse 49

तस्मिन्सति श्वासप्रश्वासयोर्गतिविच्छेदः प्राणायामः ॥ ४९ ॥

tasmin satiśvāsa praśvāsayoḥ

gativicchedaḥ prāṇāyāmaḥ

Once this is accomplished, breath regulation, which is the separation of the flow of inhalation and exhalation, is attained.

Verse 50

वाह्याभ्यन्तरस्तम्भवृत्तिः देशकालसङ्ख्याभिः परिदृष्टो दीर्घसूक्ष्मः ॥ ५० ॥

bāhya ābhyantara stambha vṛttiḥ deśa kāla

saṁkhyābhiḥ paridṛṣṭah dīrgha sūkṣmaḥ

It has internal, external and restrictive operations, which are regulated according to the place, time and accounting, being prolonged or hardly noticed.

Verse 51

वाह्याभ्यन्तरविषयाक्षेपी चतुर्थः ॥ ५१ ॥

bāhya ābhyantara viṣaya ākṣepī caturthaḥ

That which transcends the objective, external and internal breath regulation is the fourth type of breath infusement techniques.

Verse 52

ततः क्षीयते प्रकाशावरणम् ॥ ५२ ॥

tataḥ kṣīyate prakāśa āvaraṇam

From that is dissipated, the mental darkness which veils the light,

Verse 53

धारणासु च योग्यता मनसः ॥ ५३ ॥

dhāraṇāsu ca yogyatā manasaḥ

and from that, is attained the state of the mind for linking the attention to a higher concentration force or person.

Verse 54

स्वविषयासम्प्रयोगे चित्तस्य स्वरूपानुकार इवेन्द्रियाणां प्रत्याहारः ॥५४॥

svaviṣaya asaṁprayoge cittasya svarūpāanukāraḥ

iva indriyāṇāṁ pratyāhāraḥ

**The withdrawal of the senses, is as it was,
their assumption of the form of mento-emotional energy
when not contacting their own objects of perception.**

Verse 55

ततः परमा वश्यतेन्द्रियाणाम्॥५५॥

tataḥ paramā vaśyatā indriyāṇām

**From that accomplishment comes the highest degree
of control of the senses.**

CHAPTER 3: VIBHŪTI PĀDA

Glory Displayed

Verse 1

देशबन्धश्चित्तस्य धारणा॥१॥

deśa bandhaḥ cittasya dhāraṇā

**Linking of the attention to a concentration force
or person, involves a restricted location
in the mento-emotional energy.**

Verse 2

तत्र प्रत्ययैकतानता ध्यानम्॥२॥

tatra pratyayaḥ ekatānatā dhyānam

**When in that location,
there is one continuous threadlike flow
of one's instinctive interest, that is the effortless linking
of the attention to a higher concentration force or person.**

Verse 3

तदेवार्थमात्रनिर्भासं स्वरूपशून्यमिव समाधिः ॥ ३ ॥

tadeva arthamātranirbhāsaṁ

svarūpaśūnyam iva samādhiḥ

**That same effortless linkage of the attention
when experienced as illumination
of the higher concentration force or person,
while the yogi feels as if devoid of himself,
is *samādhi* or continuous effortless linkage of his attention
to the special person, object, or force.**

Verse 4

त्रयमेकत्र संयमः ॥ ४ ॥

trayam ekatra saṁyamaḥ

The three as one practice are the complete restraint.

Verse 5

तज्जयात्प्रज्ञालोकः ॥ ५ ॥

tajjayāt prajñālokaḥ

**From the mastery of that complete restraint
of the mento-emotional energy, one develops the illuminating insight.**

Verse 6

तस्य भूमिषु विनियोगः ॥ ६ ॥

tasya bhūmiṣu viniyogaḥ

The practice of this complete restraint occurs in stages.

Verse 7

त्रयमन्तरङ्गं पूर्वेभ्यः ॥ ७ ॥

trayam antaraṅgaṁ pūrvebhyaḥ

**In reference to the preliminary stages of yoga,
these three higher states concern the psychological organs.**

Verse 8

तदपि बहिरङ्गं निब�जस्य ॥ ८ ॥

tadapi bahiraṅgaṁ nirbījasya

**But even that initial mastership
of the three higher stages of yoga,
is external in reference to meditation,
which is not motivated by the mento-emotional energy.**

Verse 9

व्युत्थाननिरोधसंस्कारयोरभिभवप्रादुर्भावौ निरोधक्षणचित्तान्वयो निरोधपरिणामः ॥ ९ ॥

vyutthāna nirodha saṁskārayoḥ

abhibhava prādurbhāvau nirodhakṣaṇa

cittānvayaḥ nirodhapariṇāmaḥ

**When the connection with the mento-emotional energy momentarily ceases
during the manifestation
and disappearance phases when there is expression
or suppression of the impressions, that is the restraint
of the transforming mento-emotional energy.**

Verse 10

तस्य प्रशान्तवाहिता संस्कारात् ॥ १० ॥

tasya praśāntavāhita saṁskārāt

**Concerning this practice of restraint,
the impressions derived cause a flow of spiritual peace.**

Verse 11

सर्वार्थतैकाग्रतयोः क्षयोदयौ चित्तस्य समाधिपरिणामः ॥ ११ ॥

sarvārthatā ekāgratayoḥ kṣaya udayau

cittasya samādhipariṇāmaḥ

**The decrease of varying objectives in the mento-emotional energy
and the increase of the one aspect within it,
are the changes noticed
in the practice of continuous effortless linking of the attention
to higher concentration forces, objects or persons.**

Verse 12

ततः पुनः शान्तोदितौ तुल्यप्रत्ययौ चित्तस्यैकाग्रतापरिणामः ॥ १२ ॥

tataḥ punaḥśānta uditau tulya pratyayau

cittasya ekāgratāpariṇāmaḥ

Then again, when the mind's content is the same as it was when it is subsiding and when it is emerging, that is the transformation called "having one aspect in front of or before the attention".

Verse 13

एतेन भूतेन्द्रियेषु धर्मलक्षणावस्थापरिणामा व्याख्याताः ॥ १३ ॥

etena bhūtendriyeṣu dharma lakṣaṇa avasthā

pariṇāmāḥ vyākhyātāḥ

By this description of the changes, quality and shape, the two changing conditions of the states of matter, as well as of the sensual energy, were described.

Verse14

शान्तोदिताव्यपदेश्यधर्मानुपाती धर्मी ॥ १४ ॥

śānta udita avyapadeśya dharma anupātī dharmī

When the collapsed, emergent and latent forces reach full retrograde, that is the most basic condition.

Verse 15

क्रमान्यत्वं परिणामान्यत्वे हेतुः ॥ १५ ॥

krama anyatvaṁ pariṇāma anyatve hetuḥ

The cause of a difference in the transformation is the difference in the sequential changes.

Verse 16

परिणामत्रयसंयमादतीतानागतज्ञानम् ॥ १६ ॥

pariṇāmatraya saṁyamāt atīta anāgatajñānam

From the complete restrain of the mento-emotional energy in terms of the three-fold transformations within it, the yogi gets information about the past and future.

Verse 17

शब्दार्थप्रत्ययानामितरेतराध्यासात्सङ्करस्तत्प्रविभागसंयमात्सर्वभूतरुतज्ञानम्॥ १७॥

śabda artha pratyayānām itaretarādhyāsāt

saṅkaraḥ tatpravibhāga saṁyamāt

sarvabhūta rutajñānam

From the complete restraint of the mento-emotional energy in relation to mental clarity, regarding the intermixture resulting from the superimposing one for the other, of sound, its meaning and the related mentality, knowledge about the language of all creatures is gained.

Verse 18

संस्कारसाक्षात्करणात्पूर्वजातिज्ञानम्॥ १८॥

saṁskāra sākṣātkaraṇāt pūrvajātijñānam

From direct intuitive perception of the subtle impressions stored in the memory, the yogi gains knowledge of previous lives.

Verse 19

प्रत्ययस्य परचित्तज्ञानम्॥ १९॥

pratyayasya paracittajñānam

A yogi can know the contents of the mental and emotional energy in the minds of others.

Verse 20

न च तत्सालम्बनं तस्याविषयीभूतत्वात्॥ २०॥

na ca tat sālambanaṁ tasya aviṣayī bhūtatvāt

And he does not check a factor which is the support of that content, for it is not the actual object in question.

Verse 21

कायरूपसंयमात्तद्ग्राह्यशक्तिस्तम्भे चक्षुःप्रकाशासम्प्रयोगेऽन्तर्धानम्॥ २१॥

kāya rūpa saṁyamāt tadgrāhyaśakti

stambhe cakṣuḥ prakāśa asaṁprayoge 'ntardhānam

From the complete restraint of the mento-emotional energy in relation to the shape of the body, on the suspension of the receptive energy, there is no contact between light and vision, which results in invisibility.

Verse 22

एतेन शब्दादि अन्तर्धानम् उक्तम्

etena śabdādi antardhānam uktam

By this method, sound and the related sensual pursuits, may be restrained, which results in the related non-perceptibility.

Verse 23

सोपक्रमं निरुपक्रमं च कर्म तत्संयमादपरान्तज्ञानमरिष्टेभ्यो वा॥ २३॥

sopakramaṁ nirupakramaṁ ca karma

tatsaṁyamāt aparāntajñānam ariṣṭebhyaḥ vā

Complete restraint of the mento-emotional energy in relation to current and destined cultural activities results in knowledge of entry into the hereafter. Or, the same result is gained by the complete restraint in relation to portents.

Verse 24

मैत्र्यादिषु बलानि॥ २४॥

maitryādiṣu balāni

By complete restraint of the mento-emotional energy in relation to friendliness, he develops that very same power.

Verse 25

बलेषु हस्तिबलादीनि॥ २५॥

baleṣu hasti balādīni

**By complete restraint
of the mento-emotional energy in relation to strength,
the yogin acquires strength of an elephant.
The same applies to other aspects.**

Verse 26

प्रवृत्त्यालोकन्यासात्सूक्ष्मव्यवहितविप्रकृष्टज्ञानम्॥ २६ ॥

pravṛitti āloka nyāsāt sūkṣma

vyavahita viprakṛṣṭajñānam

**From the application of supernatural insight
to the force producing cultural activities,
a yogi gets information about what is subtle, concealed
and remote from him.**

Verse 27

भुवनज्ञानं सूर्ये संयमात्॥ २७॥

bhuvanajñānaṁ sūrye saṁyamāt

**From the complete restraint of the mento-emotional energy
in relation to the sun god or the sun planet,
knowledge of the solar system is gained.**

Verse 28

चन्द्रे ताराव्यूहज्ञानम्॥ २८॥

candre tārāvyūhajñānam

**By complete restraint of the mento-emotional energy,
in reference to the moon or moon-god,
the yogi gets knowledge about the system of stars.**

Verse 29

ध्रुवे तद्गतिज्ञानम्॥ २९॥

dhruve tadgatijñānam

**By the complete restraint of the mento-emotional energy in relation to the
Pole Star, a yogi can know
of the course of planets and stars.**

Verse 30

नाभिचक्रे कायव्यूहज्ञानम्॥ ३०॥

nābhicakre kāyavyūhajñānam

**By complete restraint of the mento-emotional energy
in relation to the focusing on the navel energy-gyrating center,
the yogi gets knowledge about the layout of his body.**

Verse 31

कण्ठकूपे क्षुत्पिपासानिवृत्तिः॥ ३१॥

kaṇṭhakūpe kṣutpipāsā nivṛttiḥ

**By the complete restraint of the mento-emotional energy
in focusing on the gullet,
a yogi causes the suppression of hunger and thirst.**

Verse 32

कूर्मनाड्यां स्थैर्यम्॥ ३२॥

kūrmanāḍyāṃ sthairyam

**By the complete restraint of the mento-emotional energy
in focusing on the kurma nāḍi subtle nerve,
a yogi acquires steadiness of his psyche.**

Verse 33

मूर्धज्योतिषि सिद्धदर्शनम्॥ ३३॥

mūrdhajyotiṣi siddhadarśanam

**By the complete restraint of the mento-emotional energy
as it is focused
on the shining light in the head of the subtle body,
a yogi gets views of the perfected beings.**

Verse 34

प्रातिभाद्वा सर्वम्॥ ३४॥

prātibhād vā sarvam

**By complete restraint of the mento-emotional energy,
while focusing on the shining organ of divination
in the head of the subtle body,
the yogin is able to know all reality.**

Verse 35

हृदये चित्तसंवित्॥ ३५॥

hṛdaye cittasaṁvit

By the complete restraint of the mento-emotional energy as it is focused on the causal body in the vicinity of the chest, the yogi gets thorough insight into the causes of the mental and emotional energy.

Verse 36

सत्त्वपुरुषयोरत्यन्तासङ्कीर्णयोः प्रत्ययाविशेषो भोगः परार्थत्वात्स्वार्थसंयमात्पुरुषज्ञानम्॥ ३६॥

sattva puruṣayoḥ atyantāsaṁkīrṇayoḥ
pratyayaḥ aviśeṣaḥ bhogaḥ parārthatvāt
svārthasaṁyamāt puruṣajñānam

Experience results from the inability to distinguish between the individual spirit and the intelligence energy of material nature, even though they are very distinct. By complete restraint of the mento-emotional energy while focusing on self-interest distinct from the other interest, a yogi gets knowledge of the individual spirit.

Verse 37

ततः प्रातिभश्रावणवेदनादर्शास्वादवार्ता जायन्ते॥ ३७॥

tataḥ prātibha śrāvaṇa vedana
ādarśa āsvāda vārtāḥ jāyante

From that focus is produced smelling, tasting, seeing, touching and hearing, through the shining organ of divination.

Verse 38

ते समाधावुपसर्गा व्युत्थाने सिद्धयः॥ ३८॥

te samādhau upasargāḥ vyutthāne siddhayaḥ

Those divination skills are obstacles in the practice of continuous effortless linkage of the attention to a higher concentration force, object or person. But in expressing, they are considered as mystic perfectional skills.

Verse 39

बन्धकारणशैथिल्यात्प्रचारसंवेदनाच्च चित्तस्य परशरीरावेशः ॥ ३९ ॥

bandhakāraṇa śaithilyāt pracāra

saṁvedanāt ca cittasya paraśarīrāveśaḥ

The entrance into another body is possible
by slackening the cause of bondage
and by knowing the channels of the mento-emotional energy.

Verse 40

उदानजयाज्जलपङ्ककण्टकादिष्वसङ्ग उत्क्रान्तिश्च ॥ ४० ॥

udānajayāt jala paṅka kaṇṭakādiṣu asaṇgaḥ utkrāntiḥ ca

By mastery over the air which rises from the throat into the head, a yogi can
rise over or not have contact
with water, mud or sharp objects.

Verse 41

समानजयाज्ज्वलनम् ॥ ४१ ॥

samānajayāt jvalanam

By conquest of the samāna digestive force,
a yogi's psyche blazes or shines with a fiery glow.

Verse 42

श्रोत्राकाशयोः सम्बन्धसंयमाद्दिव्यं श्रोत्रम् ॥ ४२ ॥

śrotra ākāśayoḥ saṁbandha saṁyamāt divyaṁ śrotram

By the complete restraint of the mento-emotional energy,
while focusing on the hearing sense and space,
a yogin develops supernatural and divine hearing.

Verse 43

कायाकाशयोः सम्बन्धसंयमाल्लघुतूलसमापत्तेश्चाकाशगमनम् ॥ ४३ ॥

kāya ākāśayoḥ saṁbandha saṁyamāt

laghutūlasamāpatteḥ ca ākāśagamanam

By the complete restraint of the mento-emotional energy,
while linking the mind to the relationship
between the body and the sky and linking the attention
to being as light as cotton fluff,
a yogi acquires the ability to pass through the atmosphere.

Verse 44

बहिरकल्पिता वृत्तिर्महाविदेहा ततः प्रकाशावरणक्षयः ॥ ४४ ॥

bahiḥ akalpitā vṛttiḥ mahāvidehā tataḥ
prakāśa āvaraṇakṣayaḥ

By the complete restraint of the mento-emotional energy which is external, which is not formed, a yogi achieves the great bodiless state. From that the great mental darkness which veils the light, is dissipated.

Verse 45

स्थूलस्वरूपसूक्ष्मान्वयार्थवत्त्वसंयमाद्भूतजयः ॥ ४५ ॥

sthūla svarūpa sūkṣma anvaya arthavatva
saṁyamāt bhūtajayaḥ

By the complete restraint of the mento-emotional energy, while linking the attention to the gross forms, real nature, subtle distribution and value of states of matter, a yogi gets conquest over them.

Verse 46

ततोऽणिमादिप्रादुर्भावः कायसम्पत्तद्धर्मानभिघातश्च ॥ ४६ ॥

tataḥ aṇimādi prādurbhāvaḥ kāyasaṁpat
taddharma anabhighātaḥ ca

From minuteness and other related mystic skills, come the perfection of the subtle body and the non-obstruction of its functions.

Verse 47

रूपलावण्यबलवज्रसंहननत्वानि कायसम्पत् ॥ ४७ ॥

rūpa lāvaṇya bala vajra saṁhananatvāni kāyasaṁpat

Beautiful form, charm, mystic force, and diamond-like definition come from perfection of the subtle body.

Verse 48

ग्रहणस्वरूपास्मितान्वयार्थवत्त्वसंयमादिन्द्रियजयः ॥ ४८ ॥

grahaṇa svarūpa asmitā anvaya arthavattva

saṁyamāt indriyajayaḥ

From the continuous effortless linkage of the attention to sensual grasping, to the form of the sensual energy, to its identifying powers, to its connection instinct and to its actual worth, a yogi acquires conquest over his relationship with it.

Verse 49

ततो मनोजवित्वं विकरणभावः प्रधानजयश्च ॥ ४९ ॥

tataḥ manojavitvaṁ vikaraṇabhāvaḥ pradhānajayaḥ ca

Subsequently, there is conquest over the influence of subtle matter and over the parting away or dispersion of the mento-emotional energy, with the required swiftness of mind.

Verse 50

सत्त्वपुरुषान्यताख्यातिमात्रस्य सर्वभावाधिष्ठातृत्वं सर्वज्ञातृत्वं च ॥ ५० ॥

sattva puruṣa anyatā khyātimātrasya

sarvabhāva adhiṣṭhātṛtvaṁ sarvajñātṛtvaṁ ca

Only when there is distinct discrimination between the clarifying perception of material nature and the spiritual personality, does the yogi attain complete disaffection and all-applicative intuition.

Verse 51

तद्वैराग्यादपि दोषबीजक्षये कैवल्यम् ॥ ५१ ॥

tadvairāgyāt api doṣabījakṣaye kaivalyam

By a lack of interest, even to that (discrimination between the clarifying mundane energy and the self) when the cause of that defect is eliminated, the absolute isolation of the self from its lower psyche, is achieved.

Verse 52

स्थान्युपनिमन्त्रणे सङ्गस्मयाकरणं पुनरनिष्टप्रसङ्गात्॥ ५२॥

sthānyupanimantraṇe saṅgasmayākaraṇaṁ

punaraniṣṭa prasaṅgāt

On being invited by a person from the place one would attain if the body died, a yogi should be non-responsive, not desiring their association and not being fascinated, otherwise that would cause unwanted features of existence to arise again.

Verse 53

क्षणतत्क्रमयोः संयमाद्विवेकजं ज्ञानम्॥ ५३॥

kṣaṇa tatkramayoḥ saṁyamāt vivekajaṁ jñānam

By the continuous effortless linkage of the attention to the moment and to the sequence of the moments, the yogi has knowledge caused by the subtle discrimination.

Verse 54

जातिलक्षणदेशैरन्यतानवच्छेदात्तुल्ययोस्ततः प्रतिपत्तिः॥ ५४॥

jāti lakṣaṇa deśaiḥ anyatā anavacchedāt

tulyayoḥ tataḥ pratipattiḥ

Subsequently, the yogi has perception of two similar realities which otherwise could not be sorted due to a lack of definition in terms of their general category, individual characteristics and locations.

Verse 55

तारकं सर्वविषयं सर्वथाविषयमक्रमं चेति विवेकजं ज्ञानम्॥ ५५॥

tārakaṁ sarvaviṣayaṁ sarvathāviṣayaṁ

akramaṁ ca iti vivekajaṁ jñānam

The distinction caused by subtle discrimination is the crossing over or transcending of all subtle and gross mundane objects in all ways they are presented, without the yogi taking recourse to any other sequential perceptions of mind reliance.

Verse 56

सत्त्वपुरुषयोः शुद्धिसाम्ये कैवल्यमिति॥ ५६॥

sattva puruṣayoḥ śuddhi sāmye kaivalyam iti

When there is equal purity between the intelligence energy of material nature and the spirit, then there is total separation from the mundane psychology.

CHAPTER 4: KAIVALYA PĀDA:

Segregation Accomplishment

Verse 1

जन्मौषधिमन्त्रतपःसमाधिजाः सिद्धयः॥ १॥

janma auṣadhi mantra tapaḥ samādhijāḥ siddhayaḥ

The mystic skills are produced
by taking birth in particular species,
by taking drugs, by reciting special sounds,
by physical bodily austerities
or by the continuous effortless linkage of the attention
to a higher concentration force, object or person.

Verse 2

जात्यन्तरपरिणामः प्रकृत्यापूरात्॥ २॥

jātyantara pariṇāmaḥ prakṛtyāpūrāt

The transformation from one category to another
is by the saturation of the subtle material nature.

Verse 3

निमित्तमप्रयोजकं प्रकृतीनां वरणभेदस्तु ततः क्षेत्रिकवत्॥ ३॥

nimittaṁ aprayojakaṁ prakṛtīnāṁ

varaṇabhedaḥ tu tataḥ kṣetrikavat

**The motivating force of the subtle material energy
is not used except for the disintegration of impediments,
hence it is compared to a farmer.**

Verse 4

निर्माणचित्तान्यस्मितामात्रात्॥ ४॥

nirmāṇacittāni asmitāmātrāt

**The formation of regions within the mento-emotional energy,
arises only from the sense of identity
which is developed in relation to material nature.**

Verse 5

प्रवृत्तिभेदे प्रयोजकं चित्तमेकमनेकेषाम्॥ ५॥

pravṛtti bhede prayojakaṁ cittam ekam anekeṣām

**The one mento-emotional energy is that which is very much used
in numberless different dispersals of energy.**

Verse 6

तत्र ध्यानजमनाशयम्॥ ६॥

tatra dhyānajam anāśayam

**In that case, only subtle activities which are produced
from the effortless linkage of the attention to a higher reality
are without harmful emotions.**

Verse 7

कर्माशुक्लाकृष्णं योगिनस्त्रिविधमितरेषाम्॥ ७॥

karma aśukla akṛṣnaṁ yoginaḥ trividham itareṣām

**The cultural activity of the yogis
is neither rewarding nor penalizing,
but others have three types of such action.**

Verse 8

ततस्तद्विपाकानुगुणानामेवाभिव्यक्तिर्वासनानाम्॥ ८॥

tataḥ tadvipāka anuguṇānām

eva abhivyaktiḥ vāsanānām

Subsequently from those cultural activities there is development according to corresponding features only, bringing about the manifestation of the tendencies within the mento-emotional energy.

Verse 9

जातिदेशकालव्यवहितानामप्यानन्तर्यं स्मृतिसंस्कारयोरेकरूपत्वात्॥ ९॥

jāti deśa kāla vyavahitānām api ānantaryaṁ smṛti saṁskārayoḥ ekarūpatvāt

Even though circumstances are separated by status, location and time, still the impressions which form cultural activities and the resulting memories, are of one form and operate on a timely sequence.

Verse 10

तासामनादित्वं चाशिषो नित्यत्वात्॥ १०॥

tāsām anāditvaṁ ca āśiṣaḥ nityatvāt

Those memories and impressions are primeval, without a beginning. Energies of hope and desire are eternal as well.

Verse 11

हेतुफलाश्रयालम्बनैः सङ्गृहीतत्वादेषामभावे तदभावः॥ ११॥

hetu phala āśraya ālambanaiḥ saṅgṛhītatvāt

eṣām abhāve tad abhāvaḥ

They exist by what holds them together in terms of cause and effect, supportive base and lifting influence. Otherwise if their causes are not there, they have no existence.

Verse 12

अतीतानागतं स्वरूपतोऽस्त्यध्वभेदाद्धर्माणाम् ॥ १२ ॥

atīta anāgataṁ svarūpataḥ

asti adhvabhedāt dharmāṇām

There is a true form of the past and future, which is denoted by the different courses of their characteristics.

Verse 13

ते व्यक्तसूक्ष्मा गुणात्मानः ॥ १३ ॥

te vyakta sūkṣmāḥ guṇātmānaḥ

They are gross or subtle, all depending on their inherent nature.

Verse 14

परिणामैकत्वाद्वस्तुतत्त्वम् ॥ १४ ॥

pariṇāma ekatvāt vastutattvam

The actual composition of an object is based on the uniqueness of the transformation.

Verse 15

वस्तुसाम्ये चित्तभेदात्तयोर्विभक्तः पन्थाः ॥ १५ ॥

vastusāmye cittabhedāt tayoḥ vibhaktaḥ panthāḥ

Because of a difference in the mento-emotional energy of two persons, separate prejudices manifest in their viewing of the very same object.

Verse 16

न चैकचित्ततन्त्रं वस्तु तदप्रमाणकं तदा किं स्यात् ॥ १६ ॥

na ca ekacitta tantraṁ ced vastu

tat apramāṇakaṁ tadā kiṁ syāt

An object is not dependent on one person's mento-emotional perception. Otherwise, what would happen if it were not being perceived by that person?

Verse 17

तदुपरागापेक्षित्वाच्चित्तस्य वस्तु ज्ञाताज्ञातम्॥ १७॥

taduparāga apekṣitvāt cittasya vastu jñāta ajñātam

**An object is known or unknown,
all depending on the mood and expectation
of the particular mento-emotional energy
of the person in reference to it.**

Verse 18

सदा ज्ञाताश्चित्तवृत्तयस्तत्प्रभोः पुरुषस्यापरिणामित्वात्॥ १८॥

sadā jñātāḥ cittavṛttayaḥ tatprabhoḥ

puruṣasya apariṇāmitvāt

**The operations of the mento-emotional energy
are always known to that governor
because of the changelessness of that spirit.**

Verse 19

न तत्स्वाभासं दृश्यत्वात्॥ १९॥

na tat svābhāsaṁ dṛśyatvāt

**That mento-emotional energy is not self-illuminative
for it is rather only capable of being perceived.**

Verse 20

एकसमये चोभयानवधारणम्॥ २०॥

ekasamaye ca ubhaya anavadhāraṇam

It cannot execute the focus of both at the same time.

Verse 21

चित्तान्तरदृश्ये बुद्धिबुद्धेरतिप्रसङ्गः स्मृतिसङ्करश्च॥ २१॥

cittāntaradṛśye buddhibuddheḥ

atiprasaṅgaḥ smṛtisaṅkaraḥ ca

**In the perception of mento-emotional energy
by another such energy, there would be an intellect
perceiving another intellect independently.
That would cause absurdity and confusion of memory.**

Verse 22

चितेरप्रतिसङ्क्रमायास्तदाकारापत्तौ स्वबुद्धिसंवेदनम्॥ २२॥

citeḥ apratisaṁkramāyāḥ tadākārāpattau svabuddhisaṁvedanam

The perception of its own intellect occurs when it assumes that form in which there is no movement from one operation to another.

Verse 23

द्रष्टृदृश्योपरक्तं चित्तं सर्वार्थम्॥ २३॥

draṣṭṛ dṛśya uparaktaṁ cittaṁ sarvārtham

The mento-emotional energy which is prejudiced by the perceiver and the perceived, is all-evaluating.

Verse 24

तदसङ्ख्येयवासनाभिश्चित्रमपि परार्थं संहत्यकारित्वात्॥ २४॥

tat asaṅkhyeya vāsanābhiḥ citram

api parārthaṁ saṁhatyakāritvāt

Although the mento-emotional energy is diversified by innumerable subtle impressions, it acts for the sake of another power because of its proximity to that other factor.

Verse 25

विशेषदर्शिन आत्मभावभावनाविनिवृत्तिः॥ २५॥

viśeṣadarśinaḥ ātmabhāva bhāvanānivṛttiḥ

There is total stopping of the operations of mento-emotional energy for the person who perceives the distinction between feelings and the spirit itself.

Verse 26

तदा हि विवेकनिम्नङ्कैवल्यप्राग्भारञ्चित्तम्॥ २६॥

tadā hi vivekanimnaṁ kaivalya prāgbhāraṁ cittam

Then, indeed, the mento-emotional force is inclined towards discrimination and gravitates towards the total separation from the mundane psychology.

Verse 27

तच्छिद्रेषु प्रत्ययान्तराणि संस्कारेभ्यः ॥ २७ ॥

tat cchidreṣu pratyayāntarāṇi saṁskārebhyaḥ

Besides that, in the relaxation of focus, other mind contents arise in the intervals. These are based on subtle impressions.

Verse 28

हानमेषां क्लेशवदुक्तम् ॥ २८ ॥

hānam eṣāṁ kleśavat uktam

As authoritatively stated, the complete removal of these is like the elimination of the mento-emotional afflictions.

Verse 29

प्रसङ्ख्यानेऽप्यकुसीदस्य सर्वथा विवेकख्यातेर्धर्ममेघः समाधिः ॥ २९ ॥

prasaṁkhyāne api akusīdasya sarvathā
vivekakhyāteḥ dharmameghaḥ samādhiḥ

For one who sees no gains in material nature, even while perceiving it in abstract meditation, one has the super discrimination. One attains the continuous effortless linkage of the attention to higher reality which is described as knowing the mento-emotional clouds of energy which compel a person to perform according to nature's way of acting for beneficial results.

Verse 30

ततः क्लेशकर्मनिवृत्तिः ॥ ३० ॥

tataḥ kleśa karma nivṛttiḥ

Subsequently there is stoppage of the operation of the mento-emotional energy in terms of generation of cultural activities and their resulting afflictions.

Verse 31

तदा सर्वावरणमलापेतस्य ज्ञानस्यानन्त्याज्ज्ञेयमल्पम्॥ ३१॥

tadā sarva āvaraṇa malāpetasya

jñānasya ānantyāt jñeyam alpam

**Then, because of the removal
of all mental darkness and psychological impurities,
that which can be known through the mento-emotional energy,
seems trivial in comparison
to the unlimited knowledge available
when separated from it.**

Verse 32

ततः कृतार्थानां परिणामक्रमसमाप्तिर्गुणानाम्॥ ३२॥

tataḥ kṛtārthānāṁ pariṇāmakrama samāptir guṇānām

**Thus, the subtle material nature, having fulfilled its purpose,
its progressive alterations end.**

Verse 33

क्षणप्रतियोगी परिणामापरान्तनिर्ग्राह्यः क्रमः॥ ३३॥

kṣaṇa pratiyogī pariṇāma

aparānta nirgrāhyaḥ kramaḥ

**The process, of which moments are a counterpart,
and which causes the alterations,
comes to an end and is clearly perceived.**

Verse 34

पुरुषार्थशून्यानां गुणानां प्रतिप्रसवः कैवल्यं स्वरूपप्रतिष्ठा वा चितिशक्तिरिति॥ ३४॥

puruṣārtha śūnyānāṁ guṇānāṁ

pratiprasavaḥ kaivalyaṁ

svarūpapratiṣṭhā vā citiśaktiḥ iti

**Separation of the spirit
from the mento-emotional energy (*kaivalyam*)
occurs when there is neutrality
in respect to the influence of material nature,
when the yogi's psyche
becomes devoid of the general aims of a human being.
Thus at last, the spirit is established in its own form
as the force empowering the mento-emotional energy.**

END

Part 2

An Approach to Patañjali's Yoga Sūtras

Chapter 1

Samādhi Pāda:

Transcendence Accomplishment

1. *Now Śrī Patañjali gave the explanation of yoga and its practice.*
2. *Yoga is accomplished when as a yogin, you can stop the creative urges of your mind and emotions.*
3. *Then you can become familiar with your bare self.*
4. *But otherwise, whatever you do is regulated by the urges.*
5. *There are five types of those creative urges. Each type has troublesome and non-troublesome interactions.*
6. *The five types are experienced when you gage external things correctly, when you gage them incorrectly, when you imagine anything, when you sleep and when you experience memory.*
7. *Your correct assessments occur by accurate sense perception, by efficient analysis or by using a reliable reference.*
8. *When you gage something incorrectly, that occurs through false information or by mistaking one factor for something else.*
9. *When you hear of something or read of it, ideas concerning it usually form. When these concepts misrepresent the actual thing, that misconception is imagination.*
10. *Sleep is that creative urge which operates without your awareness.*
11. *Memory operates anytime you visualize something which was experienced before.*
12. *By not having an interest in the mental ideas and emotional feelings, you may develop the power to stop their influence.*
13. *You should persistently cultivate that lack of interest.*

14. *However you should be reverential in the practice and it must be sustained for a long time.*

15. *Note well, that the lack of interest in one's own ideas and emotions is achieved only by one who has mastery over his psychological nature. Such a person would not crave things mundane which are perceived by his own senses or which is heard of by his own ears.*

16. *Please realize that the required lack of interest is exhibited when one attains a resistance to urges which usually compel one to fulfill mundane desires. That lack of interest results in the development of a thorough awareness of the spiritual self.*

17. *At first, after you develop that lack of interest, you will notice that your attention becomes linked to higher psychological states, but there will still be some analysis, reflection, inner joy and focus on self-consciousness.*

18. *Periodically and with good luck, you will experience the transcendence in which the memory of things mundane seems not to exist at all.*

19. *That will give you a glimpse of the status of the released souls, who are diffused into the subtle material nature requiring no gross existence and those divine beings who exist without a subtle or super subtle material body. Their mind and emotion does not comprise of subtle energies of material nature.*

20. *Since you have neither the diffused status nor the divine one, and since you still have a fixation with the memory of things mundane, your success in cultivating the required lack of interest hinges on confidence in what Śrī Patañjali recommends. You would be required to have stamina. You should train yourself to retain any transcendental experiences, even the slightest. You should study this text so as to recognize the characteristics of samādhi which is continuous and spontaneous contact between your attention and someone or some energy which is beyond your normal range of perception. By this, a profound insight will develop in your psyche.*

21. *Know with certainty that those of you who practice forcefully in a very intense way, will be masterful yogis in the near future.*

22. *But not everyone can apply themselves with intensity. One person might be mediocre. Another might practice infrequently.*

23. *There is a special method to be mentioned. That is the profound religious meditation upon the Supreme Lord.*

24. *This person is that special individual who is not affected by troubles, actions, developments or by subconscious motivations, which are based on the urgings of subtle material nature.*

25. *He is, for all practical purposes the ultimate knower. He is the most experienced person.*

26. *This God, being unconditioned by time, is the teacher even of the ancient masters of yoga, the pioneers of the process of release.*

27. *The teachers before me designated the sacred syllable AUM (Oṁ) as being related to Him.*

28. *Many ancient teachers constantly repeated and murmured AUM (Oṁ) for realizing it's effects and meaning.*

29. *Thus when uttered correctly, one's sense energy develops the urge to turn away from objects outside of one's material body. The sense energy then seeks psychological inner objects. Thus the extrovert tendency which is an obstacle to progress, is greatly decreased.*

30. *The obstacles to the practice of yoga are: physical and mental diseases, idleness, doubts about the power of the practice, inattentiveness while practicing, lack of energy to invest in an intense practice, proneness to sensuality in terms of always being drawn to forms in this world, mistaken views due to the inability to side-step cultural activities and scattered mental and emotional energy which is due to being influenced by the subtle material energy.*

31. *It would be necessary to remove the tendency for distracted states of mind. These come about by distress, depression, nervousness and labored breathing. All of which are triggered by impulsive emotional states.*

32. *To remove any of these obstacles, one should practice a standard method, which was effective for a more advanced yogi and which he recommends.*

33. *When the obstacles to the practice of yoga temporarily subside or when they are removed altogether, an abstract meditation ensues. In that state, the creative urges disappear. This is directly related to the successful cultivation of friendliness, compassion, cheerfulness and non-responsiveness to happiness, distress, virtue and vices.*

34. *That abstract meditation may be caused by practicing a method of breath manipulation wherein the vital energy of the gross and subtle body is enhanced, causing the creative urges to subside, so that the higher nature is experienced.*

35. *One may attain fusion to higher states or steadiness of mind by directing the mind towards a supernatural or spiritual object. Such an object would be just as real and objective as a physical one.*

36. *That may be achieved by attaining sorrowless and spiritually-luminous states.*

37. *One may attain super-consciousness by linking one's attention to a person who is without craving.*

38. *In some cases, super-consciousness may occur after one takes recourse to dream experiences or to the dreamless sleep.*

39. *It may be achieved by a spontaneous linkage of the attention to a higher concentration force or person which was dearly desired.*

40. *The mastery over the functions and movements of the urges, results in the control of one's relationship to the smallest portions of energy or to the largest conglomerations.*

41. *For the great reduction of the urges in your mind and emotions, one has to sort between the perceiver in the mind, the flow of ideas or images, which are perceived by him and the objects from which the perception originated. This is similar to knowing the status of a transparent jewel, the light which it absorbs from a colorful source, and that colorful source itself. In that comparison the perceiver is like the jewel. His ideas and images are like the colored light which is reflected in the jewel.*

42. *Even in ordinary usage of consciousness, one may deliberately link one's attention to a higher concentration force by a careful observation of how the mind-attention mechanism operates when a word, it's meaning and the knowledge of the object alternate within the mind, blending as it were, with one of those facets permeating with the other.*

43. *Even though analysis is useful in material existence, it does not serve the purpose in higher yoga practice. In fact such analysis is discarded completely in the highest stages. When the memory is completely purified where it no longer reminds the self to pursue vices and when the inquiring inquisitive nature disappears as it were, then the higher concentration forces and the divine personalities are experienced objectively.*

44. *One may investigate very subtle objects after dropping the usual analysis, and after mastering the linkage of the attention as stated above.*

45. *But the insight gained by that mystic research terminates, when one becomes linked to the higher concentration force which has no gross characteristics and which is not directly linked to a gross object.*

46. *Initially, all of this is motivated by the creative urges, in the sense that they caused the inquiring tendency in the first place. Thus the previous descriptions were of higher experiences which were to a degree, motivated, because the spirit made contact with the creative urges of the mental and emotional energies.*

47. *In the advanced states however, those urges lose their hold on the self. Thus that self is no longer motivated by them and no longer reacts to them, either for fulfilling the urges or for becoming indifferent to them. Thus the motivations come from the Supreme Soul to whom the limited soul becomes linked. That association brings on clarity and serenity.*

48. *There, with that competence, the yogi develops the reality-perceptive insight, which is so natural to the Supreme Soul and which the limited soul develops in the supreme association.*

49. *This is different to the normal perception, which is based on what is heard of, what is reasoned out in the material world, since that limited perception is restricted to a partial aspect of an object and never does it reveal comprehensively.*

50. *Once the association of Supreme Soul is repeatedly attained, the impressions of that contact which forms in the mind, acts as the preventer of the other impressions which used to contravene yoga practices.*

51. *When there is linkage of the attention to the higher concentration force, this must be effortless and continuous (not with effort and not momentarily). When it is like that it is considered to be samādhi, the highest stage of yoga. In that state there is a complete departure from the memory and so its power of reminding the self of its contents is nullified completely. The self then becomes freed.*

ā

Chapter 2

Sādhana Pāda:

Practice Accomplishment

1. *Kriya yoga is strongly recommended because it is definite. It is a hands-on personal process. It is not reliant on mere good luck nor on accidental process. Kriya yoga has scientific austerity, careful introspective study of the psyche and religious meditation on the Supreme Lord, as it's practice.*
2. *That kriyā yoga causes a reduction of the mental and emotional conflicts and their short-termed or long-termed negative effects. It is the definite way for attaining samādhi, which is the continuous effortless linkage of the attention to higher dimensions and their contents*
3. *There are five general headings of the mental and emotional conflicts which are stored in the psyche. These are the inability to know the difference between one's spirit and its subtle sensing tools, the compelling tendency to react to other influences, the tendency to link with other factors emotionally, the strong urge to dislike certain other factors, and the instinctive fear of death which sponsors a strong focus on mundane existence.*

4. *The inability to know the difference between one's spirit and its subtle sensing tools, is not just that lack of knowledge, but it serves as a mental and emotional environment, which is productive of and supportive of the other conflicts of identity, and energy. These conflicting energies may be dormant, reduced, appearing periodically or expanding fully.*

5. *That spiritual ignorance is revealed to someone when he realized that what he considered to be eternal was temporary, and what was pure was actually impure, what was joyful was in fact distressful and what was spiritual was mundane.*

6. *The compelling tendency to react to other influences occurs when one cannot distinguish between the viewing-sensing power and what is seen through it.*

7. *The impulsive urge to link with other factors emotionally creates as a result, a craving for repeated contact with those factors and a devoted attachment to any pleasure experienced by such contact.*

8. *The strong urge to dislike certain factors arises as a need for conflict and disharmony. It is an attachment to distress.*

9. *The instinctive fear of death is the subtle body's way of showing its dislike for having to repeatedly give up gross forms in an unpleasant way. To counteract the effects of this, the subtle form exhibits a strong focus on mundane existence. These energies operate even in the psyche of a wise man.*

10. *The mental and emotional conflicts are to be nullified by squelching their eruptions so that when they arise within the mind or emotions, their urges are inhibited or forced back into dormancy or potentiality.*

11. *The mental or emotional eruptions are to be squelched by developing a meditation habit whereby the attention effortlessly links to a higher concentration force or person.*

12. *Impressions of everything encountered do lodge in the mind and are stored there but this stored energy is itchy and troublesome. An advanced yogi may perceived those stored impressions which erupts into mental and emotional distress and is even felt by persons who are not yogis.*

13. *Those bodies which are assumed as well as the various climatic and geographic environments come about on the basis of those stored impressions. They are the origin. Thus the control of that stored energy is vital in terms of liberation of any limited being.*

14. *With those bodies functioning in the outcome-environments like this earth, we perform austerities which produce a culture or way of life. And this in turn causes happiness and distress as results, all occurring on the basis of merits and demerits which are defined by the relationship of the energies.*

15. *An advanced yogi has a special discriminating ability, whereby he can sort between his spirit and his psychological viewing aids. Thus he recognizes the potential for distress which cultural activity and the resulting impressions pose. There will be circumstantial changes which are beyond the performer's control and which may aid or frustrate his enterprise. He must exert himself on many occasions. He must submit to impulsive motivations from time to time, and he must react to some clashing aspects whether he wants to or not. Finally, he cannot at all times suppress the urges which grow out of his mind and emotions.*

16. *But distress which is not manifested is to be avoided. Thus one should develop power to thwart the impressions which would produce that.*

17. *Remember that the cause which can definitely be adjusted is the indiscriminate association of the observer and what is perceived. But since that linkage is impulsive and most natural, efforts will have to be made to change it.*

18. *What is perceived in this world with this psychology is of the nature of the mundane elements and the sense organs, and is formed in clear perception, action or stability. Its purpose is to give experience or to allow liberation. But to gain liberation, one has to abandon the need for the experiences in this world.*

19. *Some of the experiences afforded by material nature occur in clear perception, some in the fervor of action, some in any of the states of stability which make one form regrettable decisions. These experiences may be specific, regular, indicated before hand, or not anticipated at all.*

20. *Even though the perceiver is the pure extent of his consciousness, his conviction, once formed in any way, is patterned by what he perceived.*

21. *The individual spirit who is involved in what is seen exists here for either purpose. He may either accept the experience presented to him and react to it as he is urged and biased, or he may side-step the experiencing mechanism and move in the direction of liberation.*

22. *The experiences have little impact on one to whom its purpose is fulfilled but it has a common effect on all others, and keeps them occupied and enthralled.*

23. *Even though the conjunction of the individual spirit and his psychological energy is condemned, still its ultimate purpose is justified, when the person attains liberation. Then he appreciates that it afforded him the objective experience of his own form through blending and then contrasting itself with his core self.*

24. *Always keep in mind that the inability to know the difference between one's spirit and it's sensing tools, is the very cause of their conjunction in the first place. Kriya yoga is designed to remove that inability.*

25. *One must practice the kriyā discipline because it affords a detachment whereby the perceiver is separated from his sensing tools.*

26. *The unification with the sensing tools is to be avoided. If achieved, one develops the discriminative insight, which affords one freedom from identity with the urges of the mind and emotions.*

27. *There are seven stages of progress when developing the discriminative insight, which gives one the ability to differentiate between the self and it's sensing tools.*

28. *The radiant organ of perception becomes available to one who has consistently practiced the kriyā yoga process. It is experienced when there is elimination of the psychological impurities.*

29. *Restraining from vices and sensual addictions, becoming habituated to a disciplined life which accelerates yoga, doing bodily postures which enhances health, performing breath enrichment and control processes, removing one's attention from the things pertaining to this existence, shifting one's attention to higher concentration forces or persons, holding one's attention there long enough for it to become habituated to the higher forces or persons, and experiencing the resultant fusion of the attention into the higher dimension encountered.*

30. *The **moral restraints** consist of the following:*

<u>Non-violence:</u> The avoidance of violence towards other life forms, the avoidance of psychological violence towards other spiritual entities, the practice of a calm, detached mood as professed by Śrī Krishna in the Bhagavad-gīta, if one is duty bound to discipline or apply violence to anyone.

<u>Realism:</u> The practice of studying the situations carefully before acting or reacting to them. The practice of assessing the defects of one's intellect to gage its reliability in perceiving truth. Relieving oneself of the need for a favorable or palatable truth.

<u>Non-stealing:</u> Curing oneself of the natural urge to steal by carefully observing and monitoring the psychological mechanisms ofstealing which is innate to nature.

<u>Sexual non-expressiveness</u> which results in the perception of spirituality (brahman): Becoming detached from expressive sexuality and from normal exhibitions and demonstrations of sexuality either as a male or female. Investing the energy usually used in sexuality for the perception of spirituality.

<u>Non-possessiveness:</u> Carefully studying the sense of possession. Suppressing it effectively while studying methods of its eradication and spiritually supportive uses.

31. *Even though one may be pressured to adjust the moral restraints, one should strive to side-step those causes and justifications for deviation. The pressures come on from the status, the location, the time and the condition. Since the moral restraints are applicable in all stages of yoga, they are the great commitment for all yogis.*

32. *The recommended behaviors are as follows*

<u>Purification:</u> Psychic cleansing which is achieved by mastery of kuṇḍalini yoga for purifying the subtle body and its energies.

<u>Contentment:</u> This is the practice of detachment from desire for the mundane life. It means to find an effective way of changing one's nature to eradicate the desire for mundane experiences.

<u>Austerity:</u> This means to practice kriyā yoga under the guidance of a more advanced yogi. These austerities should suppress unwanted desires to the point of eliminating them. Such desires are those which cause extroversion and which discourage the quest for liberation.

<u>Profound meditation on the Supreme Lord:</u> One can meditate on the Person God, if one has a functional relationship with Him. Over all, this is impractical for most practitioners since they either have an imaginary relationship with their preferred deity or a very meager connection. To be realistic one has to develop a relationship with a person who is more advanced on this spiritual path laid out by Śrī Patañjali.

33. *There may be doubts about the claims of yoga made in this text of Śrī Patañjali and made in other yoga books, however one should cast these doubts aside and practice. When the doubts arise, one should ignore the doubtful ideas and push ahead with practice.*

34. *One may doubt that one can exist without committing some minimal violence. For instance, even ifone refrains from eating animal flesh, one will have to eat something else, vegetables or fruits for example. And in that case there will be violence against trees, insects and microbes. Still one should minimize such violence and hold faith that ultimately it can be removed by transfer to another dimension where the violence will be absent. If one does not succeed at yoga practice, the implication is that one will be condemned to material existence, with endless distress and continued misidentification with the mundane energy in any of its gross or subtle formations.*

35. *When a yogi is firmly established in non-violence, that is exhibited by his life style. Then even hostile creatures abandon their aggressive stance in his presence.*

36. *When a yogi is established in realism, his actions serve as a basis for desired results. He is not easily frustrated because he acts in accordance with reality, is subordinate to it, respects it and rarely makes unrealistic plans in attempts to contravene it.*

37. *When the yogi has subdued the stealing tendency in human nature, material existence endeavors to serve him. Thus it seems that all precious things become available to him.*

38. *When the yogi has practiced effective methods of sex activity reduction and elimination, his vigor to perform yoga increases proportionately. Thus his perception of spirituality is actuated.*

39. *Due to the development of non-possessiveness, the yogi intuits into the causes of his birth. By mystic skill he reviews actions from past lives which caused him to take the present birth.*

40. *From purification of the subtle body, comes a disgust for one's own gross form and lack of desire to associate sexually with others.*

41. *Purification of the subtle energy results in a great reduction in emotional needs. From that stability one finds it easy to link the attention to one concentration force or person. After much practice one acquires conquest of the sensual energy. One gets vision of the spirit and becomes fit for abstract meditation.*

42. *With the reduction of sensual life in this world, with a developed resistance to desires, one gains contentment. From that, the very best in happiness is obtained.*

43. *Kriya yoga austerities which are highlighted by mystic actions in and with the subtle body, do result in elimination of emotional impurities. That gives perfection of the subtle form in which the troublesome, vice-seeking sensual energy is housed.*

44. *An in-depth mystic research into the nature of the subtle body causes the yogi to make contact with more advanced mystics. This leads to communication with divine beings, and eventually he gets in touch with the cherished divine beings, one of whom is the Supreme Lord .*

45. *From the profound religious meditation upon the Supreme Lord or upon any of the divine beings, comes a full time communion with that divinity.*

46. *As for bodily posture, it should be steady and comfortable.*

47. *When mastered, it results in relaxation of the effort to subdue the body and make it serve the spiritual aims. That assists in the quest of meeting with the infinite.*

48. *Once the body is mastered, comfortable or uncomfortable climate, pleasant or unpleasant emotions, no longer bother the person.*

49. *Once this is accomplished, the body's anxiety for air is greatly decreased, then there are pauses between the flow in inhalation and exhalation.*

50. *Breathing has internal, external and restrictive operations, which are regulated according to the place, time and accounting, being prolonged or hardly noticed. A change in lifestyle affects all this.*

51. *But a more advanced condition is realized, which has nothing to do with physical breathing. This is the energy consumption of the subtle body. That regulation of the subtle energy or prāṇa is the fourth type of prāṇāyāma energy intake.*

52. *When a yogi shifts his attention to that subtle plane of consciousness, the darkness within his mind becomes dissipated, resulting in perception of light in real subtle objects,*

53. *and the establishment of always being able to link his attention to a higher concentration force or person.*

54. *The self should learn how to subsist on the bare sensual energy by itself without its usage procuring objects in this world. This is called pratyāhār or sensual energy withdrawal. After mastering this, the yogin notices that the withdrawal of the senses is as it were, their assumption of the form of unformed psychological energy which is quiescent when it is not contacting the objects of perception.*

55. *From that accomplishment comes the highest degree of control of the senses because they are powered by the inner sensual energy which a human being identifies as his emotions and mental force.*

Chapter 3

Vibhūti Pāda:

Glory Displayed

1. *The yogi must be so familiar with the realm of mind and emotions, that he should begin to recognize where thoughts, ideas, images and memories arise. Their particular location in the mind environment and emotional atmosphere should be known. Then he may practice the sixth stage of yoga, which is linking of the attention to a concentration force or person through a restricted location in the mento-emotional space.*

2. *But in the seventh stage of yoga, the next stage, that of dhyāna, the yogi experiences that there is a continuous threadlike flow of his instinctive interest to the selected location in the mind or emotions. This is the effortless linkage of the attention to a higher concentration force or person.*

3. *When, however, that sense of effortless linkage of the attention joins continually to a particular location in the mind or emotions or outside into a higher dimension, it is the highest stage of yoga, that of samādhi. It may be a link to a greater yogi or to a divinity. This is experienced as illumination of the higher concentration force or person while the yogi feels as if devoid of his conditioned self.*

4. *The three higher stages of yoga, when practiced in sequence, are considered as the complete restraint; then the sixth stage directly progresses into the seventh and seventh into the eighth and final stage.*

5. *By regular practice of the sequential three higher stages, one gains mastery over the mental and emotional urges, and then the illuminating insight becomes available for usage.*

6. *But this development occurs in stages.*

7. *This higher yoga concerns voluntary control over the psychological organs in the mind and the creative urges in the emotions.*

8. *But even that initial mastership of the three higher stages of yoga is external in reference to meditation which is not motivated by the mental and emotional energy. Therefore you should strive to reach the advanced stages.*

9. *It may be asked: What is the description of the mind and emotions when the creative urges cease? The answer is this: The mind energy and emotional feelings periodically assume of their own accord, a stillness wherein there is no activity. This happens just after an idea or image subsides, and just before another one begins. The interim period may be long or momentary. When this happens impulsively, a yogi has no control over it, but he should still observe it and focus sharply on the blank interval. He should carefully note the location where the idea or image subsides. He should attach his attention to that place in the mind or emotion environment. When practicing however, he should, with attention, suppress any emerging idea or image and hold his mind or emotion in that blank state so that no other idea or image expresses itself.*

10. *When one learns how to use the attention to suppress any emerging idea or image, and to hold the mind and emotions in that blank state, that mastership causes a flow of spiritual peace. Impressions from that restraining activity do enter the memory. Those records of it, aid, and support the yogi, giving him more and more power over the impulsive creative urges.*

11. *When a yogi first gets a foothold on this mastership, he notices a decrease of the various impulsive objectives of the mind and emotions and an increase in the blank duration which occurs between the emergence and the dissolution of ideas.*

12. *The blankness of the mind and emotions is the desired objective for that initial samādhi practice, even though perception will develop later in it.*

13. *By this practice one gets personal experience of the changes, the quality, shape, changing conditions of the various states of matter and the sensual energy. Thus the mental and emotional provinces are clarified and are no longer a muddlement or vague environment. Nor does one confuse oneself with it.*

14. *When the emerging, manifesting, collapsing or not-yet-manifested ideas, images or emotions push back into the mental or emotional energy, and when that energy has a blankness or quiescence, that is the most basic condition.*

15. *But when there is expression of ideas, images or emotional feelings, these are usually different because of the sequential changes in the emotional energy which produces them.*

16. *When the yogi repeatedly pushes back the images or emotions into the mental and emotional energy, he gains access to the deeper layers of the memory, even to those from previous lives and he gains perception of those future possibilities which would be based on past impressions.*

17. *The yogi removes himself from biases which relate to sound and when he can steady his attention on that alone, getting beyond words, sounds and their formation, he makes contact with the object being described by any creature. Thus their different languages do not confuse his perception.*

18. *The yogi gains knowledge of his previous lives by developing direct intuitive perception of the subtle impressions stored in his own or another's memory.*

19. *Though he can know the mental or emotional content of a person, he should not seek to use that skill. Unless he is advised to do so by a senior yogi, he should not exercise that skill.*

20. *The tendency of the memory and imagination, is to check, recheck, create and recreate opinions and conclusions. An advanced yogi eliminates this tendency because it hampers higher yoga. Thus he does not allow his mind to project one idea after another in an endless sequence which entertains or keeps one occupied without any increased control over the emotions.*

21. *When the receptive energy of the subtle body is curbed, the yogi develops a resistance to social contact. This causes him to have some invisibility.*

22. *This imperceptibility may be applied to the other sensual perceptions.*

23. *By applying his attention to current or destined cultural activities, when no other ideas, images or memories occur in the mind, the yogi gains insight into the hereafter, or he may apply his attention to supernatural occurrences which cause his perception of worlds in other dimensions.*

24. *By applying his attention to friendliness within his nature and in the subtle cosmic environment, he develops universal benevolence.*

25. *By applying his attention to strength, personally or generally, he acquires the power of an elephant. This type of application is effective in other aspects.*

26. *When after much practice, a yogi develops the supernatural insight he would, of course, apply it to the force which produces cultural activities. Thus he gets information about what is subtle, concealed and what is remote from him.*

27. *He may apply his supernatural insight to the sun god or the sun planet. Thus knowledge about the solar system is gained.*

28. *From an application to the moon or moon-god, he gets knowledge about the system of stars.*

29. *By application to the Pole Star he can know of the course of the planets and stars.*

30. *By supernaturally focusing on the navel energy-gyrating center, the yogi gets knowledge about the layout of his subtle body.*

31. *By focusing on the gullet, he causes the suppression of appetite.*

32. *By focusing on the kurmanadi nerve which runs from below the gullet down the inner center of the subtle body, he acquires steadiness of his psyche.*

33. *By focusing on the shinning light in the subtle head, he gets views of the perfected beings.*

34. *By focusing on the shining organ of divination in the head of the subtle form, he gets the ability to know all reality.*

35. *By focusing on the causal body in the vicinity of the chest, he gets thorough insight into the cause of the mental and emotional energies.*

36. *Experience in the material world results from the inability to distinguish between the individual spirit and the intelligence energy of material nature, even though they are in fact, very distinct. By complete restraint of the mental and emotional energies while focusing on self-interest distinct from the other concerns, a yogi gets knowledge of the individual spirit.*

37. *From that focus is produced supernatural smelling, tasting, seeing, touching and hearing, through the shining organ of divination*

38. *But those divination skills may prove to be obstacles in advanced yoga practice. But to worldly people they are considered as spectacular powers.*

39. *The entrance into another's body is possible by slackening the cause of bondage to cultural activities, and by knowing the channels which the mental and emotional energies use to entertain and dominate the self.*

40. *By mastery over the air which rises from the throat into the head, in the subtle body, a yogi can cause his gross form to rise over or not have contact, with water, mud or sharp objects.*

41. *By conquest of the digestive force in the gross body, a yogi's subtle form blazes or shines with a fiery glow.*

42. *By special focusing on the hearing sense and space, a yogin develops supernatural and divine hearing.*

43. *By linking the mind to the relationship between the body and the sky and linking the attention to being as light as cotton fluff, a yogi acquires the ability to objectively pass his subtle form through the atmosphere.*

44. *By restraining his response to the mental and emotional energy, which is universal, a yogi achieves the great bodiless state. From that, the great mental darkness which veils subtle light is dissipated.*

45. *By restraining his mind and emotions, while linking the attention to gross forms, real nature, subtle distribution and supersubtle states of matter, a yogi gets conquest over them.*

46. *From the assumption of minuteness and other related mystic skills, come the perfection of the subtle body and the non-obstruction of its functions.*

47. *Beautiful form, charm, mystic force, diamond-like definition come from the perfection of the subtle body. This is attained by mastership of kuṇḍalini yoga.*

48. *From supernatural linkage to sensual grasping, to the form of the sensual energy, to its identifying powers, to its connection instinct and to its actual worth, a yogi acquires conquest over his relation with the sensual energy.*

49. *Subsequently, he progresses into conquest over the influence of subtle matter and over the parting away or dispersion of the mental and emotional forces, having the required swiftness of mind.*

50. *Only when there is distinct discrimination between true perception of material nature and the spiritual personality, does the yogi attain complete disaffection from the same nature and all-applicative intuition to whatever he encounters.*

51. *By a lack of interest, even to that skill, when the cause of that defect is eliminated, the absolute isolation of the self from the lower psyche, is achieved.*

52. *On being invited by a person from the gross or subtle mundane place one would attain, if the body died, a yogi should be non-responsive, not desiring their association and not being fascinated, otherwise that would cause unwanted features of existence to arise again, and he would again take birth in this world or appear in a dimension near to this one, from which he would be transferred here again.*

53. *By supernatural linkage of his attention to the moment in time and to the sequence of moments, the yogi has detailed supernatural information.*

54. *Subsequently, the yogi clearly distinguishes between two similar realities which otherwise, could not be sorted due to lack of definition in terms of their general category, individual characteristic and location.*

55. *Thus the yogin need no longer take recourse to the normal methods of perception and analysis. For him the distinction caused by subtle discrimination is the crossing over or transcending of all subtle and gross mundane objects in all ways they are presented.*

56. *When by mastership of kriyā yoga, there is equal purity between the intelligence energy of material nature and the spirit, then there is total separation from the error-prone, spiritually-misleading mundane psychology.*

Chapter 4

Kaivalya Pāda:

Segregation Accomplished

1. *The mystic skills are demonstrated on the material plane through the various abilities of the varying species of life one may assume. Each species facilitates a particular ability of the subtle body. One may be empowered with a mystic skill by taking drugs which alter the chemistry of a particular form. Skills may be exhibited after pronouncing certain special sounds which affect the constitution of a body. Physical austerities may change a body to make it do what is normally impossible for the particular species. And supernatural linkage of one's mystic attention may affect changes which are unusual for one's body.*

2. *The transformation from one life form to another or from one dimension to another, from one existential status to another, occurs by saturation of the subtle body with the energy from that other species, dimension or status that is to be adopted.*
3. *The motivating force of the subtle material energy, whereby it appears to inspire the yogi to endeavor for liberation, is not used except for the disintegration of impediments, hence it is compared to a farmer who is not the real cause of growth of cultivated plants.*
4. *A yogi is shown how the various parts of his mind and emotions come into existence because of the involuntary application of his sense of identity to the subtle material nature.*
5. *The one mento-emotional energy is that which is very much used in numberless different dispersals of energy, which occur as ideas and images, arising from memory and sense perception.*
6. *In that case, only subtle activities which are produced from linkage to higher realities, are without harmful emotions; for the others are rooted in the subtle material nature, which always affords reversals.*
7. *Due to their effective detachment and their ability to push the emerging ideas and images back into the pad of the mind or the territory of the emotions, the cultural activity of the advanced yogins is neither rewarding nor penalizing, but others have three types of such action.*
8. *Subsequently for those cultural activities of common people, there is development according to corresponding features only, bringing about the manifestation of the tendencies within the mento-emotional energy, which causes harmful emotions to be experienced by them.*
9. *Even though circumstances are separated by status, location and time, still the impressions which form cultural activities and the resulting memories, are of one form and operate on a full time sequence. Thus all who are involved in worldly life meet with unfavorable circumstances and are fatigued by favorable occasions, which endorse the vices which bleed out their sensual energies.*
10. *Those memories and impressions are primeval without a beginning. Hope and desire energies are eternal as well. Thus the proposal which makes sense, recommends a removal of the individual spirit from this unalterable environment.*

11. *The memories, the impressions, the hope and desire energies, exist by what holds them together in terms of what produced them and what they generate, as well as the supportive basis and the lifting influences which reinforce their production. Otherwise, if their causes were not in existence, they would have no register at all. Thus without supernatural perception and action one cannot become freed from their influence. Hence the practice of kriyā yoga is essential.*

12. *There is a true form of the past and future, which is denoted by the different courses of their particular characteristics. And one is subjected to the future unless one escapes from time's dominance.*

13. *The manifestations which are to a greater degree preset, are gross or subtle, all depending on their inherent nature.*

14. *The actual composition of an object is based on the uniqueness of the transformation which produced it, but this can only be viewed supernaturally.*

15. *Because of a difference in the prejudices of the mento-emotional energy of the two persons, separate opinions manifest in their viewing of the very same object.*

16. *An object is not dependent on one person's view of it; otherwise what would happen if it were not being perceived by that viewer? Would it cease to exist? But we find that this is not so.*

17. *An object is known or unknown, all depending on the mood and expectation of the particular mental and emotional energy of the viewer in reference to it. Thus each person must endeavor separately and individually for liberation.*

18. *The operations of the mind and emotions are always conducted by empowerment taken from the governing spirit. This is because of the spirit being a perpetual energy source. However, the spirit is usually bewildered and is entertained by the usage of his powers.*

19. *The separation of the mind and emotions are not self-generated by the mind nor the emotions. For these are only capable of being perceived by a real viewer. It is like a viewing instrument which cannot see for itself even though it is useful to the vision of a human being.*

20. *It cannot by itself execute the focus of itself or something else.*

21. *If it were possible for the mind or emotions to view themselves, then one mind would perceive another mind independently without involvement with a spirit or one emotional reserve would interact with another in the same way. That is not possible. It is an absurd idea.*

22. *The perceptions of a spirit's intellect occurs when the intellect operates to create an image but as soon as the image begins to dissolve, it seems as if the intellect itself vanishes.*

23. *When the mental and emotional forces are quieted, they do not display a prejudiced reaction. Under these conditions, their biases remain dormant. But as soon as there is an activation of the urges, the predispositions are displayed. These are attitudes and responses which were created previously by interactions of the perceiver, his sense energy and what was perceived.*

24. *Although the mind and emotions seem to combine to exhibit habits and unique behaviors, still those exhibitions only entertain the perceiver. It is that seer whose radiant energy causes the activation. The mind and emotions absorb his energy to entertain him.*

25. *When someone can distinguish between himself and his auxiliary shadow-self, his detachment or ability to distance himself from the sensuality, empowers him to push away the creative urges which may arise in his psyche.*

26. *Then a strange but glorious observation is made. One notices that the troublesome and once hard-to-control mind and emotions, begin acting cooperatively, as if to actually please the self and do as told. It exhibits a habit of discrimination, loosing its impulsive tendency, and it gravitates towards total separation from the self, a thing which before it was fearful of.*

27. *However, whenever the self relaxes vigilance, that now-cooperative psychology is again forced into the old behaviors, which were based on the old subtle impressions.*

28. *When the yogi applies an effective method to remove the old impressions, his resulting condition is exactly like that experienced, when the mental and emotional afflictions are no longer actuated.*

29. *The super discrimination, the highest degree of disinterest, is achieved by one who sees no gain in material nature, even in very abstract but potent conditions. Such a person attains an insight whereby he perceives the mento-emotional clouds of energy which dictate the laws of responsibility. Subsequently, he can side-step such obligations.*

30. *Unless instructed by a divine being, he stops the participation of his auxiliary shadow-self, which has the mind and emotions as its chief components. These are restrained from generating further cultural activities. Thus ending potential afflictions.*

31. *Obviously then, the yogin considers his former insights and feelings to be trivial, when compared to his newly-earned visions.*

32. *Thus the subtle material nature having served a useful purpose, its progressive alterations which sometimes perplexed and sometimes entertained the spirit, come to an end.*

33. *The once free and own-way (aniruddha) auxiliary self stops its mental, sensual and emotional dominance, those rhythmic displays which the self was once forced to enjoy or endure.*

34. *When he sheds off the human type of character which was a combination of mentality, sensuality and emotions, he gains a neutrality in reference to the subtle material nature. That separation from his auxiliary self, is established. Thus he discovers his segregated real self, which empowers the auxiliary shadow character*

Part 3

Yoga Sūtras: Verses, Translation and Commentary

Chapter 1

Samādhi Pāda:

Transcendence Accomplishment

Verse 1

अथ योगानुशासनम्॥ १ ॥

atha yogānuśāsanam

atha – now; yogānuśāsanam = yoga – yoga and its practice + ānuśāsanam – explanation

This is the explanation of yoga and its practice.

Commentary:

Śrī Patañjali began by the term *atha* which means now or at this time, I will do something. He took the task of giving the explanation of yoga and its practice, because before this time such an explanation was not laid out in an academic way. He gave the syllabus for yoga, thus breaking the monopoly of all those teachers who mastered yoga and who taught it to their students bit by bit over the years.

Whatever *Śrī Patañjali* would say would be standard. It cannot be changed merely by a difference in philosophy. Just as a gasoline combustion engine manufactured in Japan will be quite similar to one manufactured in Germany, so yoga practice will be the same everywhere, because the human body is the same in each case, and the way of changing the subtle form which produced that gross one is also the same.

Verse 2

योगश्चित्तवृत्तिनिरोधः ॥ २ ॥

yogaḥcittavṛtti nirodhaḥ

yogaḥ – the skill of yoga; cittavṛtti = citta – mento-emotional energy + vṛtti – vibrational mode; nirodhaḥ – cessation, restraint, non-operation.

The skill of yoga is demonstrated by the conscious non-operation of the vibrational modes of the mento-emotional energy.

Commentary:

Yoga is something personal and practical. It is not a group effort. Each student of yoga has to achieve the states all by himself or herself. Thus in a sense, yoga is an isolated and lonely course. This is the reason for the poor response of the public to the call to take up hard-core yoga austerities. People like company but yoga requires the company of one's self only. One must work with one's psyche only to be successful in yoga.

There were many attempts to translate the word chitta. Some say it is the mind, some say it is the energy in the mind. Some say it is the consciousness. These terms, though accurate to a degree bring with them a certain vagueness which covers the meaning even more.

To understand chitta we have to consider two aspects, those of thinking and feeling. Whatever energy is used for thinking is chitta, and whatever is used for feeling is chitta. It is chitta through which we think and feel. To understand chitta one has to become concerned with psychological locations. Where does your thinking take place? When a thought arises in which energy is it illustrated in the mind? When you have an emotional response to something real or imaginary, in which part of your psyche does that take place? What sort of energy is used to develop and transmit emotion? Whatever correct answer one would give to any of these questions would identify the chitta energy. Chitta is the mento-emotional energy in which our thoughts are formed and are disintegrated. It is the energy in which our feelings are formed and in which the same feelings subside to nothingness.

By convention it is discovered that the vibrational energy of the mind always keeps moving in one way or the other. Thus some spiritual masters conclude that it would be impossible to comply with this stipulation of *Patañjali* for the non-operation of the mento-emotional force in the psyche. They have dismissed *Patañjali* as being an impractical theorist. The solution they say is to engage the mind in spiritual topics, never giving it the chance to dwell on ordinary subjects, which are apart from the transcendence. However, human convention is not everything. When a yogin gets experience beyond the dimension of this world, he can afford to heed *Patañjali*, and strive for the non-operation of the mental-emotional force in this dimension of consciousness. Somehow by his own endeavor and by divine grace, a yogin's mento-emotional force becomes stilled. It stalls for a time and turns into a divine vision which perceives the chit akasha, the sky of consciousness, the world known otherwise as akshardam, brahma and vaikuṇṭha. When this happens, the yogi understands what *Śrī Patañjali* explained in this verse 2 of his *sūtras*.

Śrīla Yogeshwarananda *Yogirāja* indicated that *Śrī Patañjali* should not have suggested that it was possible to completely quiet the mento-emotional force, for indeed, it is not possible to stop it from vibrating altogether, but rather one may quiet it in one dimension while it continues to operate in another. It cannot be quieted in all of its phases because even after the dissolution of the universe, the *prāṇa*, or subtle mundane energy keeps shifting quietly for many millions of years. This slight movement, might in reference, be considered to be static but it does have a vibrational consistency.

Verse 3

तदा द्रष्टुः स्वरूपेऽवस्थानम्॥ ३॥

tadā draṣṭuḥ svarūpe avasthānam

tadā – then; draṣṭuḥ – the perceiver; svarūpe – in his own form; avasthānam – is situated.

Then the perceiver is situated in his own form.

Commentary:

When the mento-emotional energy has reached the state of quiescence, the perceiver within that energy, experiences himself by himself, alone without those influences. This is the state of *svarūpa*, or his own form.

So long as that mento-emotional energy vibrates actively, the perceiver is not allowed to reflect on himself. He is instead, drawn into concerns other than myself. Thus he responds carelessly since his sense of identity was diverted to something else. *Śrī Patañjali* gave this statement about the situation in the spiritual self, *swarūpe*, to give encouragement and to generate interest in self-realization. After all, if one does not realize one's essential self, one must identify with objects or energies which are not the self.

Verse 4

वृत्तिसारूप्यमितरत्र ॥ ४ ॥

vṛtti sārūpyam itaratra

vṛtti – the mento-emotional energy; sārūpyam – with the same format, conformity; itaratra – at other times.

At other times, there is conformity with the mento-emotional energy.

Commentary:

The perceiver, even though he is different to the mento-emotional energy, is not allowed to show autonomy or independence when that energy is active in its concern for things in this dimension. The perceiver is forced as it were, to conform to the dictates of that mento-emotional force. He is forced to use the same format as the energy irrespective of a deliberate or non-deliberate interest into this dimension and its corresponding higher or lower locales. The perceiver is forced to identify with that ideation energy. It is only when its vibrations cease of their own accord or are suppressed by him or by another force, that he may realize the self.

Verse 5

वृत्तयः पञ्चतय्यः क्लिष्टा अक्लिष्टाः ॥ ५ ॥

vṛttayaḥ pañcatayyaḥ kliṣṭā akliṣṭāḥ

vṛttayaḥ – the vibrations in mento-emotional energy; pañcatayyaḥ – fivefold; kliṣṭākliṣṭāḥ = kliṣṭā – agonizing + akliṣṭāḥ – non-troublesome.

The vibrations in the mento-emotional energy are five-fold, being agonizing or non-troublesome.

Commentary:

Śrī Patañjali has not given a middle designation or a mixed status for the mento-emotional vibrations. He simply stated that there were five types of these vibrations; some causing agony and some which are not troublesome. This is to be realized in mystic yoga practice so that the yogi becomes expert at recognizing the various moods of his mind and emotions. An ignorance of the operations of the mental and emotional energy, will cause the self to trail behind the mental and emotional moods. This will invariably lead to haphazard rebirths and responsibility for wreckless acts. Ignorance of one's psychology and of how it operates, is costly to the living entity.

As stated in the second verse of these *sūtras*, the skill of yoga is demonstrated by non-vibration of the mento-emotional energies. When the yogi ceases the vibrations, the energy converts into being a supernatural vision with which he sees into the chit akash, the sky of consciousness, the spiritual environment. The yogin was given the chitta energy for that purpose but due to his ineptness he was not able to use it appropriately. Instead it served him for imagining and analyzing mundane energy. *Śrī Patañjali* will tell us something more about the five vibrationial modes of the mental and emotional energy.

Verse 6

प्रमाणविपर्ययविकल्पनिद्रास्मृतयः ॥ ६ ॥

pramāṇa viparyaya vikalpa nidrā smṛtayaḥ

pramāṇa – correct perception; viparyaya – incorrect perception; vikalpa – imagination; nidrā – sleep; smṛtayaḥ – memory.

They are correct perception, incorrect perception, imagination, sleep and memory.

Commentary:

This means that we have to recognize five kinds of vibrational activities of the mento-emotional energy. According to *Śrī Patañjali* whatever occurs in the mental and emotional energy must be one of a combination of the five vibrations. A yogin should know these thoroughly. If one does not understand the workings of his mind and feelings, he cannot become liberated. One cannot become liberated from an ignorance of these.

We are endowed with the mento-emotional energy and it is restricted to those five kinds of vibrations which produce either correct perception, false perception, imagination, sleep and memory. All these psychological functions occur in the chitta energy. That is its capability when focused into this dimension. The problem with this is that the living entity cannot always be in a position to know what is taking place within his own mind and emotions. In most persons, the operations occur faster than the entity is able to perceive. Thus the entity sees the conclusions or feels such conclusions and does not understand what is taking place until after it has occurred or until after he or she has reacted beneficially or unbeneficially to them.

Let us take for example the operation of sleep. One may fall asleep and not know it until after the sleep mode has terminated. A man for instance, who drives a car in a tired state, would realize that he fell asleep at the wheel after his car had crashed into a tree and he awoke in a badly damaged body in a hospital. The operations are impulsively performed in the mind and emotions. This impulsiveness is a handicap for the living entity.

Now I will discuss these five operations one by one:

Correct Perception:

The most interesting feature of this operation is our dependence upon it. The question arises as to why we need a psychological tool for correct perception. Why is it that we could not perceive reality without having to use the mento-emotional energy? The question is this: If as this *sūtra* indicates, we are dependent on the correct perception vibrational mode of the mind, then how can we restrict the energy so that it does not shift into the mode which gives us incorrect perception or unrealistic imagination? As we consider these *sūtras*, we will see if *Śrī Patañjali* dealt with these questions. Otherwise each yogi will have to get answers from another authority and from his own valid research.

The only thing we know for certain is this: the mento-emotional energy is capable of five kinds of operations. Furthermore, normally we do not control this, but rather this happens reflexively. What yoga process gives us the ability to control this either absolutely or partially?

Incorrect Perception:

The problem with false perception is that within the energy itself, there is a tendency not to recognize the vibrations which cause false perception, but rather to try to correct such perception by various haphazard applications. Therefore we have to train the psychology in a different way, in a totally new way, so that it becomes concerned only with recognizing the vibrational state from which false perceptions are derived. This means that we have to advance to higher yoga in *dhāraṇā* linkage of the mind to higher concentration forces.

It is not false perceptions that are the problem but rather the vibrations in the energy which cause the wrong views in the first place. We have to strive to recognize these vibrations and to stop them, so that the mind may function only with the vibrations which produce correct or true perceptions. This will take repeated practice, because the vibrations which produce false perceptions are naturally occurring. It is not a matter of suppressing these undesirable vibrations, even though a yogi will have to suppress them from time to time. It is rather a feat for the yogi to cause the mind and feelings not to vibrate in that way. This would require a mastership of *prāṇāyāma* and a strong development of vigilance and acute dispassion. These aspects will be discussed in detail elsewhere in this commentary. It is mentioned by *Śrī Patañjali*.

SPECIAL NOTE:

Two persons in particular requested that I write this translation and commentary of Śrī Patañjali Muni's Yoga Sūtras. Those persons are Srila Yogeshwaranand Yogirāja who has departed from his physical body and Sir Paul Castagna, who to this date (Jan. 2003) still uses a physical form. Srila Yogeshwarananda, thought that I was duty bound to write such a translation and commentary and that it would benefit me. Sir Paul Castagna thought that I would further break open the meaning of the sūtras. In any case I now thank these two individuals for their pushing and tugging.

Śrī Patañjali Maharshi is not an ordinary person. And though I was reluctant to translate and comment on this classic work on yoga and its practice, still I benefited from this task which my teacher Srila Yogeshwarananda and my colleague Sir Paul Castagna motivated me to begin and complete.

Imagination:

The curbing of the imagination faculty is the key to a successful *dhāraṇā* practice. This *dhāraṇā* is the sixth stage of yoga, that of linking the attention to a higher concentration force. The process of willful non-operation of the vibrational capacity of the mento-emotional energy has to do with curbing the impulsive nature of the imagination faculty of the buddhi organ in the head of the subtle body. Hence the checking of the impulsive operation of this faculty is the key to mastery of the *dhāraṇā* practice.

Śrī Krishna told Arjuna that for those living entities who are embodied, this technique is hard to attain:

kleśo 'dhikataras teṣām avyaktāsakta-cetasām

avyaktā hi gatir duḥkhaṃ dehavadbhir avāpyate

The mental exertion of those whose minds are attached to the invisible existence is greater. The goal of reaching that invisible reality is attained with difficulty by the human beings. (Gītā 12.5)

For a person who is used to gross and subtle mundane objects and who is sensually inclined to enjoying such objects, a preliminary procedure is given by the yogi masters. This is the process of focusing on sanctified objects in this world. After some time when the student develops detachment from this world, he is introduced to the method of directly shifting his attention from this world to the chit akash, the sky of consciousness. This begins with the naad sound *kriyā* which was given to Uddhava in the eleventh canto of *Śrīmad Bhāgavatam*:

hṛdy avicchinnam oṁkāram ghaṇṭā-nādaṁ bisorṇa-vat

prāṇenodīrya tatrātha punaḥ samveśayet svaram

In the heart chakra, the Oṁ sound which is like the continuous peal of a bell, resonates continually, like a fibre in a lotus stalk. Raising it by using the vitalizing energy, one should blend that sound with the musical tones. ((Śrīmad Bhāgavatam 11.14.34)

When the imagination faculty is fully curbed, it develops into the eye of consciousness, which is called *jnāña* chaksus or *jnāña* dipah. When this eye opens one sees into the chit akash, the sky of consciousness. When one is steady in using this eye, one's spiritual life is sealed. That is an objective of yoga practice.

Sleep:

The vibration of sleep cannot be eliminated altogether but its negative aspects may be curtailed by a yogin through mastery of *prāṇāyāma* and expertise in the *dhāraṇā* linkage of the attention to higher concentration forces. According to *Śrīla* Yogeshwarananda, sleep is a permanent requirement for the subtle and causal forms. These bodies require sleep for rejuvenation. Even the cosmic god, the Hiranyagarbha personality, has to sleep from time to time, thus shutting down his energies which flow into this material world.

However, a yogin should curtail the negative aspects of sleep by learning how to keep his subtle body fully charged with fresh *prāṇa* and with energies which come in from higher dimensions.

Memory:

The vibration of memory is ever-active and functions automatically on the basis of promptings which come to it from the mento-emotional chamber. Memory circuits are triggered by impressions which arise in the imagination, as well as from the other three vibrational powers of true perception, false perception and sleep. A yogin has to learn how to shut off the automatic switch which causes the memory to be activated. If he fails to do this, he will be unable to reach the stage of *samādhi* which is the highest level of yoga practice.

Verse 7

प्रत्यक्षानुमानागमाः प्रमाणानि ॥ ७ ॥

pratyakṣa anumāna āgamāḥ pramāṇāni

pratyakṣanumānāgamāḥ = pratyakṣa – direct but correct perception + anumāna – correct analysis + āgamāḥ – correct reference; pramāṇāni – true perception, correct perception.

Correct perception may be acquired directly, by correct analysis or by correct reference.

Commentary:

Even though this is obvious, *Śrī Patañjali* alerts us in this verse, that we have to learn how to recognize when our intellect functions in this mode of operation. Everyone understands that when false information is used there will be incorrect conclusions. Analysis, when applied to false information, results in false conclusion, which leads to incorrect insight. It is the same with reference. A reference may be the wrong one, or it may be inaccurate, hence the use of it will lead to false conclusions. Direct perception may be incorrect. *Pratyakṣa* is a combination of prati and akshah, but aksha means perception. When that perception is correct, it is prati-aksha, *pratyakṣa* . For true perception a yogin must have an accurate intellect and also have accurate information from outside his intellect. It is not just reliant on his intellect. It is reliant on getting accurate information outside the intellect. However, if the yogin's intellect is sufficiently surcharged with higher concentration forces, he will recognize the incorrect and unreliable information. He will not use such information to produce wrong conclusions. A yogi must be in the right position to get the right information. This is achieved by mystic maneuvers. This all means that there is more for accurate perception; more is required besides the purity of the psyche of the yogi. He has to get himself into a position from which he can use his accurate buddhi organ to perceive correctly.

An astronomer may have an accurate telescope but still he cannot take an accurate reading on a very cloudy night unless he can go beyond the cloud formations. He has to put himself in the proper positions to use the accurate instrument. Correct perception may be acquired directly only if the yogin has a reality-perceiving intellect and is in the proper position to use it.

Correct perception can be acquired directly by insight developed by correct analysis after getting some facts but this is solidified only after the yogin can take that analysis to the point of getting the direct sight of it. Furthermore, by correct reference, a yogin may form certain correct conclusions but that is not sufficient because it is not direct sensual observation. Therefore it is incomplete. He will have to develop himself further to reach the stage of true direct sensual perception of the supernatural and spiritual realities.

Finally, a yogin has to develop himself in such a way as to sort out the various true and erroneous perceptions of his intellect. Then he may suppress and gradually eliminate the faulty parts and the motivations which support defective perception.

Verse 8

विपर्ययो मिथ्याज्ञानमतद्रूपप्रतिष्ठम् ॥ ८ ॥

viparyayaḥ mithyājñānam atadrūpa pratiṣṭham

viparyayaḥ – incorrect perception; mithyājñānam = mithyā – false + jñānam – information; atadrūpa = atad – not this + rūpa – form; pratiṣṭham – positioned, based.

Incorrect perception is based on false information and on perception of what is not the true form.

Commentary:

The vibrational mode which produces a firm conviction about something that is incorrect is caused by the perception of false information and on perceiving what is not the true form (*atadrūpa*).

The willingness of the buddhi organ in accepting the information given to it by the senses is the root of this problem. The reliance of the buddhi on the sensual energies must be broken by the yogin. This can be achieved by perfecting the *pratyāhār* 5th stage of yoga practice, where the sensual energies are withdrawn from their interest into the subtle and gross mundane world. The strength of the senses which is their ability to keep the buddhi organ under subjugation is based on the extrovert tendencies of the organ. Thus if that tendency is squelched, the senses lose their authority over the organ and it becomes independent of them. This is mastered by *pratyāhār* practice.

The perception of the sensual energies is operated with the energy of fuel of the *prāṇa* which is subtle air. When the yogi practices *prāṇāyāma* and is able to take in a higher grade of *prāṇa*, his senses become purified and they no longer make so many erroneous judgments which they force the buddhi to accept. Thus the yogi becomes freed from incorrect perceptions.

Verse 9

शब्दज्ञानानुपाती वस्तुशून्यो विकल्पः ॥ ९ ॥

śabdajñāna anupātī vastuśūnyaḥ vikalpaḥ

śabdajñāna – written or spoken information; anupātī – followed by; vastuśūnyaḥ – devoid of reality, without reality; vikalpaḥ – imagination.

Verbal or written information, which is followed by concepts which are devoid of reality, is imagination.

Commentary:

It is important to understand that the same imagination faculty which can mislead the living entity or cause him to come to the wrong conclusion, is the very same psychic organ which he must use to see into the superphysical world. Even though *Śrī Patañjali* listed only five modes of operation for this tool, still, when it is shifted off from this world it can be used for superphysical perceptions. Therefore it can be used in the mode of correct perceptions for spiritual insights.

When it is used as motivated by false verbal or written information, it develops ideas, conceptions and the like, which cause an imagination which has no basis in reality. But since the living entity is dependent on it, he accepts its picturizations, sounds and impressions as if such notions were a reality. Thus he makes mistakes. He has to learn to recognize when his buddhi organ has adopted a submissive acceptance of incorrect information.

Verse 10

अभावप्रत्ययालम्बना वृत्तिर्निद्रा ॥ १० ॥

abhāva pratyayaḥ ālambanā vṛttiḥ nidrā

abhāva – absence of awareness; pratyayaḥ – conviction or belief as mental content; ālambanā – support, prop, means of conversion; vṛttiḥ – vibrational mode; nidrā – sleep.

Sleep is the vibrational mode which is supported by the absence of objective awareness.

Commentary:

There are various types of sleep but the true sleep is when the mind has no content, such that one feels as if one was barely existing during the sleep. This is realized not during that state but after it. During such sleep the living entity becomes disconnected from his buddhi organ. But when he is connected to it again, he realizes that he was barely connected to his discrimination and sense of objectivity.

We may consider that the *vṛttis* or vibrational modes of the mental and emotional energy are fivefold in normal consciousness. It is like a car which has a set of five gears, with a neutral function. The reverse function is comparable to the operational mode of memory. Memory has to do with recalling something from the past. The other modes or gears are all forward vibrations, which *Śrī Patañjali* gave as correct perception, false perception, imagination, and sleep.

Verse 11

अनुभूतविषयासम्प्रमोषः स्मृतिः ॥ ११ ॥

anubhūta viṣaya asaṁpramoṣaḥ smṛtiḥ

anubhūta – the experience; viṣaya – the object; asaṁpramoṣaḥ – retention; smṛtiḥ – memory.

Memory is the retained impression of experienced objects.

Commentary:

Memory has to do with the past and therefore it might be compared to the reverse gear in an automobile. In reverse, the driver travels on the path traversed before. Memory must be curbed by a yogin, because otherwise he would never be free from the mental impressions which have formed in his conscious and subconscious mind. These impressions vent themselves into the conscious mind and are appropriated by the buddhi intellect organ for usages in further imaginations, which lead to actions of interference in the material world. This interference brings on liabilities for which the yogin is held responsible. If one does not quell, or quiet off completely the memory and disconnect from it, he cannot become liberated. Thus a yogin has to get a method for neutralizing this function in the mento-emotional energy.

Verse 12

अभ्यासवैराग्याभ्यां तन्निरोधः ॥ १२ ॥

abhyāsa vairāgyābhyāṁ tannirodhaḥ

abhyāsa – effective yoga practice; vairāgyābhyāṁ = non-interest, a total lack of concern, non-interference; tan = tat – that; nirodhaḥ – cessation, restraint, non-operation.

That non-operation of the vibrational modes is achieved by effective practice in not having an interest in the very same operations.

Commentary:

Śrī Patañjali Mahamuni *Yogirāja* gave me a hint regarding this verse. By telepathy he sent this clarification:

"Those who are advanced should continue practicing with firm faith so that their connection with the lower operational modes of the mental and emotional energies decreases daily. They need not read any more of these sūtras which I wrote down so long ago.

"However those who are not so advanced should read further and take hints according to their particular progressions. In this verse twelve, these sūtras are concluded, but dull students need to hear more from the teacher. They should listen to more of the verses. This book ends in this verse twelve for those who are advanced, but others should read on for more hints on practice."

To wipe out one's connection with the *vṛttis* or the operational modes, we need to be detached from the very same operations or modes. That is all we need to do. However, for those of us who are not so advanced we need to hear more. Basically speaking we have to enter into the neutral mode and from there into higher concentration energies which cause sensual perception into the chit akash, the sky of consciousness.

Vairāgya has come to be translated as detachment or non-attachment. However it is more than that. It is a total lack of interest and an attitude of non-interference in cultural activities. One gets hints about this as one progresses in yoga. One is shown the way by other great yogins like *Śrī Patañjali*.

Verse 13

तत्र स्थितौ यत्नोऽभ्यासः ॥ १३ ॥

tatra sthitau yatnaḥ abhyāsaḥ

tatra – there, in that case; sthitau – regarding steadiness or persistence; yatnaḥ – endeavor; abhyāsaḥ – practice.

In that case, practice is the persistent endeavor (to cultivate that lack of interest).

Commentary:

The related practice is hereby defined. It must be persistent and requires endeavor (*yatnaḥ*). One has to cultivate that lack of interest because by nature, the mind and emotions are extroverted and have self-conceited mentality. The self-conceited mentality is used to enjoy privately in the psychology in a perverted and harmful way. All this must be curbed effectively.

Verse 14

स तु दीर्घकालनैरन्तर्यसत्कारासेवितो दृढभूमिः ॥ १४ ॥

sa tu dīrghakāla nairantarya
satkāra āsevitaḥ dṛḍhabhūmiḥ

sa = sah – that; tu – but; dīrgha – long; kāla – time; nairantarya – uninterrupted, continuous; satkāra – reverence, care, attention; āsevitaḥ – sustained practice, aggressive interest; dṛḍha – firm; bhūmiḥ – ground, foundation, basis.

But that is attained on the firm basis of a continuous reverential sustained practice which is executed for a long time.

Commentary:

What was acquired over millions and millions of births will take some time for its removal from the psyche. It will not go away overnight. Thus this yoga course is not the same as the easy paths of salvation.

Verse 15

दृष्टानुश्रविकविषयवितृष्णस्य वशीकारसञ्ज्ञा वैराग्यम्॥ १५॥

dṛṣṭa ānuśravika viṣaya vitṛṣṇasya
vaśīkārasaṁjñā vairāgyam

dṛṣṭa – what is seen or perceived directly; ānuśravika – what is conjectured on the basis of scripture or valid testimony; viṣaya – an attractive object; vitṛṣṇasya – of one who does not crave; vaśīkāra – through control; saṁjñā – consciousness, demeanor, mind-set; vairāgyam – non-interest.

The non-interest in the operations of the mento-emotional energy is achieved by one who has perfect mastery in consciousness and who does not crave for what is perceived or what is heard of in the mundane existence.

Commentary:

To silence the mento-emotional energy one has to stop craving the subtle and gross existence. Any craving triggers a renewed interest in this world and its activities. That activates the five vibrational operations, which were listed before as correct perception, incorrect perception, imagination, memory and sleep.

Verse 16

तत्परं पुरुषख्यातेर्गुणवैतृष्ण्यम्॥ १६॥

tatparaṁ puruṣakhyāteḥ guṇavaitṛṣṇyam

tat – that; paraṁ – highest (non-interest); puruṣa – of the spiritual person; khyāteḥ – of a thorough awareness; guṇa – features of material nature; vaitṛṣṇyam – freedom from desire.

That highest non-interest occurs when there is freedom from desire for the features of material nature and thorough awareness of the spiritual person.

Commentary:

This does not come about easily. This is why *Śrī Patañjali* alerted the student yogis that it will take a long time (*dīrgha kāla*) for them to attain success. This cultivation of non-interest is said to be part of *rāja* yoga, but that does not mean that one can get it by avoiding *āsana* and *prāṇāyāma* practice.

Puruṣa, the spiritual personality and *prakṛti*, the gross and subtle material nature, display a liking for one another. It is not an easy task for anyone to nullify this affinity. A complete transformation in the psychology would be required for one to develop the full non-interest in the subtle or gross mundane energy.

Verse 17

वितर्कविचारानन्दास्मितारूपानुगमात्सम्प्रज्ञातः ॥ १७॥

vitarka vicāra ānanda asmitārūpa
anugamāt saṁprajñātaḥ

vitarka – analysis; vicāra – deliberation, reflection; ānanda – introspective happiness; asmitārūpa – I-ness self-consciousness; anugamāt – by accompaniment, occurring with; saṁprajñātaḥ – the observational linkage of the attention to a higher concentration force.

The observational linkage of the attention to a higher concentration force occurs with analysis, reflection and introspective happiness or with focus on self-consciousness.

Commentary:

Suddenly and without warning, *Śrī Patañjali* jumped from the cultivation of non-interest in the mundane world to the observational linkage of the attention to higher concentration force. If a yogin is successful at stopping the ordinary functions of his mento-emotional energies, he will enter a neutral stage from which his attention will be linked to or fused to higher concentration forces in the sky of consciousness, the chit akasha.

In the beginning the yogi will be affected by four other forces from this side of existence. These are the analytical power of the intellect, the reflective mood of it, the introspective happiness which is felt during *pratyāhār* sensual withdrawal practice and the I-ness or self-consciousness which has directed the attention to be linked to the higher concentration force.

Some other commentators categorized *saṁprajñāta* as a type of *samādhi*. In other words it has come down in the yogic disciplic succession that *saṁprajñātaḥ* is a type of *samādhi* or a lower stage of the eighth and final level of yoga practice. However, this writer wants to inform readers that *saṁprajñāta* is part of *dhāraṇā* practice which is the sixth stage of yoga. In that stage the linkage is deliberate and is done by the yogi by the mystic force applied. In the next stage, that of *dhyāna*, the yogi is able to realize his sense of identity and its forceful application. He finds that his will power is drawn into the higher concentration force of it's own accord. In the eighth stage, that of *samādhi*, his will is not only effortlessly drawn but it is continually pulled like that for a long time, for over half hour or so.

In the stage of *samādhi*, he loses himself more and more, because he does not have to exert his will or deliberation. Thus he becomes relaxed. His mystic power loses tension and application because it is effortlessly pulled into and fused to the higher concentration force.

In the *saṁprajñāta* observational linkage, the yogin sometimes finds that he must analyze what he is linked to. This is preliminary. All yogis go through these stages one by one as they progress and one does not move from lower to a higher stage until one has integrated the lower progression. At first when the deliberate linkage occurs, there is an analysis of what one is linked to, as to what level it is on and as to its value, as to what it will evolve into and as to the extent of transcendence.

After this one reflects on it, for the purpose of integrating it fully for the sake of being able to explain it to others at a later date. Many of the writings of this writer were made on the basis of due reflection in this stage. It is for the integration of the writer himself and use later on in teaching and explaining. After one advanced beyond this, one reaches a stage of introspective happiness. This is due to full *pratyāhār* when one loses interest in others and totally pulls in all sensual energies and is able to direct oneself purely without looking back for others.

When this stage is completed, one reaches a stage of self-awareness in feeling the limits of one's spiritual radiation. At this stage one links up with the cosmic buddhi and the cosmic sense of identity, which are bright lights on the supernatural planes of existence. This causes an enrichment of one's personality and a surcharging of one's spirituality. If one is not careful at this stage, one may attract many disciples, thus bring one's spiritual practice to an end.

Student yogins must remember that *saṁprajñāta* absorption is observational. That is its flaw. However it is part of the course of development. One must perform it and do so carefully so that one can reach a higher stage. On any stairway, some steps might be slippery, some might be rough, some might have partial treaders, but regardless on has to use all of them if one is to go higher. Thus one should not feel that he can bypass the *saṁprajñāta* stage of absorption. If one completes it properly one will progress upward without having to come down again.

Verse 18

विरामप्रत्ययाभ्यासपूर्वः संस्कारशेषोऽन्यः ॥ १८ ॥

virāmapratyayaḥ abhyāsapūrvaḥ
saṁskāraśeṣaḥ anyaḥ

virāma – losing track of, dropping; pratyayaḥ – objective awareness, opinions and motives of mind content; abhyāsa – practice; pūrvaḥ – previous, before; saṁskāraśeṣaḥ = saṁskāra – impression in the mento-emotional energy + śeṣaḥ – what is remaining; anyaḥ – other.

The other state is the complete departure from the level where the remaining impressions lie in the mento-emotional energy.

Commentary:

The previous practice of losing track of one's opinions and motives, results in the other state which is awareness of remaining impressions left in the mento-emotional energy.

Most commentators agree that this is the stage of *asaṁprajñāta samādhi* or a state of fusion to a higher plane without maintaining any opinions or motivations.

Provided that one has had a previous practice of repeatedly losing track of one's opinions and motivations, one can attain this other state in which there is awareness of the remaining impressions in their seed form as they exist in the mind compartment and in the emotions. The yogi must repeatedly practice to attain this, as *Śrī Patañjali* told us of the long practice (*dīrgha kāla*) required. In this state there is no foothold on any form or forms, and therefore the yogi has to be very determined, patient and persistent.

Verse 19

भवप्रत्ययो विदेहप्रकृतिलयानाम्॥ १९॥

bhavapratyayaḥ videha prakṛtilayānām

bhava – inherent nature, psychology; pratyayaḥ – mental content, objective awareness; videha – bodiless persons; prakṛtilayānām – of those who are diffused into subtle material nature.

Of those who are diffused into subtle material nature and those who exist in a bodiless state, their psychology has that content.

Commentary:

This is another jolt put to us by *Śrī Patañjali*, as he explained why one yogi gets a certain advancement, which is different from another and why without any current practice, some persons attain the benefits of yoga. In this case, those who are diffused into the subtle material nature without any effort on their part, without endeavor, are able to do so because of their inherent nature. A question remains as to whether this is the inherent nature of the spirit or of the psyche which is allied to it.

Śrī Patañjali answered that question by throwing at us the word *pratyayaḥ*, which means their mental content, the psychological make-up. However, even though it is not their spirits, still they have to adhere to that nature.

Certain other individuals attain the bodiless state and remain in material nature. They sometimes take birth but are unable to remain tied down to a material body due to their inherent tendency to be bodiless.

Bengali Baba, in his commentary on these *sūtras* stated that the *videhas*, the bodiless ones, are the persons who after performing virtuous actions such as Agnihotra ceremonies of the Vedas, attain the state of freedom, which is similar to absoluteness. He referred to Māṇḍukopaniṣad, Chapter 2 Part 1. He wrote that they are not to return to human life but they will become presiding officers in future creations. He cited King Suratha who will be the eighth Manu after the reign of the current Manu who is Vaivasvata.

Such persons attain a permanent status as small-time gods of these worlds. They have no need at all to take a gross body. They either use a subtle body or no type of material body at all, but their energy affects this creation.

Verse 20

श्रद्धावीर्यस्मृतिसमाधिप्रज्ञापूर्वक इतरेषाम्॥ २०॥

śraddhā vīrya smṛti samādhiprajñā
pūrvakaḥ itareṣām

śraddhā – confidence; vīrya – vigor, stamina; smṛti – introspective memory; samādhi – continuous effortless linkage of the attention to a higher concentration force; prajñā – profound insight; pūrvakaḥ – previously practiced; itareṣām – for others.

For others, confidence, stamina, introspective memory, the continuous effortless linkage of the attention to a higher concentration force, and profound insight, all being previously mastered, serve as the cause.

Commentary:

These are the requirements for those who want full success in attaining what *Śrī Patañjali* described in the second *sūtra*.

yogaḥ cittavṛtti nirodhaḥ

The skill of yoga is demonstrated by the conscious non-operation of the vibrational modes of the mento-emotional energy. (Yoga Sūtra 1:2)

One must have confidence in the practice of yoga and be satisfied with it to such an extent that one becomes attached to it above everything else and will do it to completion. If one does not have such confidence one will be stalled at the lower stages, one will give up the practice and take a position here or there in the material world, or one might become detached from gross existence but remain attached to subtle mundane life.

One must have stamina which arises with sufficient vigor to spur one to practice. There are many energies which contravene, or undermine yoga practice. If one does not have the stamina, one will be influenced by a negative force and will give up the practice.

One must practice *samādhi* repeatedly. *Samādhi* is the continuous effortless linkage of the attention to any of the higher concentration forces, which a yogi experiences. He must practice repeatedly.

The yogin must have profound insight gained through development of the buddhi intellect organ which sees beyond the material world into the superphysical planes and beyond.

Śrī Patañjali though acknowledging those persons who are natural mystics, wrote these *sūtras* expressively for those yogis who are endeavoring with such stamina that they will adhere to yoga, life after life until they reach the culmination. There are many people who without any record of yoga practice in their current or perhaps even in their past lives, are able to switch themselves to psychic or supernatural levels. But these persons rely on their inherent nature either to be accustomed to being bodiless, or to being diffused into particular subtle phases of material nature (*prakṛtilāya*).

Verse 21

तीव्रसंवेगानामासन्नः ॥ २१ ॥

tīvrasaṁvegānām āsannaḥ

tīvra – very intense; saṁvegānām – regarding those who practice forcibly; āsannaḥ – whatever is very near, what will occur soon.

For those who practice forcefully in a very intense way, the skill of yoga will be achieved very soon.

Commentary:

Even though *Śrī Patañjali* stated that yoga is attained after a long time, he qualified that statement by saying that it is achieved shortly by those who have intense speedy practice. In fact one cannot conclude yoga practice in any life without intensity and persistence. It is impossible otherwise.

Verse 22

मृदुमध्याधिमात्रत्वात्ततोऽपि विशेषः ॥ २२ ॥

mṛdu madhya adhimātratvāt tataḥ api viśeṣaḥ

mṛdu – slight; madhya – mediocre; adhimātratvāt – from intense; tataḥ – then; api – even; viśeṣaḥ – rating.

Then there are even more ratings, according to intense, mediocre, or slight practice.

Commentary:

Yoga practice yields results according to the intensity of correct practice. One person might practice intensely with the wrong methods. His result will be the realization of the incorrect practice. Another person might practice very little with the correct method but he too might not get the results because his practice does not have much forcefulness.

Śrī Patañjali Maharshi gave four rates. Very intense (*tīvra saṁvega*), intense (*adhimātratvā*), mediocre (*madhya*), and slight (*mṛdu*).

Verse 23

ईश्वरप्रणिधानाद्वा ॥ २३ ॥

īśvara praṇidhānāt vā

īśvara – The Supreme Lord; praṇidhānāt – derived from profound religious meditation; vā – or.

Or by the method of profound religious meditation upon the Supreme Lord.

Commentary:

Śrī Patañjali in an abrupt statement gave an alternative method (*vā* - or), which is the profound religious meditation upon the Supreme Lord. Readers who want to inquire further into the meaning and application of this verse may check on the root words in Sanskrit to find out what that word *praṇidhāna* means. One should first check the root word *dha*, which meant to put, to lay upon, to fix upon, to hold, to contain, to seize. Then check *nidhana*, which means putting down, depositing, or a place where anything is placed. Then check *praṇidhāna*.

This indicates very profound and a deep laying of the mind upon the Supreme Lord. This is very deep meditation. If one can achieve that without doing yoga practice, one would be demonstrating that culmination of yoga, or one would have the mastery of yoga, even without practice.

Verse 24

क्लेशकर्मविपाकाशयैरपरामृष्टः पुरुषविशेष ईश्वरः ॥ २४ ॥

kleśa karma vipāka āśayaiḥ aparāmṛṣṭaḥ
puruṣaviśeṣaḥ Īśvaraḥ

kleśa – affliction, troubles; karma – action; vipāka – developments; āśayaiḥ – by subconscious motivations; aparāmṛṣṭaḥ – unaffected; puruṣa – person; viśeṣaḥ – special; īśvaraḥ – Supreme Lord.

The Supreme Lord is that special person who is not affected by troubles, actions, developments or by subconscious motivations.

Commentary:

Less there be argument about it, *Śrī Patañjali* clarified what he meant by the Supreme Lord, the *īsvara*, as the person who is ever free from all afflictions, actions and developments in the material world and from subconscious motivations. Such a person wherever he may be found, would cause the devotee to enter into the higher consciousness for being free from the normal operations of the mento-emotional energy provided the devotee could do as instructed in the previous verse:

īsvara praṇidhānāt vā

"Or by the method of profound religious meditation upon the Supreme Lord." (Yoga Sūtra 1:23)

Verse 25

तत्र निरतिशयं सर्वज्ञबीजम्॥ २५ ॥

tatra niratiśayaṁ sarvajñabījam

tatra – there, in Him; niratiśayaṁ – unsurpassed; sarvajña – all knowing; bījam – origin.

There, in Him, is found the unsurpassed origin of all knowledge.

Commentary:

This is a further description of the Supreme Lord. *Śrī Patañjali* has carefully not named this Lord as Krishna or Shiva or Brahma, or anyone else. He gave that Lord's special characteristics through which He may be identified.

Verse 26

स पूर्वेषामपि गुरुः कालेनानवच्छेदात्॥ २६ ॥

sa eṣaḥ pūrveṣām api guruḥ kālena anavacchedāt

sa = sah – He; eṣaḥ – this particular person; pūrveṣām – of those before, previous authorities, the ancient teachers; api – even; guruḥ – the spiritual teacher; kālena – by time; anavacchedāt – unconditioned.

He, this particular person being unconditioned by time, is the guru even of the ancient teachers, the previous authorities.

Commentary:

In case there is doubt about this Supreme Person, *Śrī Patañjali* informs us that God is the teacher even of the ancient authorities from before. He is ever-existing and is ever the supreme master and supreme teacher of everyone.

Verse 27

तस्य वाचकः प्रणवः॥ २७॥

tasya vācakaḥ praṇavaḥ

tasya – of him; vācakaḥ – what is denoted or named; praṇavaḥ – the sacred syllable āuṁ (Oṁ).

Of Him, the sacred syllable *āuṁ* (*Oṁ*) is the designation.

Commentary:

Oṁ is the standard designation given to the Supreme Being by the Vedic sages, who went beyond this world before. In the *Bhagavad-gītā*, *Śrī* Krishna identified Himself with this *āuṁ* (*Oṁ*).

Verse 28

तज्जपस्तदर्थभावनम्॥ २८॥

tajjapaḥ tadarthabhāvanam

taj = tat – that sound; japaḥ – murmuring; tadarthabhāvanam = tat = that + artha – value + bhāvanam – with deep feelings.

That sound is repeated, murmured constantly for realizing its meaning.

Commentary:

A whimsical repitition of *āuṁ* (*Oṁ*) will not serve the purpose. The japa murmuring has to be done with deep feeling and intense concentration. This leads into a deeper state of mind and to a quietude in which reverberates the sounds which come in from the supernatural world. These sounds are the actual *āuṁ* (*Oṁ*) and the yogi recognizes them after purifying his mento-emotional energy through *prāṇāyāma* and a lack of interest in the material world.

A key factor is to disengage the gears of memory from the engine of the buddhi organ. For so long as the memory runs on automatically, the yogi cannot be free from the chatter and picturizations of the mind. Thus he will not experience what comes from the supernatural and spiritual world.

Verse 29

ततः प्रत्यक्चेतनाधिगमोऽप्यन्तरायाभावश्च॥ २९॥

tataḥ pratyakcetana adhigamaḥ api
antarāya abhāvaḥ ca

tataḥ – thence, what is resulting; pratyak – backwards, inwards, in the opposite direction; cetana – sense consciousness; adhigamaḥ – accomplishment; api – also; antarāya – obstacle; abhāvaḥ – not existing; ca – and.

As a result there is an inwardness of the sense consciousness and the disappearance of obstacles to progress.

Commentary:

The result of chanting Oṁkara is given here as the attainment of the stage of *pratyak* (*pratyāhāra*), which is the internalization of the sense consciousness. Usually this consciousness courses outward into the subtle and gross material world. If *āuṁ* (*Oṁ*) is repeated properly, one may develop introspection so that the same outward going sense energy turns back and begins to flow inwards.

This causes conservation of psychological energy in the realms of thinking and feeling. Thus the mento-emotional energy is restrained and conserved. The yogi then gets a boost of pranic charge and experiences supernatural and spiritual realities. This leads into *dhāraṇā* practice which is the sixth stage of yoga.

As soon as one has mastered the internalization of the sense consciousness, many obstacles goes away, because one is lifted out of the dimension where such hindrances exist. One transcends them. The obstacles remain for others who have not advanced to that stage.

Verse 30

व्याधिस्त्यानसंशयप्रमादालस्याविरतिभ्रान्तिदर्शनालब्धभूमिकत्वानवस्थितत्वानि

चित्तविक्षेपास्तेऽन्तरायाः॥ ३०॥

vyādhi styāna saṁśaya pramāda ālasya avirati
bhrāntidarśana alabdhabhūmikatva
anavasthitatvāni cittavikṣepaḥ te antarāyāḥ

vyādhi – disease; styāna – idleness; saṁśaya – doubt; pramāda – inattentiveness; ālasya – lack of energy; avirati – proneness to sensuality; bhrāntidarśana – mistaken views; alabdhabhūmikatva – inability to maintain the progress made, not holding the ground (bhumi); anavasthitatvāni – unsteadiness in the progression; cittavikṣepaḥ – scattered mental and emotional energy; te – these; antarāyāḥ – obstacles.

These obstacles are disease, idleness, doubt, inattentiveness, lack of energy and proneness to sensuality, mistaken views, inability to maintain the progress attained, unsteadiness in progression, scattered mental and emotional energy.

Commentary:

Pratyāhār practice which was described in the previous verse as being the main benefit from the murmuring of the *āuṁ* (*Oṁ*) sound, is the turning point in the practice of a yogi. If he masters that, there is really no turning back for him. He will thereafter consolidate the progress. Those who do not master *pratyāhār* are subjected to numerous types of discouragement in yoga practice. It is mainly because they did not master *prāṇāyāma*.

Under a false notion (*bhrāntidarśana*), a neophyte gets an idea that he does not have to do any painstaking strenuous *prāṇāyāma*. Thus he neglects a very important stage and is unable to change out the lower pranic energies in his subtle body.

Let me go over the obstacles one by one.

Disease (*vyādhi*)

Disease is an obstacle to any yogi who acquires a gross body for the practice of yoga. That body is our means of deliverance but if it is unhealthy, our minds and emotions will be disturbed in such a way as to cause us to desist from practice for sometime. However a yogi should be realistic. He is a limited being and he should not expect that his human form will always be free from disease.

Some yogis, the advanced ones, maintain the practice even with disease. This is to maintain the habit of the practice. If one passes on from a diseased body and does not attain liberation, one will carry to the next human body the tendency to do yoga, which will be an asset in the new form. Thus even if there is disease, a yogin should maintain whatever portion of the practice he can do with the diseased form.

One who has passed the seventh stage of yoga, that of *dhyāna*; effortless linkage of the attention to the higher concentration forces, is not put down by disease, but others definitely are. Since one's liberation is reliant on the status of one's human body, one should do as much as possible to protect the body from disease.

Laziness / Idleness (*stāyana*)

By constitution some persons do not have much determination. Their minds are fickle. Such persons come to a yoga class for quick liberation. Without understanding the requirement, they adopt the view that everyone can attain liberation in a jiffy or that a great yogin should be able to liberate everybody.

The truth is that everyone cannot become liberated because by constitution some spirits do not have the gomsha or inner drive to work for liberation.

However a person who is by nature idle-minded might become liberated if his atma or spirit is connected existentially to a great yogin. By proximity to that great yogin, an idle-minded person might become liberated. If a boat has got too small of an engine, then a tug which is a small boat with an overly-powerful engine can pull it along. Similarly if another boat has a large enough engine which is defectively operating, it too can be pulled by a powerful tug. It is a question of how long such a tug would pull the powerless boat. How long can a great yogi drag an idle-minded disciple?

Idle mindedness can be overcome after long long practice, especially in *prāṇāyāma* and *pratyāhār*, which are breath infusion and sensual restraints. It is the outpouring of the sensual energies which cause a person to have a scattered mind. This is why in the last *sūtra*, *Śrī Patañjali* indicated that if one chants the *Oṁkara* one could develop internalization.

Doubt (*saṁśaya*)

Doubt is removed by personal experience of spiritual truths. Such experience comes after persistent practice. Some student yogis are doubtful by instinct. Even after having a few experiences, they remain troubled about the aim of yoga. This stresses their minds and causes them to go slower in the progressions.

A doubtful student will leave the path unless he or she is sustained in the practice by the association of a great yogin.

Inattentiveness (*pramāda*)

This is related to idleness, and is based on innate tendencies having to do with the scattering energies of the mind. It is by mastery of *pratyāhār*, the fifth stage of yoga, that this is achieved. Inattentiveness is a state of mind which is driven by certain types of pranic forces which latch on to a particular living entity. If he or she can change that pranic energy, taking in a more concentrated type, the inattentiveness goes away.

Lack of energy (*ālasya*)

In yoga one has to endeavor. If there is a lack of energy, there will be no progress.

Proneness to sensuality (*avirati*)

This is also driven by the type of pranic energy in the mind. Hence the need for *prāṇāyāma* and *pratyāhār* practice to change the nature of the mind by changing the energy content. The mental and emotional energy which we use has certain inherent capabilities.

Mistaken views (*bhrāntidarśana*)

Mistaken views come about according to the status of the buddhi organ which is used for analyzing. That organ, regardless of its accurate or inaccurate deductions, is prone to receiving information from the senses. The senses in turn accept information in a prejudiced way, depending on the type of sensual energy used and on the basis what come up in the memory circuits. Purification of the buddhi brings about a dismissal of the mistaken views and that process is called buddhi yoga which is described in detail in chapter two and three of the *Bhagavad-gītā*.

One must purify the lifeforce, the *kuṇḍalini* chakra, as well as all parts of the subtle body. One must be celibate by practicing the yoga austerities. Then the buddhi organ assumes a brighter glow and becomes capable to avoiding mistaken views. The sensual energies are purified by *prāṇāyāma* and *pratyāhār* practice.

Not being able to maintain the progress made (*alabdhabhūmikatva*)

A person who takes to yoga and who by association with a great yogi, makes some progress, may not be able to maintain the advancement. He or she might digress into a lower stage after sometime. This is due to the assertion of the lower nature. It is due also to the distractions which come by virtue of the power of the memory. Instead of shedding off previous negative tendencies, the person is motivated by these, because of the probing and prompting of the memory circuits. Thus the person becomes distracted from yoga and is driven to live a life which is similar to the one used by non-yogis. Thus whatever progress is made is lost for the time being, when the lower tendencies take over the psyche and force it to their way of operation.

Unsteadiness in progress (*anavasthitatvāni*)

Unsteadiness in progression occurs because of the force of cultural activities. These acts force their way into the life of an aspiring yogi and cause him to abandon yoga altogether or to see it as being a side feature. When the cultural activities assert themselves as the priority, the yogi is unable to maintain a consistent practice. His progression becomes sporadic and he loses faith in yoga, thinking that it will not give him the results intended.

A yogi in such a position needs to consult with a person who understandings karma yoga as it is taught in the *Bhagavad-gītā* to Arjuna. If one works under the direction of the Universal Form in helping with His duties in karma yoga, then one can ultimately be free from cultural acts, even from those which are enforced in this world by the Universal form of *Śrī* Krishna. But one must be directed by a great yogi or alternately by Lord Shiva, Lord *Balarāma*, or Lord Krishna.

Scattered mental and emotional energy (*cittavikṣepaḥ*)

There is only one way to get rid of the scattered mental and emotional energy. That is the method of *prāṇāyāma* and *pratyāhār* practice. *Pratyāhār* practice causes one not to need much association from others because by it one conserves the sensual powers and enriches oneself being less and less dependent on whimsical social associations. *Prāṇāyāma* practice makes the yogin see that it is possible to change out the lower pranic energies in the psyche for higher ones which accelerate yoga.

Verse 31

दुःखदौर्मनस्याङ्गमेजयत्वश्वासप्रश्वासा विक्षेपसहभुवः ॥ ३१ ॥

duḥkha daurmanasya aṅgamejayatva
śvāsapraśvāsāḥ vikṣepa sahabhuvaḥ

duḥkha – distress; daurmanasya – of mental depression; aṅgamejayatva – nervousness of the body; śvāsapraśvāsāḥ – labored breathing; vikṣepa – distraction; sahabhuvaḥ – occurring with the symptoms.

Distress, depression, nervousness and labored breathing are the symptoms of a distracted state of mind.

Commentary:

Physical distress, mental distress, emotional distress causing nervousness of the body and labored breathing, occur as symptoms of a distracted mind. These manifest in old age as a matter of course. To decrease these occurances consistent *āsana* and *prāṇāyāma* practice is required.

These distractions and the obstacles mentioned in the previous verse must be avoided by a yogin. He must recognize how these come about and stay away from their causes. He must know how to side-step the human association which bring on or aggravates these.

Verse 32

तत्प्रतिषेधार्थमेकतत्त्वाभ्यासः ॥ ३२ ॥

tatpratiṣedhārtham ekatattva abhyāsaḥ

tat – that; pratiṣedha – removal; ārtham – for the sake of; eka – one; tattva – standard method in pursuit of reality (tattva); abhyāsaḥ – practice.

For the removal of the obstacles, there should be the practice of a standard method used in the pursuit of the reality.

Commentary:

One has no alternative but to practise, using methods which yogis in the past were successful in applying. Each yogin has to use a method that applies to his state of development. In the *Bhagavad-gītā* also there is a similar statement about the practice:

śrī-bhagavān uvāca asaṁśayaṁ mahā-bāho mano durnigrahaṁ
calam abhyāsena tu kaunteya vairāgyeṇa ca gṛhyate

The Blessed Lord said: Undoubtedly, O powerful man, the mind is difficult to control. It is unsteady. By practice, however, O son of Kunti, by indifference to its responses, also, it is restrained. (Gīta 6.35)

Verse 33

मैत्रीकरुणामुदितोपेक्षाणां सुखदुःखपुण्यापुण्यविषयाणां भावनातश्चित्तप्रसादनम् ॥ ३३ ॥

maitrī karuṇā muditā upekṣāṇāṁ
sukha duḥkha puṇya apuṇya
viṣayāṇāṁ bhāvanātaḥ cittaprasādanam

maitrī – friendliness; karuṇā – compassion; muditā – joyfulness, cheerfulness; upekṣaṇam – indifference, neutrality, non-responsiveness; sukha – happiness; duḥkha – distress; puṇya – virtue; apuṇya – vice; viṣayāṇāṁ – relating to attractive objects; bhāvanātaḥ – abstract meditation; citta – mento-emotional energy; prasādanam – serenity.

The abstract meditation resulting from the serenity of the mento-emotional energy comes about by friendliness, compassion, cheerfulness and non-responsiveness to happiness, distress, virtue and vice;

Commentary:

This reverts back to the second verse where the skill of yoga is defined:

yogaḥ cittavṛtti nirodhaḥ

"The skill of yoga is demonstrated by the conscious non-operation of the vibrational modes of the mento-emotional energy." (Y. S. 1:2)

The turbulence in the mental and emotional energies cause the living entity to be unsettled in the material creation and to strive after that which is temporary. This causes stress and ends in frustration, because the temporary manifested energy always changes either in a favorable or unfavorable way.

For stability of that energy, one has to practise yoga for a long time, but most persons are disinclined to the austerities and do not regard yoga as the priority. This is because they are given over to the sensual energies and the promises transmitted to them by such powers, promises that are not to be fulfilled in fact.

By cultivating friendliness, by administering compassion, by maintaining a cheerful demeanor and by an overall attitude of neutrality in non-responsiveness to the movements of the lower energies, the yogin develops serenity of nature, which allows him to practice the abstract meditation through which he is allowed to break away from here and enter into the supernatural and spiritual dimensions.

Verse 34

प्रच्छर्दनविधारणाभ्यां वा प्राणस्य ॥ ३४ ॥

pracchardana vidhāraṇābhyāṁ vā prāṇasya

pracchardana – exhalation; vidhāraṇābhyāṁ – by inhalation; vā – or; prāṇasya – of the vital energy.or by regulating the exhalation and inhalation of the vital energy.

or by regulating the inhalation and exhalation of the vital energy;

Commentary:

This is the practice of *prāṇāyāma*, the fourth stage of yoga practice. This must be learned from a knowlegable yogin who practices and knows the benefits of the methods he teaches. It may be discovered by a few fortunate students of yoga.

Verse 35

विषयवती वा प्रवृत्तिरुत्पन्ना मनसः स्थितिनिबन्धिनी ॥ ३५ ॥

viṣayavatī vā pravṛttiḥ utpannā
manasaḥ sthiti nibandhanī

viṣayavatī – like normal sensuality, something different but similar to a normal object; vā – or; pravṛttiḥ – the operation; utpannā – produced, brought about; manasaḥ – of the mind; sthiti – steadiness; nibandhanī – bond, fusion.

Or fusion and steadiness of the mind is produced by the operation of the mento-emotional energy towards an object which is different to but similar to a normal thing;

Commentary:

This refers to the supernatural and or spiritual perception, which is developed in the psyche of a yogi, especially in his buddhi organ through the curbing of the imagination faculty. Then the yogi sees objects which are not of the gross and subtle material energy but which are superphysical and spiritual. Perceiving such objects brings steadiness of mind and fusion of the attention of the yogi into the higher level of reality, the chit akash.

Viṣaya is a normal sense object of this world, something to which our normal senses are usually attracted to, either for attaching itself or for repulsing itself from. *Vatī* means something that is similar, something like that. Objects in the sky of consciousness are also objects but they do not cause the self to be degraded as the objects in this world do.

The term *pravṛtti* means operation, for active function. Even though the mastership of yoga is to stop the conventional operation of the mental and emotional energies, still this means that they must be stopped on this side of existence. Hence the functioning of that energy for perception of spiritual objects causes the fusion of the mental-emotional force to a higher reality.

Verse 36

विशोका वा ज्योतिष्मती ॥ ३६ ॥

viśokāh vā jyotiṣmatī

viśokāh – sorrowless; vā – or; jyotiṣmatī – spiritually-luminous.

or by sorrowless and spiritually-luminous states;

Commentary:

The experience of various student yogis differ, but the similarity is that the experiences cause them to have faith in the practice of yoga, and it increases their drive for progress. It is not stereotyped. One person might see beyond this physical world into the sky of consciousness. Another might feel a sorrowless energy or experience sheer spiritual light.

Any of these experiences which are valid alternatives to this subtle and gross material existence, will result in the stability of mind required to put a halt to the operations of the mental and emotional energy, thus leading to personal experiences of the transcendence, and to mastership of one's interaction with this material world.

Verse 37

वीतरागविषयं वा चित्तम्॥ ३७॥

vītarāga viṣayaṁ vā cittam

vīta – without; rāga – craving; viṣayaṁ – an object or person; vā – or; cittam – mento-emotional energy.

or by fixing the mento-emotional energy on someone who is without craving;

Commentary:

One may, by association with a great yogi who is free from craving, develop stability to stop the razzy dazzy operations of the mental and emotional energies. Such associations can definitely cause this.

Verse 38

स्वप्ननिद्राज्ञानालम्बनं वा॥ ३८॥

svapna nidrā jñāna ālambanaṁ vā

svapna – dream; nidrā – dreamless sleep; jñāna – information; ālambanaṁ – taking recourse; vā – or.

or by taking recourse to dream or dreamless sleep.

Commentary:

Some yogis gain steadiness of mental and emotional energy by keeping track of their dreams and by remaining objectively conscious in dreamless sleep. Through these mystic observations they study the movements of consciousness and are able to discern reality and non-reality and to situate themselves in the state which is detached from the normal operations of the mental and emotional force. For success in this course a yogi must distance himself from his memory, because its impressions aggravate the instability of the mind and motivate the emotional energies to create picture sensations for further cultural activity in the material world.

Verse 39

यथाभिमतध्यानाद्वा ॥ ३९ ॥

yathābhimata dhyānāt vā

yatha – as, according; ābhimata – what is dearly desired; dhyānāt – from effortless linkage of the mind to a higher concentration force; vā – or.

Or it can be achieved from the effortless linkage of the mind to a higher concentration force which was dearly desired.

Commentary:

This gives the hint that through love and endearment, one may attain the cessation of the undesirable operations of the mental and emotional energy. The process of bhakti or devotion is mentioned in this verse under the term *ābhimata* which means agreeable, beloved and endearing.

Verse 40

परमाणुपरममहत्त्वान्तोऽस्य वशीकारः ॥ ४० ॥

paramāṇu paramamahattvāntaḥ asya vaśīkāraḥ

paramāṇu = parama – smallest + aṇu – atom; parama – greatest; mahattva – largeness, cosmic proportions; āntaḥ – ending, extending to; asya – of his, him; vaśīkāraḥ – mastery of the psyche.

The mastery of the psyche results in control of the relationship to the smallest atom or to cosmic scale.

Commentary:

Some commentators explain that this means the yogi gains control over what is atomic (*aṇu*) and what is cosmic (*mahatva*). However, on a close check of the Sanskrit term *vaśīkāraḥ*, this does not tally with what *Śrī Patañjali* indicated. He means that the yogi is able to control not the atomic and cosmic but rather his relationship to the same. By controlling the forces in his psyche, his psychological energies, he acquires a greater degree of control over his response to what is cosmic and atomic. Those aspects remain the same in the universe he inhabits, but his response to them changes in such a way as to set him in a position of relative immunity to their negative or spiritually detrimental influences. This occurs because of the yogin's detachment, his lack of interest as described in text 12 and 15.

While a human being is almost compelled to react in a preset way to a set of circumstances or to a type of energy, the yogin, because he has switched his energy intake to a higher concentration force, can side-step most influences and remain in an unbiased status as conferred on him by his yoga practice.

Verse 41

क्षीणवृत्तेरभिजातस्येव मणेर्ग्रहीतृग्रहणग्राह्येषु तत्स्थतदञ्जनता समापत्तिः ॥ ४१ ॥

kṣīṇavṛtteḥ abhijātasya iva maṇeḥ grahītṛ
grahaṇa grāhyeṣu tatstha tadañjanatā samāpattiḥ

kṣīṇa – great reduction; vṛtteḥ – concerning the mento-emotional operations; abhijātasya – of what is produced all around or transparent; iva – like; maṇeḥ – of a gem; grahītṛ – perceiver; grahaṇa – flow perception; grāhyeṣu – in what is perceived; tatstha – basis foundation; tad = tat – that; añjanatā – assuming the nature of or characterization of (añj – to smear with, to mix with); samāpattiḥ – linkage fusion.

In regards to the great reduction
of the mento-emotional operations,
there is fusion of the perceiver, the flow of perceptions
and what is perceived,
just like the absorption of a transparent jewel.

Commentary:

This happens also in ordinary experiences, when a person becomes totally preoccupied as it were with gross objects or an endearing feeling. Thus what is so special about a yogin who achieves this after much practice at greatly reducing the impulsive operations of his mento-emotional energy?

There must be a difference in the accomplishment of the yogi. For one thing, the ordinary person is driven impulsively. He has not practiced to stop the automatic operations of his mental and emotional energies. He has no control over the fusion of his consciousness with various forces to which his mind and emotions are impulsively attracted. He does not have the purity in psyche, which the yogi earned by higher yoga practice. The yogin's linkage with higher concentration forces is quite different to the ordinary man's absorption with subtle and gross energy, which is perceived by an impure psyche.

Verse 42

तत्र शब्दार्थज्ञानविकल्पैः सङ्कीर्णा सवितर्का समापत्तिः ॥ ४२ ॥

tatra śabda artha jñāna vikalpaiḥ
saṅkīrṇā savitarkā samāpattiḥ

tatra – there, in that case; śabda – word; artha – meaning; jñāna – knowledge concerning something; vikalpaiḥ – with option, alternative, doubt, uncertainty; saṅkīrṇā – blending together, mixed; savitarkā – thoughtfulness, reasoning, deliberation; samāpattiḥ – fusion, linkage.

In that case, the deliberate linkage
of the mento-emotional energy
to a higher concentrating force occurs when a word, its meaning and the
knowledge of the object
alternate within the mind, blending as they was.

Commentary:

There are various types of linkage between the yogin's partially or fully purified attention and some other person or force. It might be a person or force residing in his psyche or one that is exterior to it. When that linkage occurs with the analytical organ being operative, then it is called deliberative linkage or *savitarkā samāpattiḥ*. *Śrī Patañjali* defined each type of higher linkage to clarify the various levels of accomplishment of a yogi and to remove any vagueness regarding lower accomplishment and higher yoga.

Verse 43

स्मृतिपरिशुद्धौ स्वरूपशून्येवार्थमात्रनिर्भासा निर्वितर्का॥ ४३ ॥

smṛtipariśuddhau svarūpaśūnya iva
arthamātranirbhāsā nirvitarka

smṛti – memory; pariśuddhau – on complete purification; svarūpa – essential nature of something; śunya – devoid of; iva – as if; artha – meaning; mātra – only; nirbhāsā – shining; nirvitarka – fusion or linkage without deliberation or analysis.

Non-analytical linkage of the attention
to a higher concentration force
occurs when the memory is completely purified
and the essential inquiring nature disappears as it were,
so the value of that higher force shines through.

Commentary:

This is a description of what a yogi experiences when he engages in non-analytical linkage of his attention to a higher concentration force with a purified memory and when he finds that the analytical urges of the buddhi organ cease functioning, then he discovers the value of the higher concentration force or person to which he is linked.

Readers should not get frustrated because these are very complicated explanations given by *Śrī Patañjali*. After all, what he describes has to do with very subtle superphysical and spiritual phenomena. This is not easy to understand. It gives us an appreciation of the accomplishments of the great yogins.

Shudda means purity but *pari shudda* means complete, all around purity. When the memory is cleaned by a consistent and thorough practice, which results in stopping its impulsive activations and silencing its influences and biases, then the yogi is able to disarm the buddhi organ. This is the important clue in this verse.

Because the buddhi carries the weapon of analysis, it is able to blackmail and intimidate the self into cooperating with the plan of the impulsive but blind life force and the sensible but shortsighted senses. Thus when the yogin silences the weapon of analysis, he becomes freed from its harassments.

At that time the senses become powerless to bother him, because they lose the protective support of their powerful friend, the analytical intellect organ (buddhi). Thus the yogin no longer has to fight with the memory to stop it from whimsically and impulsively showing him so many impressions in their visual and audial forms. With such distractions reduced to nil, he progresses quickly and is able to move his attention into the realm of the chit akash, the sky of consciousness.

Verse 44

एतयैव सविचारा निर्विचारा च सूक्ष्मविषया व्याख्याता ॥ ४४ ॥

etayaiva savicārā nirvicāra ca
sūkṣmaviṣayā vyākhyātā

etaya – by this; eva – only; savicārā – investigative linkage of one's attention to a higher concetration force; nirvicāra – non-investigative linkage; ca – and; sūkṣma – subtle; viṣayā – object; vyākhyātā – explained.

By this, the investigative linkage and non-investigative linkage of one's attention to a higher concentration force consisting of subtler objects, was explained.

Commentary:

There is a difference between an analytical linkage and an investigative one. There is a slight difference. It depends on the yogi's interest in particular subtle phenomenea as well as on the influence of the higher concentration force to which he is linked. At a higher stage, he regards the subject of interest without the bias of analytical or investigative approach. This is called surrender to the higher concentration force, person or thing.

Verse 45

सूक्ष्मविषयत्वं चालिङ्गपर्यवसानम् ॥ ४५ ॥

sūkṣmaviṣayatvaṁ ca aliṅga paryavasānam

sūkṣma – subtle; viṣayatvaṁ – what is concerning the nature of gross objects; ca – and; aliṅga – without characteristics; paryavasānam – termination.

The insight into the subtle nature of gross objects terminates when one becomes linked to the higher concentration force which has no characteristics.

Commentary:

As far as matter is concerned, a yogin has to research into it by linking his attention to its subtle states. Ultimately, he will reach a stage where he connects with the undifferentiated status of matter, which is its ultimate stage. At that point, his research into it terminates. Yet he still has to discover the role played by the Supreme Lord (*īsvara*) in activating and manifesting matter.

Śrī Patañjali has graciously informed all student-yogins that when they reach the featureless state of the subtle material energy, they have reached the end of their research into it. But this must be discovered by each yogin during the linkage of his attention to higher concentration forces.

Verse 46

ता एव सबीजः समाधिः ॥ ४६ ॥

tā eva sabījaḥ samādhiḥ

tā – they; eva – only; sabījaḥ – with motivation from the mento-emotional energy; samādhiḥ – effortless continous linkage of the attention to a higher concentration force.

**The previous descriptions
concern the effortless and continuous linkage
of the attention to a higher concentration force,
as motivated by the mento-emotional energy.**

Commentary:

After making so much progress in higher yoga, a yogin realizes that what he was engaged in, was being motivated by the same mental and emotional energy which he endeavored to transcend. This is because he discovered that besides himself, there was a force in his psyche which derived fulfillments from the endeavors. He traces and discovers that these were a psychic motivational force which derived a pleasure from his practice.

At that stage the practice begins in earnest and the purpose of the material energy in the life of the yogi is revealed. Bowing to the mental and emotional mundane energy in his psyche he moves on in appreciation. The purpose for which the Supreme Being caused the limited self, His eternal partner, to come in contact with a mundane life force and an investigative organ called a buddhi, now becomes evident to the yogin.

Verse 47

निर्विचारवैशारद्येऽध्यात्मप्रसादः ॥ ४७ ॥

nirvicāra vaiśāradye adhyātmaprasādaḥ

nirvicāra – non-investigative linkage of one's attention to a higher concentration force; vaiśāradye – on gaining competence; adhyātma – relationship between the Supreme Soul and the limited one; prasādaḥ – clarity and serenity.

**On gaining competence in the non-investigative linkage
of one's attention to the higher concentration force,
one experiences the clarity and serenity
which results from the linkage
of the Supreme Soul and the limited one.**

Commentary:

When the yogin passes beyond the realm of material nature, his attention links up with spiritual energy in total. Then he may, if he continues to progress, gain the competence described in this verse. That causes his limited spirit to link up with the Supreme Personality. From that connection a serenity of spirit as well as a clarity of the relation between him and that Supreme Person develops.

Verse 48

ऋतम्भरा तत्र प्रज्ञा ॥ ४८ ॥

ṛtaṁbharā tatra prajñā

ṛtaṁbharā – reality-perceptive, truth discerning; tatra – there, at that time; prajñā – insight.

There with that competence,
the yogin develops the reality-perceptive insight.

Commentary:

The *ṛtaṁbharā* buddhi is called by different terms elsewhere in the Vedic literatures like the *Bhagavad-gītā*. It is termed as *jnāña-dipena* and *jnāña* chaksusa. This means the lighted (*dipena*) insight (*jnāña*) or the vision (chaksusa) of insight (*jnāña*). In yoga parlance it is sometimes called the cleansed brow chakra, or third eye. However this comes after much practice, when the mental and emotional energy (*citta*) is silenced, when it stops vibrating in reference to the subtle and gross material energy and when it becomes stabilized and converts the imagination orb into exacting visual insight.

Śrīla Yogeshwara of Gangotri, that great yogin, rated this *ṛtaṁbharā* buddhi highly. He recommended its development. *Śrī Patañjali* clarified that until one reaches the stage of *nirvicara samādhi*, that of non-investigative linkage of one's attention to a highter concentration force in the chit akash, one cannot develop this *ṛtaṁbharā* buddhi.

Verse 49

श्रुतानुमानप्रज्ञाभ्यामन्यविषया विशेषार्थत्वात् ॥ ४९ ॥

śruta anumāna prajñābhyām
anyaviṣayā viśeṣārthatvāt

śruta – what is heard; anumāna – what is surmised or reasoned out; prajñābhyām – from the two methods of insight; anya – other; viṣayā – object; viśeṣa – particular aspect; arthavāt – because of an object.

It is different from the two methods of insight
which are based on what is heard and what is reasoned out,
because those are limited to a particular aspect of an object.

Commentary:

Direct perception with the reality-perceptive insight is different to conventional perception which is based on what is heard or read of and what is surmised or reasoned out on the basis of lower sense perception. This is because in lower sense perception, the mind can only deal with one aspect at a time. It then presents this to the buddhi organ for analysis and comparison. Then through prejudiced notions one forms opinions. This is haphazard.

Verse 50

तज्जः संस्कारोऽन्यसंस्कारप्रतिबन्धी॥५०॥

tajjaḥ saṁskāraḥ anyasaṁskāra pratibandhī

taj = tat – that; jaḥ – which is produced from; saṁskāraḥ – the impressions; anya – other; saṁskāra – impression; pratibandhī – the preventer, that which effectively suppresses something else.

That impression which is produced from the reality-perceptive insight, acts as the preventer of the other impressions.

Commentary:

Śrī Patañjali's Sanskrit language and dissection of yoga practice is precise. Let us say for example that a car shifts into second gear at 25 miles per hour. The driver might never realize the fact. However, the engineer who designed the transmission or another observant person would know of the 25 mile per hour speed shifting requirement. Some persons who have mastered higher yoga to a degree are to an extent ignorant of the details of higher yoga practice. Unfortunately some of these persons took up the task of translating and commenting on these *sūtras*. They gave opinions that are at variance with what *Patañjali* intended.

Śrī Patañjali composed a Sanskrit grammar which means that he was very knowledgable of the language. To deal with his Sanskrit, one has to know Sanskrit grammar thoroughly. *Patañjali* was very observant of his own yoga practice and had good schooling in it. Besides he is a mahayogin from his previous births. Thus to translate and comment on his *sūtras* is a challenge for anyone. In any case, he did us a great favor by explaining the stages of higher yoga, a process which to say the least, is vague even to many of the yogins who reached the higher practice. This is because of the subtlety of the experiences and the failure of yogins to observe the minute details as *Śrī Patañjali* did. By a careful study of the information, any yogi can get some idea of where he is located on the path.

Śrī Patañjali informed us, that the impression derived from the reality-perceptive insight acts as a preventer to the other impressions in the psyche which were formed by the lower buddhi organ and which bother a student yogi.

This information is significant, because in higher yoga one wonders when and where, one will get rid of the impressions which arise repeatedly in the mind and jar one loose from the prescribed focus. The answer is that until one develops the reality-perceptive insight as stipulated here, one will not be able to completely suppress the distracting impressions. One will have to tolerate them to a degree and use other partial controlling methods. This clears misconceptions and gives the student yogi hope that a time will come when the bothersome memories will be suppressed.

Verse 51

तस्यापि निरोधे सर्वनिरोधान्निर्बीजः समाधिः ॥५१॥

tasyāpi nirodhe sarvanirodhāt nirbījaḥ samādhiḥ

tasya – of that (preventative impression); āpi – also; nirodhe – on the non-operation; sarva – all; nirodhāt – resulting from that non-operation; nirbījaḥ – not motivated by the mento-emotional energy; samādhiḥ – continuous effortless linkage of the attention to the higher concentration force

The continuous effortless linkage of the attention to the higher concentration force which is not motivated by this mento-emotional energy, occurs when there is a non-operation, even of that preventative impression which caused the suppression of all other lower memories.

Commentary:

When all the impressions cease to be activated, when they all seem to be finished for good, then the highest contemplation occurs. That is a contemplation which is not motivated from this end of existence. It is controlled by and operated by the spiritual level of existence, from the other side of life, the chit akash.

Traditionally this first chapter is called *samādhi pāda*, which means the chapter defining *samādhi*. The Second chapter is usually called sādhana *pāda*, which deals with the practice of yoga. That is of special interest to the student yogis. After describing the higher yoga, the so-called *rāja* yoga, *Śrī Patañjali* described the practice of yoga as it is. Anyone who calls himself a yogi or aspires for that honor, should pay close attention to the second chapter.

Chapter 2

Sādhana Pāda:

Practice Accomplishment

Verse 1

तपःस्वाध्यायेश्वरप्रणिधानानि क्रियायोगः ॥ १ ॥

tapas svādhyāya Īśvarapraṇidhānāni kriyāyogaḥ

tapaḥ – austerity; svādhyāya – study of the psyche; īśvarapraṇihānāni = īśvara – Supreme Lord + praṇidhānāni – profound religious meditation; kriyāyogaḥ – dynamic yoga practice.

Austerity, study of the psyche and profound religious meditation on the Supreme Lord is the dynamic *kriyā* yoga practice.

Commentary:

There are many *Vaiṣṇava* teachers who deride *Śrī Patañjali* as an impersonalist. This is because they misunderstand these *sūtras* and have a negative bias towards yoga. Even though *Śrīla Vyāsadeva*, his son Shuka and others like *Nārada*, themselves being leading *Vaiṣṇavas*, did perfect the dynamic *kriyā* yoga practice, still today many *Vaiṣṇava* leaders who hail in their name, denounce the very process as being devoid of bhakti or devotion to *īsvara*. Thus they ridicule it as being useless.

However, it is clear that this dynamic *kriyā* yoga practice was taught to Uddhava by *Śrī* Krishna in their final conversation. The three aspects mentions, namely austerity (*tapaḥ*), study of the psyche (*svādhyāya*) and profound religious meditation upon the Supreme Lord (*Īśvarapraṇidhānāni*) are absolutely essential for the liberation of a living being. Whether one cultivates this by long practice, as *Śrī Patañjali* described or one does so effortlessly as *Śrī* Caitanya *Mahāprabhu* did, it will still be necessary in one way or the other. There is no avoiding this. Ultimately it must be done.

Those who do the dynamic *kriyā* practice and who avoid the profound religious meditation upon the Supreme Lord, must substitute a profound type of religious meditation toward the yogi guru who gives them techniques. Ultimately, the offering of devotion to that person reaches the Supreme Lord, either directly or through the chain of siddhas, who ultimately must be connected to that ultimate teacher, the spiritual master of the ancient yogis. The profound religious meditation cannot be avoided in the course of dynamic *kriyā* yoga. This explains why someone may become a siddha even though he is not an avowed devotee of that Supreme Lord. It is because that person has an indirect but very effective connection to the Godhead.

Verse 2

समाधिभावनार्थः क्लेशतनूकरणार्थश्च॥ २॥

samādhi bhāvanārthaḥ kleśa tanūkaraṇārthaś ca

samādhi – continuous effortless linkage of the attention to a higher concentration force or person; bhāvana – producing; arthaḥ – for the value or purposes of; kleśa = mento-emotional afflictions; tanū – thought-reducing; karaṇa – cause, causing; arthaś = arthaḥ – for the value of purpose; ca – and.

It is for the purpose of producing continuous effortless linkage of the attention to a higher concentration force and for causing the reduction of the mental and emotional afflictions.

Commentary:

Without the reduction of the mental and emotional afflictions, there can be no *samādhi* or continuous effortless linkage of the attention to a higher concentration force or person. This is because the afflictions serves as effective distractions which keep the buddhi organ engaged in lower pursuits, effectively baring it from focusing into higher places of consciousness. The dynamic *kriyā* yoga is necessary. It is the only process, which systematically reduces the mental and emotional botherations and gradually puts the psyche at a distance from them. It does not postpone them nor put them into dormancy nor drown them out with sounds and picturizations. It brings them to an end.

Verse 3

अविद्यास्मितारागद्वेषाभिनिवेशाः क्लेशाः॥ ३॥

avidyā asmitā rāga dveṣa abhiniveśaḥ kleśāḥ

avidyā – spiritual ignorance; asmitā – misplaced identity; rāga – a tendency of emotional attachment; dveṣa – impulsive emotional disaffection; abhiniveśaḥ – strong focus on mundane existence which is due to an instinctive fear of death; kleśāḥ – the mento-emotional afflictions.

The mental and emotional afflictions are spiritual ignorance, misplaced identity, emotional attachment, impulsive emotional disaffection and a strong focus on mundane existence, which is due to an instinctive fear of death.

Commentary:

The prime cause of the mental and emotional afflictions is spiritual ignorance (*avidyā*). Unfortunately this ignorance is primeval for many of the living entities who end up in the material creation. They have no idea of their spiritual whereabouts. They assume that their existence is mundane. By not understanding their essential self (*svā-bhava*), they are subjected to endless mis-identities, on and on and on. It is by the grace of a guru that one gets some idea about the essential self. It is by the example of a guru that one makes the endeavor to release the self.

The misplaced self identity (*asmitā*) causes numerous afflictions in the day to day existence. By it, one attaches one's psychological energy to persons and things in a harmful way. It is by yoga discipline that one develops the power to control the sense of identity, so that it may focus only on higher realities and ultimately cause one to be situated in a permanent non-painful condition.

The tendency for emotional attachment (*ragā*) is an impulse which is curbed after one has mastered the *pratyāhār* fifth stage of yoga practice, consisting of withdrawing the sensual energies from their external pursuits and conserving that energy within the psyche for application to higher realities.

The impulsive emotional disaffection occurs on the basis of justified or unjustified biases acquired in the present and past lives. It is impulsively performed and is hard to control. By higher yoga, one can bring this to an end.

The strong focus on mundane existence, which is due to an instinctive fear of death (*abhiniveśaḥ*) is removed by the realization of the self. One must gain mystic experiences whereby one finds oneself in one's subtle body when it is separated from the gross one. Gradually by repeated experiences of this sort, one loses the instinctive fear of death and finds that it is no longer necessary to maintain a strong focus on material existence, since one will definitely survive the perishable body. These five causes of the mental and emotional afflictions must be removed before one can enter *samādhi* on a regular basis.

Verse 4

अविद्या क्षेत्रमुत्तरेषां प्रसुप्ततनुविच्छिन्नोदाराणाम्॥ ४॥

avidyā kṣetram uttareṣāṁ prasupta
tanu vicchina udārāṇām

avidyā – spiritual ignorance; kṣetram – field, existential environment; uttareṣāṁ – of the other afflictions; prasupta – dormant; tanu – reducted; vicchina – alternating, periodic; udārāṇām – expanded.

Spiritual ignorance is the existential environment for the other afflictions, in their dormant, reduced, periodic or expanded stages.

Commentary:

Spiritual ignorance (*avidyā*) is the root cause of the mental and emotional distresses which come upon a living entity, and which is perceived as an impediment by aspiring yogins. The other afflictions form on the basis of spiritual ignorance. These four others arise in the psychological environment of a person who is spiritually-ignorant of his self-identity, due to having not experienced it objectively and due to having a strong focus on gross existence.

Verse 5

अनित्याशुचिदुःखानात्मसु नित्यशुचिसुखात्मख्यातिरविद्या ॥ ५ ॥

anitya aśuci duḥka anātmasu nitya
śuci sukha ātma khyātiḥ avidyā

anitya – not eternal, temporary; aśuci – not clean, not pure; duḥkha – distress; anātmasu – in what is not the spirit; nitya – eternal; śuci – pure; sukha – happiness; ātma – spirit; khyātiḥ – what is known or identified; avidyā – spiritual ignorance.

Spiritual ignorance is exhibited when what is temporary, impure, distressful and mundane, is identified respectively as being eternal, pure, joyful and spiritual.

Commentary:

This exhibition is rooted in the strong focus on gross existence which is due to an instinctive fear of death (*abhiniveśaḥ*, verse 3). By that focus one mistakes what is temporary, feeling that it is or can be permanent, if it is maintained by one's interest in it. One feels that what is impure can be purified by external means and by decorations. One does not recognize what is distressful but instead feels that it is joy-yielding. One mistakes what is not the spirit for the spirit. For example, one feels that one's body is oneself, and that it might be possible for one to live as the body forever.

Verse 6

दृग्दर्शनशक्त्योरेकात्मतेवास्मिता ॥ ६ ॥

dṛg darśanaśaktyoḥ ekātmatā iva asmitā

dṛg = dṛk – supernatural vision; darśana – what is seen; śaktyoḥ – of the two potencies; ekātmatā – having one nature, identical; iva – as if, seems to be; asmitā – mistaken identity.

Mistaken identity occurs when the supernatural vision and what is seen through it, seem to be identical.

Commentary:

The drig shakti or drik shakti is the supernatural visionary power which emits from the spirit itself. It is not what is seen, even though it is the medium which is used directly or in conjunction with other perceiving instruments. Hence it is mistaken identity when one feels that what is seen is identical to his own vision.

First of all, the supernatural vision is experienced as one's attention on this level of existence. On this level one uses a subtle and gross instrument for focusing one's attention. The subtle instrument is the buddhi which is the brain of the subtle body. The gross instrument is the brain, and it's auxiliary nerves. When the attention is focused through the subtle reality, it suffers from inaccuracy. Therefore it is a mistake to think that it is true vision or direct perception.

Verse 7

सुखानुशयी रागः ॥७॥

sukha anuśayī rāgaḥ

sukha – happiness; anuśayī – connected to, devotedly attached to; rāgaḥ – craving.

Craving results from a devoted attachment to happiness

Commentary:

A yogin must study his own psychology to see how it operates. He should take steps to curb it for success in yoga. Every yogi is required to pay attention to his own nature, to find its defects and to alter it in the interest of progress.

Human nature develops cravings by being devotedly attached to happiness. Happiness is derived from sensual contact in terms of smelling, tasting, seeing, touching and hearing. In the *pratyāhār* sensual withdrawal stages, a yogi gets to understand how he becomes attached to various types of happiness and how his attachments develops into craving, which forms compulsive habits. Each yogi must systematically review his own conduct to understand this. Then he should correct himself.

Verse 8

दुःखानुशयी द्वेषः ॥८॥

duḥkha anuśayi dveṣaḥ

duḥkha – distress; anuśayi – connected to, devotedly attached to; dveṣaḥ – impulsive emotional disaffection.

Impulsive emotional disaffection results from a devoted attachment to distress.

Commentary:

Impulsive emotional disaffection is manifest as an instinctive dislike for something or someone. One can become habituated to such disaffection. This results in a cynical attitude and abhorrence towards one object or the other. It destroys yoga practice.

Distress, though painful on the emotional level, maybe liked by someone. Thus the person is drawn into distressful situations again and again to derive the emotional satisfaction caused by linking the emotions to painful situations. All this should be discovered by a yogin, so that he can wean himself from distress and its causes.

Verse 9

स्वरसवाही विदुषोऽपि तथारूढोऽभिनिवेशः ॥९॥

svarasavāhī viduṣaḥ 'pi tatha rūḍho 'bhiniveśaḥ

svarasavāhī = sva – own + rasa – essence + vāhī – flow, current, instinct for self-preservation (svarasavāhī – its own flow of energy of self preservation); viduṣaḥ – the wise man; 'pi = api – also; tatha – just as, so it is; rūḍho = rūḍhah – developed produced; 'bhiniveśaḥ = abhiniveśaḥ – strong focus on mundane existence due to instinctive fear of death.

**As it is, the strong focus on mundane existence,
which is due to the instinctive fear of death,
which is sustained by its own potencies,
and which operates for self-preservation,
is developed even in the wise man.**

Commentary:

Even though wise, a person has to curb his instinctive life force. This is why the mastership of *kuṇḍalini* yoga is necessary before one can attain salvation. It is due to the natural sense of self-preservation, which is present in the subtle body, which is instinctively fearful of not having a gross form and of having to leave such a form permanently.

Unless one effectively resists the life force in the subtle body, his wisdom or knowledge can do nothing to remove the strong fear of death. The resistance is acquired by intake of higher pranic energies, through *prāṇāyāma* and other methods which form parts of the *kriyā* yoga practice.

Mastery of the lifeforce, the *kuṇḍalini* chakra, gives the yogin the ability to infuse the subtle body with a lack of fear, due to its conscious experiences in the subtle world. When the subtle body takes a footing in the subtle existence it releases itself from dependence on this gross manifestation, and the fear of death (*abhiniveśaḥ*) departs from it.

In his translation, the Raj Yogi I.K. Taimni gave riding and dominating as the meaning of *rūḍhah*. His translation reads that *abhiniveśa* is the strong desire for life which dominates even the learned (or the wise). In his purport, he stated that the universality of *abhiniveśaḥ* shows that there is some constant and universal force inherent in life which automatically finds expression in this "desire to live".

In higher yoga one realizes this when one traces that urge to the life force in the subtle body and then to the cosmic life force which dominates or rides on the back of the psyche, dictating by urges and motivations, how it should procure gross existences, maintain these and fight to remain rooted in these.

It is only when a yogin has developed a yoga siddha body that he becomes totally free of that lifeforce impulse which forces him to procure a foot hole in the gross existences for participation in the struggle for survival in lower worlds.

Verse 10

ते प्रतिप्रसवहेयाः सूक्ष्माः ॥ १० ॥

te pratiprasavaheyāḥ sūkṣmāḥ

te – these, they; prati – opposing, reverting back; prasava – expressing, going outwards; heyāḥ – what is fit to be left or abandoned; sūkṣmāḥ – subtle energies.

These subtle motivations are to be abandoned by reverting their expression backwards.

Commentary:

This means the practice of *rāja* yoga or mystic actions which effectively curb and end off what is unwanted in the psyche and what deters the objectives of yoga.

Pratiprasava is known otherwise as the fifth stage of yoga which is *pratyāhāra* (*prati-āhāra*) reverting the sensual expressions back into the psyche, so that they do not express themselves outwards. This causes conservation of valuable psychic energy through which one develops supernatural perception.

There are many subtle motivations which are quite fit to be abandoned or left aside, to be made powerless so that they do not motivate the psyche of the yogi in a counter productive way. However one must develop the power to shut down or squelch such energies, otherwise one can say what he likes and believe whatever suits his fancy and he will still be motivated by these energies to his detriment.

Verse 11

ध्यानहेयास्तद्वृत्तयः ॥ ११ ॥

dhyānaheyāḥ tadvṛttayaḥ

dhyāna – effortless linking of the attention to the higher concentration force or person; heyāḥ – what is fit to be abandoned or left aside; tad = tat – that; vṛttayaḥ – vibrational modes of the mento-emotional energies.

Their vibrational modes are to be abandoned or ceased by the effortless linkage of the attention to a higher concentration force or person.

Commentary:

This advice is direct. It does not state that there are alternate methods for dealing with the vibrational motivations which spring from the *abhiniveśaḥ* urges which cause a yogi and others to pursue mundane life with a wanton passion which usually cannot be controlled. This is because there are no other methods but the attempt at effortless linkage of the attention to higher concentration forces or persons. This is the only method that reveals to the yogin the various parts of the psyche and the complications he faces in trying to purify his nature. The vibrational modes which apply to the lower psychic level and to the physical planes, are not to be silenced except by causing the mind to abandon those lower planes. The techniques are realized by practicing higher yoga.

Verse 12

क्लेशमूलः कर्माशयो दृष्टादृष्टजन्मवेदनीयः ॥ १२ ॥

kleśamūlaḥ karmāśayaḥ dṛṣṭa
adṛṣṭa janma vedanīyaḥ

kleśa – mento-emotional distress; mūlaḥ – root, cause; karma – cultural activities; āśayaḥ – storage, reservoir; dṛṣṭa – perceived, realized; adṛṣṭa – not perceived, not realized; janma – birth; vedanīyaḥ – what is experienced or realized.

The psychological storage of the impressions left by performance of cultural activities which is itself the cause of the mental and emotional distress, is experienced in realized and non-realized births.

Commentary:

This *karma āśayaḥ* or psychological storage-compartment which holds the compacted impressions which are left by the performance of cultural activities, is manifested to us in meditation as memory. It is very troublesome and stalls the yogi in his attempts to master *pratyāhār*, *dhāraṇā* and *dhyāna*. A yogi may be stalled for years by motivations which come out of the memory compartment. When the memory emits impressions, they are translated when they hit the mento-emotional energy, the *citta*. Then the buddhi organ takes possession of the pictures and sounds and creates further impressions, causing the psyche to create desires and motivations to act. This is the bane of higher yoga. Until a yogin can control this, he does not progress in the *dhāraṇā* and *dhyāna* practice.

Some translators have innocently translated *dṛṣṭa adṛṣṭa janma* as present and future births, but this is a mistake. *Dṛṣṭa* does not mean what is present in terms of time and *adṛṣṭa* does not mean what is not present today. *Dṛṣṭa* means observing or seeing, perceiving. *Adṛṣṭa* is the opposite, meaning births that a yogi does not objectively realize. In other words, in some births one can realize that it is a temporary circumstance one has entered into and in other births due to limited perception one does not realize this. As for instance, in the case of souls who take animal or vegetative forms. They have no idea that they are in a birth for a limited amount of time. Still, as *Śrī Patañjali* stated, the person will experience the impressions which were in his psyche, and which were left behind by his past acts in the cultural worlds. He cannot avoid those experiences even though he may not make any sense of why the impressions go through his mind.

The impressions are experienced even by animals and trees but they do not understand what they perceive. The spiritually-ignorant human beings do not understand the impressions either. They try to rationalize all of it in terms of what they remember in the present life. A yogi, by higher practice, has a big advantage, because according to his level of advancement, he may understand the impressions to a lesser or greater degree. He may also get help from his teachers, who are conversant with the forces in the psyche.

Verse 13

सति मूले तद्विपाको जात्यायुर्भोगाः ॥ १३ ॥

sati mūle tadvipākaḥ jāti āyuḥ bhogāḥ

sati – there is existing; mūle – in the cause; tat – that, it; vipākaḥ – what is resulting; jāti – species, status of life; āyuḥ – duration of life; bhogāḥ – type of experience.

In the case aforementioned, there exist the resulting effects which manifest as a particular species of life with certain duration of body and type of experiences gained in that form.

Commentary:

One develops a certain type of body with a duration for it's existence along with the experience gained through that form, on the basis of the impressions which were formed before by the performance of cultural activities. All species of life are engaged in cultural acts. The human is more deliberate. This is his only advantage. Even though one forgets the cultural acts from past lives still one's life is to a greater degree, determined by the type of cultural acts one performed previously. The psychological storage compartment holds the impressions of the past cultural acts, as motivations to take advantage of certain situations. This is done impulsively.

Verse 14

ते ह्लादपरितापफलाः पुण्यापुण्यहेतुत्वात् ॥ १४ ॥

te hlāda paritāpa phalāḥ puṇya apuṇya hetutvāt

te – they; hlāda – happiness; paritāpa – distress; phalāḥ – results; puṇya – merits; apuṇya – demerits; hetutvāt – that which causes.

They produce happiness and distress as results, on the basis of merits and demerits.

Commentary:

The impressions from previous cultural activities form happy or unhappy times according to the laws of nature, not according to what human beings believe. The rationalization of human beings, particularly the fundamental religious ones, do not necessarily tally with the laws of nature.

The merits are those which are approved by nature. The demerits form from Her disapproval. However, a living being must sometimes wait for many years, or even many thousands of years before he can enjoy or suffer for breaking or confirming to a law of nature.

His past cultural acts which left impressions in his subconscious memory (*karmāśayaḥ*) remains there until it senses a favorable circumstance for its conformity to the matching meritorious or demeritorious reaction.

Verse 15

परिणामतापसंस्कारदुःखैर्गुणवृत्तिविरोधाच्च दुःखमेव सर्वं विवेकिनः ॥ १५ ॥

pariṇāma tāpa saṁskāra duḥkaiḥ guṇavṛtti
virodhāt ca duḥkham eva sarvaṁ vivekinaḥ

pariṇāma – circumstantial change; tāpa – strenuous endeavor; saṁskāra – impulsive motivations; duḥkhaiḥ – with distress; guṇa – quality, features of material nature; vṛtti – vibrational mode of the mento-emotional energy; virodhāt – resulting from confrontation or clashing aspects; ca – and; duḥkham – distress; eva – indeed; sarvaṁ – all; vivekinaḥ – the discriminating person.

The discriminating person knows
that all conditions are distressful
because of circumstantial changes, strenuous endeavor,
impulsive motivations, clashing aspects
and the vibrational modes of the mento-emotional energy.

Commentary:

This is discrimination gained by virtue of yoga practice. It is an insight into the nature of the material world and is not a theoretical understanding of it. By this, a yogi sees the complications in the cultural activities. Thus he becomes reluctant to participate. One cannot control the features of material nature. If one does not advance into higher yoga, one cannot control the vibrational modes of one's mental and emotional energies.

Therefore a yogi has no alternative but to back away from the cultural world and harden-up himself by performing higher yoga, mastering it and then applying it while performing any remaining cultural obligations efficiently, and in a way that causes a breaking-off from the cultural circuit.

The conditions in these lower existences are always distressful either in the short or long range. That is the nature of it. There are too many circumstantial changes which a limited being can not control. He cannot at all times regulate his mind's entry into or admittance of emotional distresses. And he cannot always side-step the involuntary motivations which lead to further distress. Therefore there is no alternative but to perfect the higher yoga practice of *dhyāna* effortless linkage of his attention to higher concentration forces and persons. That is the method for getting rid of the psychological disturbances which cause instability, anxiety and emotional distress.

Verse 16

हेयं दुःखमनागतम् ॥ १६ ॥

heyaṁ duḥkham anāgatam

heyaṁ – that which is to be avoided; duḥkham – distress; anāgatam – what has not manifested.

Distress which is not manifested is to be avoided.

Commentary:

For liberation, a yogin will have to reach a stage where he can side-step all the merits and demerits which are due to him from providence but which he may side-step. Both happiness and distress which are coming on the basis of cultural activities from the past are to be avoided at all costs. However a yogin has to advance sufficiently before he can side-step these. It requires insight as to the psychological receptacles which are submissive towards the manifestation of the merits and demerits. A yogin has to close off the opening to such receptacles by practicing *kriyā* yoga.

Verse 17

द्रष्टृदृश्ययोः संयोगो हेयहेतुः ॥ १७॥

draṣṭṛdṛśyayoḥ saṁyogo heyahetuḥ

draṣṭṛ – the observer; dṛśyayoḥ – of what is perceived; saṁyogo – the indiscriminate association; heya – that which is to be avoided; hetuḥ – the cause.

The cause which is to be avoided is the indiscriminate association of the observer and what is perceived.

Commentary:

When we identify wholly and solely with what we perceive, we loose objectivity and become attached, rather than detached. This causes a misplaced identity with things which are not in our interest and which make us lose objectivity. Then we experience an impulsive interaction between the new impressions received through the senses and the old impressions stored in the memory (*karmāśayaḥ*). The analytical part of the buddhi organ then hashes over the matter and comes to a conclusion which is shown to us internally in the mind through the magical imagery of the imagination orb. Thus we again come under the spell of the function of that psychic organ.

If a yogi reaches a stage of control, whereby he stops the impulsive sensual intakes or puts a damper on them as soon as they enter the psyche, he realizes himself as being the perceiver or observer. Then he sees the operations of the senses and the machinations of his memory as being counterproductive. These interact to produce new images which he usually identifies with, to his detriment.

In higher yoga, one is trained in how to distinguish the various parts of the buddhi organ subtle mechanism and the *citta* mento-emotional energy gyrations. Then one puts an end to the impressions and their varied motivations which destroys one's ability to see beyond the material world.

Verse 18

प्रकाशक्रियास्थितिशीलं भूतेन्द्रियात्मकं भोगापवर्गार्थं दृश्यम्॥ १८॥

prakāśa kriyā sthiti śīlaṁ bhūtendriyātmakaṁ
bhogāpavargārthaṁ dṛśyam

prakāśa – clear perception; kriyā – action; sthiti – stability; śīlaṁ – form, disposition; bhūta – mundane elements; indriya – sense organs; ātmakaṁ – self, nature; bhoga – experience; apavarga – liberation; arthaṁ – value or purpose; dṛśyam – what is perceived.

What is perceived is of the nature of the mundane elements
and the sense organs
and is formed in clear perception, action or stability.
Its purpose is to give experience or to allow liberation.

Commentary:

Whatever we perceive in the subtle or gross mundane energy depends on the condition of the seeing instrument, which is the buddhi organ in the subtle body. According to how it is influenced by and powered by the modes of material nature, it allows either clear perception, impulsive action, or inertia. The purpose behind the interaction of the seer and what is seen, is experience for involvement or experience which results in either consumption or liberation.

Material nature has a purpose, either to give more and more varied pleasurable or harmful experiences or to allow liberation from both. While others hustle after what is pleasurable and try to avoid what might render pain, the yogin strives for liberation by curbing his intellect organ so that he can remain in clear perception (*prakāśa*).

Verse 19

विशेषाविशेषलिङ्गमात्रालिङ्गानि गुणपर्वाणि॥ १९॥

viśeṣa aviśeṣa liṅgamātra aliṅgāni guṇaparvāṇi

viśeṣa – that which is specific; aviśeṣa – what is regular; liṅgamātra – a mark, that which is indicated; aliṅgāni – that which has no indication; guṇa – influences of material nature; parvāṇi – phases, stages, parts.

The phases of the influences of material nature
are those which are specific, regular, indicated or not indicated.

Commentary:

By higher yoga, a yogin gets to see all this clearly: how material nature has certain over-riding phases which it shifts into by its own accord, and which the yogi can enter once he mastered *dhāraṇā* linkage of his attention to higher concentration force, either in or beyond material nature.

The specific objects are those which are perceivable on the gross plane of existence and which are highlighted to our senses because of strong attraction. The non-specific are those gross objects which exhibit mild attraction.

These are regular items like dirt. Even though a gem is a form of dirt, still it is specific. While a speck of mud or a grain of sand are regular, being non¬specific. These all have subtle counterparts, which are categorized in the same way and which can be seen through the perception of the subtle body when it is highly energised.

That which is indicated is the subtle matter which we may detect with electronic instruments or discover by mystic techniques in higher yoga. That which has no indication at all is the material energy in it's quiescent stage where it has no differentiation. It is as it were, just nothing at that stage. In higher meditation, one perceives each of these.

Verse 20

द्रष्टा दृशिमात्रः शुद्धोऽपि प्रत्ययानुपश्यः ॥ २० ॥

draṣṭā dṛśimātraḥ śuddhaḥ api pratyayānupaśyaḥ

draṣṭā – the perceiver; dṛśi – perception, consciousness; mātraḥ – measure or extent; śuddhaḥ – purity; api – but; pratyayaḥ – conviction or belief as mental content; anu – following along, patterning after; paśyaḥ – what is perceived.

The perceiver is the pure extent of its consciousness but its conviction is patterned by what it perceives.

Commentary:

In actuality the dṛśi or consciousness which spiritually emanates from the individual self, is itself that self and that self alone. However, due to it's absorbent nature, the self loses tract of itself and instead adopts patterns which form in its consciousness as conviction. On the assumption of these convictions one is motivated into cultural activities.

Śrī Patañjali Maharshi used the technical term *mātraḥ* which means a measure of or to an extent. The individual soul is limited. His consciousness radiates only to a certain extent, before it becomes attenuated or is linked to lower or higher concentration forces which help to off-set its limited range.

In the material creation, with a psychic body, the perceiver, the individual self, is itself the pure extent of its own consciousness. That is its very form. However it functions following along behind what is perceived, thus it is influenced not to realize itself by itself, but to accept itself as its perceptions. These perceptions occur when its pure consciousness is linked to a sensing mechanism. The spirit derives a correct or erroneous notion by sensual influence. By that he transmigrates from one situation to another and is implicated.

Verse 21

तदर्थ एव दृश्यस्यात्मा॥ २१॥

tadarthaḥ eva dṛśyasya ātmā

tad = tat – that; arthaḥ – purpose; eva – only; dṛśyasya – of what is seen; ātmā – individual spirit.

The individual spirit, who is involved in what is seen, exists here for that purpose only.

Commentary:

As it is, as we experience it in ourselves, and as we hear from others, this existence is meant for experiencing either ourselves as we are or ourselves as we are connected to various other sensing mechanisms. Basically speaking, a person transmigrates perceiving this or that in the material world. A person's existence here is reduced to that.

Verse 22

कृतार्थं प्रति नष्टमप्यनष्टं तदन्यसाधारणत्वात्॥ २२॥

kṛtārthaṁ prati naṣṭam api
anaṣṭaṁ tadanya sādhāraṇatvāt

kṛt – fulfilled done; ārthaṁ – purpose; prati – toward; naṣṭam – destroyed, non-existent, non-effective; api – although, but; anaṣṭaṁ – not finished, still existing, effective; tat – that; anya – others; sādhāraṇatvāt – common, normal, universal.

It is not effective for one to whom its purpose is fulfilled, but it has a common effect on the others.

Commentary:

The material world loses its effectiveness on a realized yogin. For him its purpose is fulfilled. It no longer operates on him. He no longer reacts to it as others do. For the others however it remains in effect. The others agree on its potency and place stress on it. They accept the convictions derived from it and carry on their social lives.

In a sense this statement of *Śrī Patañjali* is a denial about mass liberation. Here the liberation is individual and only for those who have retracted their spiritual energy from linkage into the subtle mundane sensing energy.

Others will remain in the material world, because its effects hold them here, utilizing their attention.

Śrī Krishna in the *Bhagavad-gītā* did not profess any mass liberation of many living entities, neither by an act of faith nor by belief or confidence. He too singled out individual yogis for liberation. This is what he said:

manuṣyāṇāṃ sahasreṣu
kaścid yatati siddhaye
yatatām api siddhānāṃ
kaścin māṃ vetti tattvataḥ

Someone, in thousands of human beings, strives for psychological perfection. Of those who endeavor, even of those who are perfected, someone knows Me in truth. (Gīta 7.3)

Verse 23

स्वस्वामिशक्त्योः स्वरूपोपलब्धिहेतुः संयोगः ॥ २३ ॥

sva svāmiśaktyoḥ svarūpa upalabdhi hetuḥ saṁyogaḥ

sva – own nature, own psyche; svāmi – the master, the individual self; saktyoḥ – of the potency of the two; svarūpa – essential form; upalabdhi – obtaining experience; hetuḥ – cause, reason; saṁyogaḥ – conjunction.

There is a reason for the conjunction of the individual self and its psychological energies. It is for obtaining the experience of its essential form.

Commentary:

This states indirectly that the living entity who has a psychological make-up can only realize his essential or spiritual nature, by first coming in contact with the subtle material nature and then differentiating himself from that mundane power.

The conjunction (*saṁyoga*) is enforced, because no limited being has the power to join himself with material nature nor to disconnect himself from it. This is why *Śrī Patañjali* acknowledged that special person who taught even the ancient yogis.

kleśa karma vipāka āśayaiḥ
aparāmṛṣṭaḥ puruṣaviśeṣaḥ Īśvaraḥ
tatra niratiśayaṁ sarvajñabījam
sa eṣaḥ pūrveṣām api guruḥ kālena anavacchedāt

He, this particular person,being unconditioned by time,is the guru even of the ancient teachers, the authorities from before. The Supreme Lord is that special person who is not affected by troubles, actions, development or by subconscious motivations.There, in Him, is found the unsurpassed origin of all knowledge.(Yoga Sūtra 1:24 - 26)

The ultimate purpose of the conjunction is for the limited beings to objectively realize their spiritual selves, apart from and distinct from the subtle material nature which they accept initially as their personal psychology.

The individual self is supposed to be the master, the swami of his psychological powers but initially he is overtaken, influenced and dominated by them. Thus he has the task of realizing what happened to his autonomy.

Verse 24

तस्य हेतुरविद्या ॥ २४ ॥

tasya hetuḥ avidyā

tasya – of it; hetuḥ – cause; avidyā – spiritual ignorance.

The cause of the conjunction is spiritual ignorance.

Commentary:

Besides the fact that there is a forced conjunction between the individual limited spirits and the mundane sensing energies, there is also an underlying reason for this, which is innate spiritual ignorance of the limited beings. They did not understand themselves initially. The Supreme Being may be blamed for putting the limited beings in peril by forcing them into conjunction with the mundane psychology, but the reason for His action is stated in this verse; being the spiritual ignorance of these limited dependents of His.

As far as the Supreme Being was concerned, the only way to free us from that ignorance was to put us in conjunction with the mundane psychology. From that position we may derive disgust (*nirvedaḥ*) with that energy and then through introspection study ourselves and our linkage with it and with His assistance, work for emancipation.

The blame placed on the Supreme Being is lifted from Him as soon as we understand we were with an innate and primeval spiritual ignorance of our true nature. The contrast between ourselves and the mundane energy is the only aspect that motivates us to realize ourselves.

Verse 25

तदभावात्संयोगाभावो हानं तद्दृशेः कैवल्यम् ॥ २५ ॥

tad abhāvāt saṁyogā abhāvaḥ
hānaṁ taddṛśeḥ kaivalyam

tad = tat – that spiritual ignorance; abhāvāt – resulting from the elimination; saṁyogā – conjunction; abhāvaḥ – disappearance, elimination; hānaṁ – withdrawal, escape; tad = tat – that; dṛśeḥ – of the perceiver; kaivalyam – total separation from the mundane psychology.

The elimination of the conjunction which results from the elimination of that spiritual ignorance is the withdrawal that is the total separation of the perceiver from the mundane psychology.

Commentary:

Yogis should take care in studying this verse, to get *Śrī Patañjali*'s definition of *kaivalyam*. This term has come down to us as meaning various forms of liberation, all depending on the spiritual sect which advocated it. However, to understand *Śrī Patañjali*, we must stick to his definitions. Clearly, *kaivalya* is defined in this verse, within the context of what *Śrī Patañjali* spoke of, which is the *saṁyoga* or conjunction between the individual spirit and his subtle mundane psychology (*sva*). This psychology is hinted at in the second verse of Chapter One, as operational *vṛttis*:

yogaḥ cittavṛtti nirodhaḥ

The skill of yoga demonstrated by the conscious non-operation of the vibrational modes of the mento-emotional energy. (Yoga Sūtra 1:2)

There is no definition here of *kaivalyam* being union with God or oneness with God or anything like that. It does not mean here that one has become God or that one has merged into the Absolute Truth. *Śrī Patañjali* in the context spoke of the complete isolation of the individual limited spirit from his psychological sensing mechanisms which are derived from material nature and his situating himself and realizing himself as his own spiritual nature in its purity by restricting himself to it and to its pure extent.

draṣṭā dṛśimātraḥ śuddhaḥ api pratyayānupaśyaḥ

The perceiver is the pure extent of his consciousness but his conviction is patterned by what is perceived. (Yoga Sūtra 2:20)

Verse 26

विवेकख्यातिरविप्लवा हानोपायः ॥ २६ ॥

vivekakhyātiḥ aviplavā hānopāyaḥ

viveka – discrimination; khyātiḥ – insight; aviplavā – unbroken, continuous; hānopāyaḥ = hana – avoidance + upāyaḥ – means, method.

The method for avoiding that spiritual ignorance is the establishment of continuous discriminative insight.

Commentary:

Vivekakhyātiḥ is discriminative insight, gained through higher yoga practice or naturally occurring as a result of actively using a yoga siddha form or a spiritual body. It is not book knowledge nor concepts derived from authoritative teachers. Most persons will have to do yoga to develop this, even though a rare few might have this naturally occurring in their yoga siddha or spiritual forms.

Spiritual ignorance (*avidyā*) which is the ignorance of the difference between one's spiritual energy and its linkage or mixture with mundane psychology, is removed by no other method besides the development of the discriminative insight.

Verse 27

तस्य सप्तधा प्रान्तभूमिः प्रज्ञा ॥ २७ ॥

tasya saptadhā prāntabhūmiḥ prajñā

tasya – of his; saptadhā – seven fold; prānta – boundary or edge + bhūmiḥ – territory, range (prāntabhūmiḥ – stage); prajñā – insight.

Concerning the development of discriminative insight, there are seven stages.

Commentary:

Śrī Patañjali clarified that in developing the discriminative insight, one moves through seven stages. It does not come overnight. One develops it step-by-step.

Verse 28

योगाङ्गानुष्ठानादशुद्धिक्षये ज्ञानदीप्तिराविवेकख्यातेः ॥ २८॥

yogāṅgānuṣṭhānāt aśuddhikṣaye
jñānadīptiḥ āvivekakhyāteḥ

yogāṅgānuṣṭhānāt = yoga – yoga process + aṅga – part + anuṣṭhānāt – from consistent practice; aśuddhiḥ – impurities; kśaye – on the elimination; jñānadīptiḥ – radiant organ of perception; āvivekakhyāteḥ = a – till, until, up to + viveka – discrimination + khyāteḥ – insight.

From the consistent practice of the parts of the yoga process,
on the elimination of the impurity,
the radiant organ of perception becomes manifest,
until there is steady discriminative insight.

Commentary:

There is really no short cut, except to practice steadily and persistently with attention from day to day. From that, the impurities gradually diminish, until they fade altogether. Then the organ of perception, the buddhi organ in the subtle body, becomes radiant. It emits a light and sees supernaturally and spiritually. This is the *jñāña dīpaḥ* or *jñānadīptiḥ*. It is also called *jñānachakshuh*. When there is consistent practice in using this vision in *dhyāna* and *samādhi* yoga, then there is steady consistent discriminative insight for the yogi, not otherwise.

Verse 29

यमनियमासनप्राणायामप्रत्याहारधारणाध्यानसमाधयोऽष्टावङ्गानि ॥ २९ ॥

yama niyama āsana prāṇāyāma pratyāhāra
dhāraṇā dhyāna samādhayaḥ aṣṭau aṅgāni

yama – moral restraints; niyama – recommended behaviors; āsana – body postures; prāṇāyāma – breath infusion; pratyāhar – sensual energy withdrawal; dhāraṇā – linking of the attention to higher concentration forces or persons; dhyāna – effortless linkage of the attention to higher concentration forces or persons; samādhayaḥ – continuous effortless linkage of the attention to higher concentration forces or persons; aṣṭau – eight; aṅgāni – parts of a thing.

Moral restraints, recommended behaviors, body posture, breath infusion,
sensual energy withdrawal, linking of the attention to higher concentration
forces or persons, effortless linkage of the attention to higher concentration
forces or persons, continuous effortless linkage of the attention
to higher concentration forces or persons
are the eight parts of the yoga system.

Commentary:

Śrī Gorakshnath in his writings gave six parts to yoga, leaving out the preliminary parts of *yama*, moral restraints and *niyama*, recommended behaviors. This is because those two are preliminary. A person who has not integrated those, must instill them in himself as he practices the advanced portions. I experienced many students who are not masterful at the preliminary stages. They should master these as they proceed or find that their lack of skill in cultural dealings causes impediments. According to the advisories and warnings issued by *Śrī* Krishna to Arjuna in the *Bhagavad-gītā*, a person who does not have an exemption from cultural activities, cannot succeed fully in yoga. Actually the sooner that a yogi can realize this, the better and more advanced he will be. If he does not cooperate with the central person in the Universal Form, with *Śrī* Krishna, he will not be able to get to the *samādhi* stage. It will be impossible.

Śrī Gorakashnath did not want the *haṭha* yogis, his students, to waste their time and energy in the moral field, in trying to perfect righteous living, but nevertheless, if one does not work his way cautiously through the cultural world, one will fail at yoga practice. We must understand that *Śrī* Gorakshnath is a birth taken by *Śrī* Skanda Kumara, the celibate son of Lord Shiva. As such he never advocates grhasta ashram but that does not mean that it has no value. We have to understand its value, just in case we require another human form. The moral restraints and recommended behaviors have their usage to keep us on the good side of King Dharma, the supernatural person who sponsors righteous life style.

Verse 30

अहिंसासत्यास्तेयब्रह्मचर्यापरिग्रहा यमाः ॥ ३० ॥

ahiṁsā satya asteya
brahmacarya aparigrahāḥ yamāḥ

ahiṁsā – non-violence; satya – realism; asteya – non-stealing; brahmacarya – sexual non-expressiveness which results in the perception of spirituality; aparigrahāḥ – non-possessiveness; yamāḥ – moral restraints.

Non-violence, realism, non-stealing, sexual non-expressiveness which results in the perception of spirituality (brahman) and non-possessiveness are the moral restraints.

Commentary:

Some authorities list other moral restraints, but these given by *Śrī Patañjali* cover the entire listing of the negative qualities which are to be avoided. This is the list of qualities which should be cultivated if they are not innate to one's character.

Ahiṁsā the attitude of genuine harmlessness towards other creatures, not just human beings. Of course a yogi has to know that the human form of life is comparatively more valuable than other species, but he should know as well that creatures who are in other life forms must fulfill their gratifications there before they could be permanently transformed to higher forms. Their lives should not be underrated. A yogi should not assume a master-of-the-species attitude. He should not harm any other creature willfully. He should situate himself circumstantially so that occasions for killing do not arise.

According to Lord Mahavira and other Tirthankaras in the Jain disciplic succession, we have no business killing other creatures. A yogin should be non-violent. If one finds that he has a violent nature or that a part of his psyche takes pleasure in harming others or in seeing others being hurt, then he should work to purify that part. Each yogin has to realize defects and work to remove them by the relevant yoga *kriyās*.

Satya or realism includes truthfulness, but for the yogin it is more than conventional honesty. It has to do with developing the deep insight described by *Śrī Patañjali* in the previous verse as *jñāña-dīptiḥ* and as *vivekakhyātiḥ*. This gives one deep insight into reality, even to perceive past lives and to properly interpret the *saṁskāra* subconscious impressions which are buried deep in memory and which surface from time to time.

Asteya or non-stealing is a must for a yogin. The tendency for stealing is innate in the subtle body. A yogin has to work with himself to eliminate it. This requires vigilance.

Brahmacarya has a conventional meaning as celibacy but it is more than that. It is an active or dynamic celibacy which is assisted by yoga practice and which results in the perception of brahman or spiritual reality. This means mastership of celibacy yoga, so that even in an adult body, the sexual urge is sublimated and does not arise to disturb the psyche. A celibate yogi should not have sexual intercourse unless he or she desires to have a child. He should ideally only have as many intercourses as there are children produced from his or her body. This is the ideal behavior. Failing in this a yogin has to work with his psyche to improve its sexual outlook, so that eventually its sexual needs are eliminated by the practice of celibacy yoga and *kuṇḍalini* yoga. Without attaining celibacy one cannot become liberated. It is not possible, because the energy of the subtle body will not be efficiently used if sexual expression continues through it. Thus one will not realize the subtle mundane existence which is preliminary for spiritual seekers.

Aparigrahāḥ or non-possessiveness has to do with understanding that whatever we encounter in the gross or subtle existence is the property of more powerful beings. The only real possession we have is the task of our purification. The critical nature within us which usually seeks external expression should be directed backward into the psyche. This redirected critical force improves our condition by the application of corrective tendencies.

Overall these moral restraints are necessary for a yogi, but he does not master these initially, even though this is listed as the first stage of yoga. He masters this a little and then he continues to get more control of his nature as he advances and sees more and more how subtle the defects are and how mystic and specific he must be to root them out.

Verse 31

जातिदेशकालसमयानवच्छिन्नाः सार्वभौमा महाव्रतम्॥ ३१॥

jāti deśa kāla samaya anavacchinnāḥ
sārvabhaumāḥ mahāvratam

jāti – status; deśa – location; kāla – time; samaya – condition; anavacchinnāḥ – not restricted by, not adjusted by; sārvabhaumāḥ – relating to all standard stages, being standard; mahāvratam – great commitment.

Those moral restraints are not to be adjusted by the status, location, time or condition. They, being the great commitment, are related to all stages of yoga.

Commentary:

Sārvabhaumā means relating to all the earth. However *bhaumā*, as a synonym, also means stage or foreground, as explained in verse 27 with the term *prāntabhūmiḥ*. In all the stages of yoga, the first stages maintain relevance. Thus the yogi never reaches a stage where he can completely ignore moral restraints, except when he is released from the material world completely.

Śrī Patañjali accredited those moral restraints as the great commitment (*mahāvrata*).

Verse 32

शौचसन्तोषतपःस्वाध्यायेश्वरप्रणिधानानि नियमाः॥ ३२॥

śauca saṅtoṣa tapaḥ svādhyāya
īśvarapraṇidhānāni niyamāḥ

śauca – purification; saṅtoṣa – contentment; tapaḥ – austerity; svādhyāya – study of the psyche; īśvara – Supreme Lord; praṇidhānāni – profound religious meditation; niyamāḥ – recommended behaviors.

Purification, contentment, austerity and profound religious meditation on the Supreme Lord are the recommended behaviors.

Commentary:

Many religious leaders ridicule *Śrī Patañjali* because he classified profound religious meditation to the Supreme Lord as part of an elementary stage in yoga practice, but just as the first stage remains relevant throughout the practices (*sārva-bhaumāh,* verse 31), so also every other stage remains in place, and is improved upon as the yogi moves to higher levels.

According to some critics, *Śrī Patañjali* hawked too much about yoga and neglected the bhakti or bhakti-yoga, giving it an insignificant place in the layout of spiritual disciplines. However if one checks the *Bhagavad-gītā* carefully, he will discover that *Śrī* Krishna, who declared Himself as the Supreme Lord, gave high precedence to yoga.

The other aspect of *Śrī Patañjali*'s treatment of devotion to God, is understood when we consider the term *pranidhānani*. *Śrī Patañjali* spoke of profound religious meditation. This is a mystic process of internal focus upon the Supreme Lord, to reach the Divinity in a totally different dimension. But why one may ask did *Śrī Patañjali* not place this as the foremost aspect of yoga practice? The reason is simple: One cannot perfect this unless one first masters yoga. The skill to do this comes only by perfecting the yoga austerities.

In the *Bhagavad-gītā*, the purpose of yoga is defined by *Śrī* Krishna in the following terms:

tatraikāgraṃ manaḥ kṛtvā yata-cittendriya-kriyāḥ

upaviśyāsane yuñjyād yogam ātma-viśuddhaye

... being there, seated in a posture, having the mind focused, the person who controls his thinking and sensual energy, should practice the yoga discipline for self-purification. (Gītā 6:12)

Śrī Krishna also explained that a yogi should commit himself to cultural activities for the sake of psychic purification:

kāyena manasā buddhyākevalair indriyair api

yoginaḥ karma kurvanti saṅgam tyaktvātma- śuddhaye

With the body, mind and intelligence, or even with the senses alone, the yogis, having discarded attachment, perform cultural acts for self-purification. (Gītā 5:11)

Śrī Patañjali does not contradict *Śrī* Krishna. In fact he reinforces what *Śrī* Krishna said.

Verse 33

वितर्कबाधने प्रतिपक्षभावनम्॥ ३३॥

vitarkabādhane pratipakṣabhāvanam

vitarka – doubt, argument; bādhane – in annoyance or disturbance; pratipakṣa – what is opposite or contrary; bhāvanam – manifesting, imagining, conceiving, considering.

In the case of the annoyance produced by doubts, one should conceive of what is opposite.

Commentary:

When there are any doubts regarding the moral restraints and the recommended behavior, a yogi should counteract that state of mind by conceiving of the opposite. In other words, sometimes a yogi is pressured by the same status, location, time or condition mentioned in verse 31. Then he may cast aside the five great commitments, feeling that he is allowed to do so because of a particular status he is awarded by providence, or because of being in a certain location, or through the time of an occurrence, or because he was pressured by certain conditions. However, *Śrī Patañjali* objects and states that the yogi should not give-in but should hold on to the principles by considering and contemplating the opposite type of actions which conflict with the five great commitments.

If a yogi remembers this instruction his course into higher yoga would be accelerated, otherwise he will be stalled in lower stages for a very long time. Sometimes a yogi gets an idea to do something which jeopardizes his practice. He may feel that he must do it to comply with a pressure of providence which is forced into his mind. Usually, such a situation will pass on even if the yogi does not satisfy the urges, but if he is rash, he will act in the wrong way and forestall his practice. Thus *Śrī Patañjali* ask that there be considerations to the contrary, anytime we get some idea to do something that is against the moral principles.

Sometimes in the astral world and in parallel dimensions a yogi is circumstantially positioned for breaking moral rules, but when he gets back into this material body and recalls the incident, he regrets or thinks that for some reason he was unable to use his discrimination. *Śrī Patañjali* mentioned this discriminative insight before under the terms of *vivekakhyātiḥ*. Unless this is developed to the extent that it is carried everywhere the yogi may go through this and into other dimensions, he will of necessity break the moral restraints here or there, whenever his discriminative insight vanishes or is weakened.

Verse 34

वितर्का हिंसादयः कृतकारितानुमोदिता लोभक्रोधमोहपूर्वका मृदुमध्याधिमात्रा दुःखाज्ञानानन्तफला

इति प्रतिपक्षभावनम्॥ ३४॥

vitarkaḥ hiṁsādayaḥ kṛta kārita anumoditāḥ lobha krodha moha pūrvakaḥ mṛdu madhya adhimātraḥ

duḥkha ajñāna anantaphalāḥ iti pratipakṣabhāvanam

vitarkaḥ – doubts; hiṁsa – violence; ādayaḥ – and related matters; kṛta – done; kārita – cause to be done; anumoditāḥ – endorsed, approved; lobha – greed; krodha – anger; moha – delusion; pūrvakaḥ – caused by, proceeded by; mṛdu – minor; madhya – mediocre; adhimātraḥ – substantial; duḥkha – distress; ajñāna – spiritual ignorance; ananta – endless; phalāḥ – results; iti – thus; pratipakṣa – opposite type; bhāvanam – considerations.

Doubts which produce violence and related actions,
which are performed, caused to be done or endorsed,
and which are caused by greed, anger and delusion,
even if minor, mediocre or substantial,
cause endless distress and spiritual ignorance as the results.
Therefore, one should consider the opposite features.

Commentary:

Violence and related actions are those which run contrary to the moral restraints of non-violence, realism, non-stealing, sexual non-expressiveness and non-possessiveness. Any ideas which run contrary to morality and which seem to justify such immoral acts are to be abandoned. If a yogin finds that he does not have the power to abandon immoral acts, then he should think deeply of the benefit of morality. This may give him the required detachment and invoke in him sufficient patience so that he restrains from vices until the impulsions pass out of his mind or loose their impulsive force.

If a moral code is to be broken at a certain time, it will be done by someone somehow because if the energy or motivation for that act, finds the yogi to be an unwilling subject, it will move away from him and influence some other person to act. A yogi should understand this. A yogi may be tricked again and again by those compulsions to do immoral acts but then after a time, he will begin to develop a resistance to those forceful motivations, which cause him to deviate. Arjuna questioned *Śrī* Krishna about this in the *Bhagavad-gīta*:

balād iva niyojitaḥ arjuna uvacā

atha kena prayukto 'yaṃ

pāpaṃ carati pūruṣaḥ

anicchann api vārṣṇeya

Arjuna said: Then explain, O family man of the Vrsnis, by what is a person forced to commit an evil even unwillingly, just as if he were compelled to do so? (Gītā 3.36)

Verse 35

अहिंसाप्रतिष्ठायां तत्सन्निधौ वैरत्यागः ॥३५॥

ahiṁsāpratiṣṭhāyāṁ tatsannidhau vairatyāgaḥ

ahiṁsā – non-violence; pratiṣṭhāyāṁ – on being firmly established; tat – his; sannidhau – presence, vicinity; vaira – hostility; tyāgaḥ – abandonment.

On being firmly established in non-violence, the abandonment of hostility occurs in his presence.

Commentary:

This charm over the violent nature of others is sometimes exhibited by great yogins. Sometimes haphazardly it is manifested in the life of student yogins. It begins in human society where people who are normally hostile to each other exhibit undue kindness even to their enemies, when they are in a presence of a yogin.

The force of the non-violent nature of the yogi may disarm and temporarily disintegrate the hostile nature of others. Sometimes this is shown when a fish-eating human being is in the presence of a great yogin. The fish-eater feels as if he cannot eat fish but must eat vegetarian or fruitarian meals. But that animal nature is again manifested when the person gets out of the range of the yogin. On the contrary however, sometimes it is seen that a great yogin has no effect on a cannibal, or flesh-eater. This is because the lower tendencies may be so strong as to resist saintly influence or it may be that the yogin assumes a sensual withdrawal attitude, intending not to adjust the life style of others.

Verse 36

सत्यप्रतिष्ठायां क्रियाफलाश्रयत्वम्॥ ३६॥

satyapratiṣṭhāyāṁ kriyāphalāśrayatvam

satya – realism; pratiṣṭhāyāṁ – on being established; kriyā – actions; phalāḥ – results; āśryatvam – what serves as a support for something else.

On being established in realism, his actions serve as a basis for results.

Commentary:

It may be contested that in all cases, a person's action serve as the basis of the results he will be afforded by providence, either for good or bad, according to what was committed. However the yogi is more conscious of his actions and their potential results than others. This is because of mystic perception in the truths of how this world operates. Thus a yogi's actions, particularly his mystic actions do confirm with reality and are consistent with realism.

In these verses instead of using the term *tistha*, *Śrī Patañjali* uses *pratistha* which means to be firmly established, not just to be initially or haphazardly established. This comes after sufficient practice or in the case of the divine beings, it is from their superior nature.

Verse 37

अस्तेयप्रतिष्ठायां सर्वरत्नोपस्थानम्॥ ३७॥

asteyapratiṣṭhāyāṁ sarvaratnopasthānam

asteya – non-stealing; pratiṣṭhāyāṁ – on firmly establishing; sarva – all; ratna – gems, precious things; upasthānam – approaching, waiting upon.

On being firmly established in non-stealing, all precious things wait to serve a yogin.

Commentary:

Still, usually a yogin is not concerned about these things. This is because his mind is fixed on the most precious thing, which is his yoga practice. Thus many opportunities for exploitation come to a yogin but he does not take advantage of them. People often wonder why a great yogi wastes his life away, and why he does not exploit all the people and resources which are in a position to be used by him. The answer is that a yogi is too preoccupied with yoga practice. A great yogin is easily discovered if one searches for the person around whom, all sorts of wealth manifest but who does not use any of that wealth and who is indifferent to it, seemingly stupid, seemingly not realizing the worth in valuables and in the cheap labor which could be derived from others.

Verse 38

ब्रह्मचर्यप्रतिष्ठायां वीर्यलाभः ॥ ३८ ॥

brahmacaryapratiṣṭhāyāṁ vīryalābhaḥ

brahmacarya – sexual non-expressiveness which results in the perception of spirituality; pratiṣṭhāyāṁ – being firmly established; vīrya – vigor; lābhaḥ – what is gained.

On being firmly established in the sexual non-expressiveness which results in the perception of spirituality, vigor is gained.

Commentary:

This means dynamic celibacy established by virtue of yoga practice in terms of *āsana* postures and *prāṇāyāma* breath nutrition methods which will be mentioned forthwith by *Śrī Patañjali*.

This is the *urdhvareta* stage where the yogi masters *kuṇḍalini* yoga and celibacy yoga.

Verse 39

अपरिग्रहस्थैर्ये जन्मकथन्तासम्बोधः ॥ ३९ ॥

aparigrahasthairye janmakathaṁtā saṁbodhaḥ

aparigraha – non-possessiveness; sthairye – in the consistent; janma – birth; kathaṁtā – how, the reason for; saṁbodhaḥ – full or correct perception regarding something.

The reason for and the correct perception of one's birth is known when there is consistent non-possessiveness.

Commentary:

When a yogi has mastered the quality of non-possessiveness in relation to this gross level of reality, his energy of appreciation shifts to the subtle reality. Thus he perceives the reason for the births he recently took. If he develops that clairvoyant skill, he comes to understand why others took up a certain body. He can know his past lives and that of others. However, if realizing that he has this skill, he becomes attracted to popularity and wants to be endearing and beloved, he might abuse himself. Thus, the skill will gradually leave him as he becomes more and more in the habit of appropriating fame in the material world.

Verse 40

शौचात्स्वाङ्गजुगुप्सा परैरसंसर्गः ॥ ४० ॥

śaucāt svāṅgajugupsā paraiḥ asaṁsargaḥ

śaucāt – from purification; svāṅga = sva – oneself + aṅga – limbs; jugupsā – aversion, disgust; parair = pariaḥ – with others; asaṁsargaḥ – non-association, lack of desire to associate.

From purification comes a disgust for one's own body and a lack of desire to associate with others.

Commentary:

True purification comes after long and hard yoga austerities. Thus the student yogi once he has earned purity of his psyche, develops a disgust for the same material body through which he worked hard to develop that purity. This is because the material body and the subtle one which caused it, has an innate tendency to absorb the pollutions which pull an ascetic down from yoga practice. As soon as a student yogi stops practice, he regresses. Even though the material body is an asset, still it always remains as a liability so long as it exists. Worse still, is the subtle body, because, until one can shed it off and take on a yoga siddha form, one is in danger of being degraded. The subtle body is worse than the gross form when it comes to adaptation and acceptance of vices.

A yogi develops a lack of desire to associate with others, except for his advanced teachers. This is because in such association he or she always runs the risks of degradation, due to susceptibility to the habits of others. People think that a yogi hates them or avoids them. Actually a yogi has no time to hate anyone because he has to attend to his practice and the energy which would be used to hate others is needed to accelerate the progress. But he develops a desire not to associate with others. This happens as a matter of course. It is a result of higher yoga practice.

Verse 41

सत्त्वशुद्धिसौमनस्यैकाग्र्येन्द्रियजयात्मदर्शनयोग्यत्वानि च॥४१॥

sattvaśuddhi saumanasya ekāgra indriyajaya
ātmadarśana yogyatvāni ca

sattva – being, nature, psyche; śuddhi – purification; saumanasya – concerning benevolence; ekāgra – ability to link the attention to one concentration force or person; indriya – sensual energy; jaya – conquest; ātma – spirit; darśana – sight, vision; yogyatvāni – being fit for yoga or abstract meditation; ca – and.

Purification of the psyche results in benevolence, the ability to link the attention to one concentration force or person, conquest of the sensual energy, vision of the spirit and fitness for abstract meditation.

Commentary:

Purification of the psyche (*sattva-śuddhi*) is possible only after celibacy yoga is mastered. Then the student yogi develops benevolence towards everyone. This is a type of detachment, but in its social application it functions as benevolence or good will towards one and all.

This student yogi develops the ability to link his mind to one concentration force in the *dhāraṇā* sixth stage of yoga practice. He masters the sensual energy by perfecting the *pratyāhār* fifth stage, and is able to begin the *dhyāna* seventh stage, to have the vision of the spirit and a fitness for abstract meditation. This is not impersonal meditation as some profess, but it is rather meditation on levels above this physical world and above the lower astral regions.

Verse 42

सन्तोषादनुत्तमसुखलाभः ॥४२॥

saṁtoṣāt anuttamaḥ sukhalābhaḥ

saṁtoṣāt – from contentment; anuttamaḥ – supreme, the very best; sukha – happiness; lābhaḥ – obtained.

From contentment, the very best in happiness is obtained.

Commentary:

This is a calm type of happiness devoid of the excitations which come from the pursuit of cravings and vices. A yogi appreciates this contentment which others dislike because it lacks excitement.

Verse 43

कायेन्द्रियसिद्धिरशुद्धिक्षयात्तपसः ॥४३॥

kāya indriya siddhiḥ aśuddhikṣayāt tapasaḥ

kāya – body; indriya – sensual energy; siddhiḥ – skill, perfection; aśuddhi – impurity; kṣayāt – from the elimination; tapasaḥ – austerity.

Austerity, resulting in the elimination of impurity produces perfection of the body and sensual energy.

Commentary:

This is the basic of results gained in the gruesome austerities of *āsana* and *prāṇāyāma*, the third and fourth stages of yoga practice. When the impurities in the subtle body are removed, one gains a skill in controlling the gross and subtle bodies as well as the sensual energy which is housed in them. This is mastered in *kuṇḍalini* yoga, celibacy yoga and purity-of-the-psyche yoga (*sattva-śuddhi*, verse 41), (*atmāśuddha*, *Gītā* 6:12).

Tapasaḥ means austerity. One may ask which austerity? This question is answered in the term *aśuddhikṣayāt*, which means the austerities which result in the elimination of *kṣayāt* or impurities.

Verse 44

स्वाध्यायादिष्टदेवतासम्प्रयोगः ॥४४॥

svādhyāyāt iṣṭadevatā saṁprayogaḥ

svādhyāyāt – from study of the psyche; iṣṭadevatā – cherished divine being; saṁprayogaḥ – intimate contact.

From study of the psyche comes intimate contact with the cherished divine being.

Commentary:

Śrī Patañjali has not named the *iṣṭadevatā*, the cherished divine personality, who the student yogi aspires to be with. However for the yogi, that person might be different than He is for some other ascetic. There are many of these divine beings who serve as cherished Lords of the limited entities.

However, when the yogi has achieved complete purity of the psyche, he gets a divine vision through which he meets the cherished deity face to face and can relate with that Personality of Godhead.

Verse 45

समाधिसिद्धिरीश्वरप्रणिधानात्॥ ४५॥

samādhisiddhiḥ īśvarapraṇidhānāt

samādhi – continuous effortless linkage of the attention to a higher concentration force or person; siddhiḥ – perfection, skill; īśvara – supreme lord; praṇidhānāt – from the profound religious meditation.

From the profound religious meditation upon the Supreme Lord comes the perfection of continuous effortless linkage of the attention to that Divinity.

Commentary:

Now all accusations upon *Śrī Patañjali* regarding his alleged ideas of impersonalism and atheism are totally denied. *Śrī Patañjali* Maharshi was undoubtedly a theist of the first order. *Śrī* B.K.S. Iyengar in his translation and commentary on the *sūtras* explained that *Patañjali* was an incarnation of Lord *Ādiśeṣa*, the divine serpentine bedstead of Lord Viṣṇu. *Patañjali*'s mother was named Goṇikā.

Verse 46

स्थिरसुखमासनम्॥ ४६॥

sthira sukham āsanam

sthira – steady; sukham – comfortable; āsanan – bodily posture.

The posture should be steady and comfortable.

Commentary:

The yoga *āsana* for meditation should be one that is steady and comfortable. Ideally, one should sit for meditation in the lotus posture, the *padmāsana*, if that posture is unsteady and uncomfortable, one should practice to improve it. During meditation one should use a posture that keeps the body steady and mind at ease. As one practices more and more, the difficult postures become easier and easier to perform.

Verse 47

प्रयत्नशैथिल्यानन्तसमापत्तिभ्याम्॥ ४७॥

prayatna śaithilya ananta samāpattibhyām

prayatna – effort; śaithilya – relaxation; ananta – endless, infinite; samāpattibhyām – meeting, encounter.

It results in relaxation of effort and meeting with the infinite.

Commentary:

Āsana is perfected when it becomes steady and comfortable, so much so that the yogin relaxes his efforts to hold the body in the posture. He shifts his attention to link it with the infinite.

Verse 48

ततो द्वन्द्वानभिघातः ॥ ४८ ॥

tataḥ dvandvāḥ anabhighātaḥ

tataḥ – then; dvandvāḥ – the dualities of happiness and distress, heat and cold; anabhighātaḥ – no shrinking, no attacking, no botheration.

From then on, there are no botherations from the dualities like happiness and distress or heat and cold.

Commentary:

When there is perfect posture of body in which the yogin attains continuous effortless linkage of his attention to a higher concentration force, or divine person, then the botheration of the mento-emotional energy which concerns happiness and distress cease for him. These continue in the life of the student yogins who are on a lower level of practice. They should master themselves through consistent effort.

Verse 49

तस्मिन्सति श्वासप्रश्वासयोर्गतिविच्छेदः प्राणायामः ॥ ४९ ॥

tasmin satiśvāsa praśvāsayoḥ
gativicchedaḥ prāṇāyāmaḥ

tasmin – on this; sati – being accomplished; śvāsa – inhalation; praśvāsayoḥ – of the exhalation; gati – the flow; vicchedaḥ – the separation; prāṇāyāmḥ – breath regulation.

Once this is accomplished, breath regulation, which is the separation of the flow of inhalation and exhalation, is attained.

Commentary:

The *prāņāyāma* cannot be mastered properly until one has mastered postures or *āsanas* but that does not mean that preliminary *prāņāyāma* cannot be learned before hand. All the stages of yoga are learned one by one or even haphazardly according to one's destiny regarding availability of knowledgeable teachers. One cannot focus properly on the vital force until one has mastered a suitable posture. This is the point but one can become familiar with the various *prāņāyāmas* before hand.

A yogin has to learn how to separate the flow of the breath, so that the inhalation is distinct from the exhalation, so that there is a pause between these. This is why the word *vicchedaḥ* was used. It means separation, cleavage, or gap. Generally, mammals breathe in and out without pause because their breath is not complete or sufficient. It is usually shallow. The out breath is rushed in to speed up the next intake of air. When one reconditions his lung apparatus, so that the intake is complete, this rush for exhalations in order to inhale again, ceases. And the separation of the intake and out breath becomes evident, along with the benefits of that for meditation.

Verse 50

वाह्याभ्यन्तरस्तम्भवृत्तिः देशकालसङ्ख्याभिः परिदृष्टो दीर्घसूक्ष्मः ॥५०॥

bāhya ābhyantara stambha vṛttiḥ deśa kāla saṁkhyābhiḥ paridṛṣṭah dīrgha sūkṣmaḥ

bāhya – external; ābhyantara – internal; stambha – restrained, suppressed, restrictive; vṛttiḥ – activity, movement operation; deśa – place; kāla – time; saṁkhyābhiḥ – with numbering accounting; paridṛṣṭah – measured, regulated; dīrgha – prolonged; sūkṣmaḥ – subtle, hardly noticeable.

It has internal, external and restrictive operations, which are regulated according to the place, time and accounting, being prolonged or hardly noticed.

Commentary:

Ideally, *prāṇāyāma* is learned from a teacher who practiced to proficiency. Such teachers are hard to find. The first accomplishment of a student yogi is to learn how to purify the nāḍīs in the subtle form. When that is achieved, he will discover other *prāṇāyāmas* automatically by the grace of the force of *prāṇa* and by the awakening of the *kuṇḍalini* chakra.

Pranayama teachers usually stress a count for alternate breathing in the ratio of 1:4:2, meaning that one should inhale through one nostril for one count, then retain the air for four counts and then exhale all air through the other nostril during two counts, such that if one starts inhaling through the right nostril alone, one will hold the air, then expel it through the left nostril. Then begin the cycle by inhaling through the left nostril, holding and expelling the air through the right nostril. Eventually one should increase the duration, so that the time for a count increases. This is done without straining the lung system. If the *nadīs* are not fully charged before one begins, and if one is not a celibate yogi, one will not be successful with this practice. There are many preliminary practices required for success in yoga. One would be fortunate if he or she could learn these from an accomplished teacher.

Verse 51

वाह्याभ्यन्तरविषयाक्षेपी चतुर्थः ॥५१॥

bāhya ābhyantara viṣaya ākṣepī caturthaḥ

bāhya – external; ābhyantara – internal; viṣaya – objective; ākṣepī – transcending; caturthaḥ – the fourth.

That which transcends the objective, external and internal breath regulation is the fourth type of breath infusement techniques.

Commentary:

In the previous *sūtra*, *Śrī Patañjali* listed three types of operations, relating to internal, external and restrictive operations of the breath. Then he gave a fourth operation having to do with transcending the objective of the preliminary three operations.

Verse 52

ततः क्षीयते प्रकाशावरणम्॥५२॥

tataḥ kṣīyate prakāśa āvaraṇam

tataḥ – thence, from that; kṣīyate – is dissipated; prakāśa – light; āvaraṇam – covering, mental darkness.

From that is dissipated,
the mental darkness which veils the light,

Commentary:

The advanced *prāṇāyāma* is done after much practice. Its mastership does not come easy. The result of it is clear to a yogi because the dark mind-space is cleared off and a brilliant light is perceived. This light is illuminating (*prakāśa*).

Verse 53

धारणासु च योग्यता मनसः॥५३॥

dhāraṇāsu ca yogyatā manasaḥ

dhāraṇāsu – for linking the attention to a higher concentration force or person; ca – and; yogyatā – being conducive for abstract meditation; manasaḥ – of the mind.

and from that, is attained the state of the mind
for linking the attention
to a higher concentration force or person.

Commentary:

Dhāraṇā practice requires a preliminary mastership in certain aspects of *prāṇa* energy control. This is why when someone sits to meditate without first doing *prāṇāyāma*, he cannot be successful even though he may imagine for himself in peace, happiness and light. One has to make the mind fit for yoga practice (*yogyatā manasaḥ*). The mind will prevent the attention from linking to a higher concentration force or person if the mind itself is not surcharged with a higher grade of pranic energy. It will be unable to make a higher linkage, except now and again, by a fluke, haphazardly. For consistent practice one must do the *āsana* with *prāṇāyāma* daily before meditation practice.

Verse 54

स्वविषयासम्प्रयोगे चित्तस्य स्वरूपानुकार इवेन्द्रियाणां प्रत्याहारः ॥५४॥

svaviṣaya asaṁprayoge cittasya svarūpāanukāraḥ
iva indriyāṇāṁ pratyāhāraḥ

sva – their own; viṣaya – objects of perception; asaṁprayoge – in not contacting; cittasya – of the mento-emotional energy; svarūpa – own form; anukāraḥ – imitation, patterning, assuming; iva – as if, as it were; indriyāṇāṁ – senses; pratyāhāraḥ – withdrawal of sensual energy and its focus on the mind.

The withdrawal of the senses, is as it was,
their assumption of the form of mento-emotional energy
when not contacting their own objects of perception.

Commentary:

In his word for word meanings, *Śrī* B.K.S. Iyengar gave as the root word for *pratyāhārah*. He gave the basic parts of that Sanskrit word as follows:

prati + ang + hr — meaning to draw towards the opposite.

When the mento-emotional energy, the *citta*, is outward bound, it is called sensual energy or *indriyāni*. But when it is inward bound it is called *citta* or emotional force. A yogin has to master that *citta* energy and reorient it so that it gives up its outward bound habit.

Verse 55

ततः परमा वश्यतेन्द्रियाणाम्॥५५॥

tataḥ paramā vaśyatā indriyāṇām

tataḥ – then, from that accomplishment; paramā – highest, greatest; vaśyatā – subdued, subjugation, control; indriyāṇām – of the sense.

From that accomplishment
comes the highest degree of control of the senses.

Commentary:

Pratyāhār practice when mastered, gives the student yogin, the qualification to practice higher yoga, which are mainly actions on the mystic plane.

Chapter 3

Vibhūti Pāda:

Glory Displayed

Verse 1

देशबन्धश्चित्तस्य धारणा ॥ १ ॥

deśa bandhaḥ cittasya dhāraṇā

deśa – location; bandhaḥ – confinement, restriction; cittasya – of the mento-emotional energy; dhāraṇā – linking of the attention to a concentration force or person.

Linking of the attention to a concentration force or person, involves a restricted location in the mento-emotional energy.

Commentary:

For higher meditation, everything is within the mental and emotional energy fields. This is the psychological environment from which a yogin can break out of this dimension to enter other parallel worlds, which are either subtle, supernatural or spiritual. It is from within the mento-emotional energy that one breaks out of this world. The paradox of it is this: the very same mental and emotional energy, which caused us to become attached to this world, can also in turn, cause liberation. The gate for exiting this world is in the same mento-emotional energy (*cittasya*).

Many people feel that a yogi enters into his own psyche, develops it, feels powerful as God and then becomes perfect. Little do they understand that from within his own psyche a yogi finds entry into parallel worlds. From particular locations, deśa, particular limiting or confining locations (*deśa bandhaḥ*), a yogi finds doorways and peep holes that give him access to other worlds, places that he might be transferred after permanently leaving his physical body.

Verse 2

तत्र प्रत्ययैकतानता ध्यानम् ॥ २ ॥

tatra pratyayaḥ ekatānatā dhyānam

tatra – there, in that location; pratyayaḥ – conviction or belief as mental content, instinctive interest; ekatānatā – one continuous threadlike flow of attention = eka – one + tānatā – thread of fiber; dhyānam – effortless linking of the attention to a higher concentration force or person.

When in that location, there is one continuous threadlike flow of one's instinctive interest, that is the effortless linking of the attention to a higher concentration force or person.

Commentary:

The key term in this verse is *pratyayaḥ*. Shivram Apte in his Sanskrit English Dictionary gave the following meanings: conviction, settled belief, trust, faith, conception, idea, and notion. I have given instinctive interest as the meaning. In any case, when that (*pratyayaḥ*) flows in a continuous threadlike motion at the place of focus, then it is the *dhyāna*, seventh stage of yoga practice.

The Raj Yogi I.K. Taimni gave stretching or streaming unbrokenly as one, as the meaning for *ekatānatā*. A student yogi would do well for himself by carefully studying the Sanskrit of this verse, because it is not sufficient to say that *dhāraṇā* is concentration, *dhyāna* is contemplation or meditation as we are accustomed to. Such definitions are too vague.

Verse 3

तदेवार्थमात्रनिर्भासं स्वरूपशून्यमिव समाधिः ॥ ३ ॥

tadeva arthamātranirbhāsaṁ
svarūpaśūnyam iva samādhiḥ

tadeva = tat – that + eva – only, alone; artha – purpose objective; mātra – only, merely; nirbhāsaṁ – illuminating; svarūpa – own form; śūnyam – empty, void, lacking; iva – as if; samādhiḥ – continuous effortless linking of the attention to a higher concentration force or person.

That same effortless linkage of the attention when experienced as illumination of the higher concentration force or person, while the yogi feels as if devoid of himself, is *samādhi* or continuous effortless linkage of his attention to the special person, object, or force.

Commentary:

Samādhi is not defined here as it is popularly described by so many meditation authorities, by those who dislike it or shun it as being impersonal. There is no word here that says that *samādhi* is a void or that it is *śūnya*. The word śūnya occurs in reference to the *svarūpa* or form of the yogi, and only in the sense that while he is in contact with the force, object or person of his interest, he is so much connected to it that his own form seems as if it were not there and that only the force, object or other person being contacted was there. The Sanskrit article *iva* means "as if".

When there is continued effortless linkage of the attention to a higher concentration force, object or person, the yogi's attention is completely or near completely given over to that higher reality, so that it feels as if he is not there (*iva śūnya*) and that only the higher reality is present with illumination (*nirbhāsaṁ*). This gives him a thorough insight into the said force, object or person.

Verse 4

त्रयमेकत्र संयमः ॥ ४ ॥

trayam ekatra saṁyamaḥ

trayam – three; ekatra – in one place, all taken together as one practice; saṁyamah – complete restraint.

The three as one practice are the complete restraint.

Commentary:

In Chapter 4 of Gita, verses 26-27, *samyama* is mentioned:

śrotrādīnī 'ndriyāni anye saṁyamāgniṣu juhvati
śabdādīn viṣayān anye indriyāgniṣu juhvati
sarvāṇī 'ndriya karmāṇi prāṇakarmāṇi capare
ātmasaṁyama yogāgnau juhvati jñānadīpite

Other yogis offer hearing and other sensual powers into the fiery power of restraint. Some offer sound and other sensual pursuits into the fiery sensual power.
Some ascetics subject the sensual actions andthe breath function to self-restraint by fiery yoga austerities, which are illuminated by experience.

Saṁ means very, quite, greatly, thoroughly, very much, all, whole, complete. *Yamaḥ* means restraint, control.

It is obvious that one has to understand the word according to how it is defined by the particular writer. *Śrī* Krishna's use of the term is similar to what *Śrī Patañjali* meant, but *Śrī Patañjali* is specific in saying that saṁyamaḥ is the combining of the three practices of higher yoga into one discipline. When *dhāraṇā*, *dhyāna* and *samādhi* are made into one technique, that is called saṁyamaḥ in *Śrī Patañjali*'s vocabulary.

From that perspective, there would be only 6 stages to yoga, namely *yama*, *niyama*, *āsana*, *prāṇāyāma*, *pratyāhār*, and *saṁyamaḥ* . In that case *saṁyamaḥ* means that one has to do the three higher stages of yoga as one practice. This actually happens when one masters *dhyāna* yoga. Sometimes in *dhyāna*, one slips back to the *dhāraṇā* stages and sometimes it progresses automatically to the *samādhi* stage. Thus *Śrī Patañjali* is correct in bridging the three higher stages. When there is success in this, the mento-emotional energy is completely restrained from its involvement in this world and in the lower subtle world.

Verse 5

तज्जयात्प्रज्ञालोकः ॥ ५ ॥

tajjayāt prajñālokaḥ

taj = tad = tat – that; jayāt – from the mastery; prajñā – insight; ālokaḥ – illuminating.

From the mastery of that complete restraint of the mento-emotional energy, one develops the illuminating insight.

Commentary:

This illuminating insight is not an understanding in the mind or mere insight or intuition. It is rather the illuminated buddhi organ in action, peering into parallel dimensions and spiritual atmospheres. With that illuminating insight, one sees visually into other worlds through one's buddhi organ and also directly through a vision which is formed by one's attention.

Verse 6

तस्य भूमिषु विनियोगः ॥ ६ ॥

tasya bhūmiṣu viniyogaḥ

tasya – of it, of this; bhūmiṣu – in stages; viniyogaḥ – application, employment, practice.

The practice of this complete restraint occurs in stages.

Commentary:

The complete restraint which is the result of mastering the three higher states of yoga does not happen instantaneously, except for those yogis who have practiced considerably in solitude. All others attain *samyama* or complete restraint of the mental and emotional energy by stages while attempting to reach the culmination of the process, which is *samādhi*. A student yogi who has a grasp on the *dhāraṇā* practice does that. Then he graduates to *dhyāna* and then to *samādhi*. Even after he reaches *samādhi*, he must sometimes begin at *dhāraṇā* and wait in his psyche for a progression to *dhyāna* and then on to *samādhi*. Sometimes for one reason or other, he struggles with the *dhāraṇā* stages and goes further. Sometimes he progresses on the *dhyāna* and goes no further, at other times, he may attain to *samādhi*. This is why *Śrī Patañjali* has alerted the student yogis that its practice occurs in stages.

Verse 7

त्रयमन्तरङ्गं पूर्वेभ्यः ॥ ७ ॥

trayam antaraṅgaṁ pūrvebhyaḥ

trayam – three; antaraṅgaṁ = antar – internal, psychological, concerning the thinking and feeling organs + aṅgaṁ – part; pūrvebhyaḥ – in reference to the preliminary stages mentioned before.

In reference to the preliminary stages of yoga, these three higher states concern the psychological organs.

Commentary:

Dhāraṇā , *dhyāna* and *samādhi* concern the psychological organs. These concern mystic practice as assisted by the physical and social practices which involve *yama*, *niyama*, *āsana*, *prāṇāyāma* and *pratyāhār*. While in the five preliminary stages there are physical actions, in the three higher stages, it is mostly mystic actions having to do with controlling, observing and operating psychological organs in the subtle body.

Verse 8

तदपि बहिरङ्गं निर्बीजस्य॥८॥

tadapi bahiraṅgaṁ nirbījasya

tadapi = that = api – even; bahiraṅga = bahir – external + aṅgaṁ – part; nirbījasya – not motivated by the mento-emotional energy.

**But even that initial mastership
of the three higher stages of yoga,
is external in reference to meditation,
which is not motivated by the mento-emotional energy.**

Commentary:

Initially a student yogi works for yoga success on the basis of disgust with the subtle and gross material energy. It is due to the impressions lodged in his mental and emotional energies. Thus in a sense he cannot strive without being motivated by those very same energies. As *Śrī Patañjali* told us, the purpose of that energy is to give us experience in the world and also to do the converse which is to motivate us to strive for liberation.

prakāśa kriyā *sthiti śīlaṁ bhūtendriyātmakaṁ*

bhogāpavargārthaṁ dṛśyam

What is perceived is of the nature of the mundane elements and the sense organs and is formed in clear perception, action or stability. Its purpose is to give experience or to allow liberation. (Yoga Sūtra 2:18)

While initially the student yogi practices *samyama*, complete restrain under motivations which comes from the mental and emotional energies, later on, as he advances, he progresses on the basis of forces, objects and persons he encounters in the spiritual atmosphere. Such motivations are free from flaws. These are termed seedless or lacking urges from this side of existence.

Verse 9

व्युत्थाननिरोधसंस्कारयोरभिभवप्रादुर्भावौ निरोधक्षणचित्तान्वयो निरोधपरिणामः॥९॥

*vyutthāna nirodha saṁskārayoḥ
abhibhava prādurbhāvau nirodhakṣaṇa
cittānvayaḥ nirodhapariṇāmaḥ*

vyutthāna – expression; nirodha – suppression; saṁskārayoḥ – of the mento-emotional impressions; abhibhava – disappearance; prādurbhāvau – and manifestation ; nirodha – restraint, cessation; kṣaṇa – momentarily; citta – mento-emotional energy; ānvayaḥ – connection; nirodha – restraint; pariṇāmaḥ – transforming effects.

**When the connection
with the mento-emotional energy momentarily ceases
during the manifestation and disappearance phases
when there is expression or suppression of the impressions,
that is the restraint of the transforming mento-emotional energy.**

Commentary:

Śrī Patañjali is respected by all advanced yogis who are aware of these yoga *sūtras*. Only persons who do no yoga and who are ignorant of the techniques, make a joke of the detailed work of *Śrī Patañjali*. One can only admire his genius.

There are many who become masters of *kriyā* yoga. Most of them do not take detailed notes of the preliminary and advanced practices. This is because those yogis are to be liberated and do not see the need to keep a record for review. However *Śrī Patañjali* saw the need. This is a detailed study of his practices. I offer respects to him.

A student yogi should note what is emotional and what is mental energy. He should note that the two energies are interchangeable under certain psychological circumstances. Furthermore even though the mental energy hold to its own integrity, showing a distinction between itself and the emotions, still the two energies do communicate with each other. Beyond that, a student should note how impressions arise and subside. Anyone who has done concentration, contemplation or meditation, knows very well that the impressions come and go of their own accord. But *Śrī Patañjali* spoke of the interval (*kṣaṇa*) between the expression of an idea in the mind and the suppression of that very same idea. At first this sounds easy. But let us think of it again.

When an idea arises in the mind, depending on its value to the emotions, it may be expanded or it may be dissipated immediately. If it is expanded, what really takes place? If it is expanded the idea ceases for a split second. The memory in conjunction with the imagination creates another idea which is associative to the one which disappeared. *Śrī Patañjali* wants us to focus on that split second cessation (*nirodhakṣaṇa*). He wants us to extend that split second to a longer, much longer period. If we could keep the mind in that state for long we would enter into *samādhi*.

Of course such a feat is easier said than done. Sometimes effortlessly, the mind remains for five or ten seconds in that blank state. Expert yogis hold the mind in that state for minutes and some do so for hours at a time. This is their accomplishment of *samādhi*. One will find that if he can hold the mind there, the imagination faculty will change into being spiritual vision, an actual illuminating sight, an eye. With the help of Lord Krishna, Arjuna had some experiences of this at Kurukshetra. When again Arjuna wanted that insight, *Śrī* Krishna with mild disappointment, declined. He said, in the *Anu Gītā* , that He could not again impart it to Arjuna because it involved a yoga siddhi which Krishna expressed at Kurukshetra for a specific purpose.

By careful study of this verse, one will get an idea of what is required for yoga success, which is the prolonging of the momentary blankness which occurs in the mind between the expression within it of one idea and another. The whole problem with meditation has to do with this.

For success, a yogi must be prepared to spend years if necessary noticing that momentarily blankness and practicing to hold the mind there. Initially, it will seem that it is impossible to stop the mind there, but by regular practice for a long time, the period for holding the mind in that state is extended.

Verse 10

तस्य प्रशान्तवाहिता संस्कारात्॥ १० ॥

tasya praśāntavāhita saṁskārāt

tasya – of this; praśānta – spiritual peace; vāhita – flow; saṁskārāt – from the impressions derived.

**Concerning this practice of restraint,
the impressions derived cause a flow of spiritual peace.**

Commentary:

When the yogi repeated practices to keep his mind in a condition of restraining, causing the transformations of the mento-emotional energy to cease, then his memory is accredited with quieting impressions, which bring on the uninterrupted flow of spiritual peace.

Verse 11

सर्वार्थतैकाग्रतयोः क्षयोदयौ चित्तस्य समाधिपरिणामः ॥ ११ ॥

*sarvārthatā ekāgratayoḥ kṣaya udayau
cittasya samādhipariṇāmaḥ*

sarvārthatā – varying objective; ekāgratayoḥ – of the one aspect before the attention; kṣaya – decrease; udayau – and increase; cittasya – of the mento-emotional energy; samādhi – the continuous effortless linkage of the attention to the higher concentration force, object or person; pariṇāmaḥ – transforming effects, change.

**The decrease of varying objectives
in the mento-emotional energy
and the increase of the one aspect within it
are the changes noticed
in the practice of continuous effortless linking of the attention
to higher concentration forces, objects or persons.**

Commentary:

We are reminded that the *samādhi* stage will come after long practice. It will come gradually over time of practicing *samyama*, as *Śrī Patañjali* defined, being the practice of *dhāraṇā* which progressed into *dhyāna*, which then changes into *samādhi*.

As one tries to practice *samādhi*, he will find that there is a decrease in the mind's many objectives and an increase of its tendency for one focus as dictated by the practice. This one focus is not a focus on a deity but rather it is the focus mentioned in verse 9 of this chapter, which is the restraint of the transformations of the mento-emotional energy.

It has nothing to do with any object or any person, divine or ordinary. It is a battle within the psychology of the yogi, for control of the psyche. It is an internal private war in the battlefield of the mind and emotions.

When the yogin notices that his mind's habits change, so that it desires more of that peace attained when it is in a void state, then he knows that he is making progress. This is not a void in the world nor in the subtle world but rather a void in his own psyche, whereby his memory does not discharge ideas which burst in the mind environment into impressions which trigger other impressions and thoughts and which torment the yogi and frustrate his efforts for psyche control.

Verse 12

ततः पुनः शान्तोदितौ तुल्यप्रत्ययौ चित्तस्यैकाग्रतापरिणामः ॥ १२ ॥

tataḥ punaḥśānta uditau tulya pratyayau
cittasya ekāgratāpariṇāmaḥ

tataḥ – then; punaḥ – again; santoditau = śānta – tranquilized, settled, subsided + uditau – and agitated, emerging; tulya – similar; pratyayaḥu – conviction or belief as mental content, instinctive interest; cittasya – of the mento-emotional energy; ekāgratā – of what is in front of one aspect before the attention; pariṇāmaḥ – transforming effects, change.

Then again, when the mind's content is the same as it was when it is subsiding and when it is emerging, that is the transformation called "having one aspect in front of or before the attention".

Commentary:

This condition of mind is related to everything which was described in this chapter so far. As the yogin gets to the stage where his mind content is no longer dominated by memories, he is able to keep his attention in a quiescent state, (*praśānta-vāhita* verse 10). However, this is maintained only by keeping the expressive and depressive restraining gyration of the mind out of contact with the memory.

At any time, when the attention is allowed to contact the memory, either by accident or as induced or deliberately, the mind content will be altered to accommodate various images and sounds (*sarvārthatā*, verse

11). That is counter productive, being regretted by the yogi, since it puts him at odds with his objective, which is to cease such mental operations completely.

The subsiding and emerging nature of the mind cannot be changed but a yogi can get relief from it by his assumption of a focus into other dimensions and by his freezing the mind by *prāṇāyāma* practice. But as soon as it is possible, the mind will be found to have reverted back to its essential nature. This is, in a sense, disgusting and it causes the yogin to feel that somehow he has got to get rid of such a mind.

It is not easy to have just one aspect in front of the attention. By nature the mind seeks to change its position by an in and out, rising and falling, creating and disintegrating function. This is the natural condition of the normal mindal stage. This is why it is necessary to do *prāṇāyāma*. By regulating the breath and by surcharging the mind with a high pressure charge of *prāṇa*, it slows down or abandons lower diversions altogether. But then again as soon as the higher pressure charge dissipates, the mind returns to its normal gyrations, except in the case of those yogins who have developed a yoga siddha body. Skeptics therefore suspect that yoga is a waste of time. They feel that no one can overcome the gyrating nature of the mind.

For the mind content to be the same when the mento-emotional energy is moving to create images as to disintegrate the same and for the mind to remain consistently blank like this for sometime, the yogin has to master the *dhāraṇā*, sixth stage of yoga practice, whereby he can link the mind to a consistent concentration force and at the same time hold on to or look through his attention energy.

The technique used for this is the one where the yogi keeps his attention locked to the subtle sound which comes in from the chit akash. Usually that is heard in the vicinity of the right ear. As a yogi hears this, he also focuses on diffused light in front of him (*ekāgratā*). There is no visual object before his attention at this time. It is merely a listening to the naad sound in the vicinity of the right ear, while looking forward through his attention which makes a slight contact with the mento-emotional energy (*citta*). When his looking action relaxes of its own accord, he sees a diffused light before him.

Śrī Patañjali already mentioned that diffusion as a covering of light. That was in Verse 52 of the last chapter.

tataḥ kṣīyate prakāśa āvaraṇam

From that is dissipated, the mental darknesswhich veils the light.

(Yoga Sūtra 2.52)

The diffused light which is actually light mixed with cloudy energy or misty force, will be separated such that the misty force or cloudy energy will disappear, leaving only light. When a yogi attains this practice, it is understood that he mastered the seventh state of yoga called *dhyāna*.

Some people think that this practice includes imagining a deity, a supernatural, or spiritual being, or imaging a subtle primal force, but that is incorrect. The yogi only needs to get his supernatural and spiritual visions to be operative. Then he sees everything in the chit akash, the sky of consciousness. He does not need to imagine any supersubtle or divine objects.

Verse 13

एतेन भूतेन्द्रियेषु धर्मलक्षणावस्थापरिणामा व्याख्याताः ॥ १३ ॥

etena bhūtendriyeṣu dharma lakṣaṇa avasthā pariṇāmāḥ vyākhyātāḥ

etena – by this; bhūta – the various states of matter; indriyeṣu – by the sensual energy; dharma – quality; lakṣaṇa – shape, characteristic; avasthā – condition; pariṇāmāḥ – changes, transformation; vyākhyātāḥ – is described.

By this description of the changes, quality and shape, the two changing conditions of the states of matter, as well as of the sensual energy, were described.

Commentary:

The whole subtle and gross material energy is effectively dealt with in this yoga practice, in the efforts of the yogi to get his psychology under control. The whole controlling effort has to do with developing a complete disinterest in the gross and subtle material energy, which is called *bhutendriya* in this verse. Our response to the mundane energy is our downfall. When we learn how to control that response and how to eventually cease responding altogether, we will get the control which we so desperately seek.

Verse 14

शान्तोदिताव्यपदेश्यधर्मानुपाती धर्मी ॥ १४ ॥

śānta udita avyapadeśya dharma anupātī dharmī

śānta – collapsed; udita - emergent; avyapadeśya – what is not to be defined, what is latent; dharma – law, sustaining force; anupātī – reach full retrogression; dharmī – most basic condition.

When the collapsed, emergent and latent forces reach full retrograde, that is the most basic condition.

Commentary:

Most commentators attribute dharmi as the *prakṛti* energy, or the most subtle form of material nature. This is correct. However, in the case of the yogi, his research into it has to do with finding a technique for abandoning it once and for all, for complete detachment and independence from it. Thus the assessment of it occurs within his psyche within the mento-emotional energy. Once he gets down to its most basic condition, or to the ultimate substratum of material nature, he can take a good look at it with supernatural vision and make his decisions for not responding to it anymore. Once he sees the course of its progression into manifestation, and retrogression out of manifestation, he will no longer be afraid of it or be attracted to it. Then it served its purpose for him and he becomes liberated quickly and definitely.

Obviously we have got some desire to be in touch with material energy. Thus it is necessary that we understand our attraction to it and eliminate that fondness for it or eradicate and dismember whatever it is that influenced us to embrace it.

Verse 15

क्रमान्यत्वं परिणामान्यत्वे हेतुः ॥ १५॥

krama anyatvaṁ pariṇāma anyatve hetuḥ

krama – sequence; anyatvaṁ – otherness, difference; pariṇāma – transformation change; anyatve – in difference; hetuḥ – cause.

The cause of a difference in the transformation is the difference in the sequential changes.

Commentary:

A student yogi may become preoccupied with the various changing scenes, which occur when the mento-emotional energy (*citta*) goes through its numerous operations. Thus he becomes bewildered, but sooner or later he will get help from a senior yogin, such that he will no longer follow the sequential changes but will instead observe the operations of the energy. The content of the operations is not important. He has to grasp this fact, if he is to acquire supreme detachment and get leverage over the transformations which occur in his mind and emotions and which keep him from achieving the supernatural and spiritual insights.

Some student yogins like infants, become spell bound by their imagination faculty and its picturizations. They make little progress in higher yoga and talk about it to their teachers. They need to understand that a fascination with the differences, in the various transformations is caused only by differences in the sequential changes and not from any thing substantial or meaningful. Whatever occurs in their silly little minds is of no consequence really. It is not the content of the mind (*pratyayaḥ*), nor the conviction or moody appetite of the mind that is relevant but rather the way the mind operates.

A person entering a film theater usually becomes enthralled with the images on the screen. But that is childish. He should be interested in the projector mechanism which causes the movie to be shown in the first place. It is the working of that mechanism that is important, not the content of the various movies which are shown through it. When a student yogi gets this understanding, he becomes freed. So long as one is attracted primarily to the mind content, one will not adhere to the instructions for higher yoga, but will instead, complain about the disciplines just as how a child cries if his parent takes him out of a movie theater before a film is finished.

The parent wants to show the child the projection apparatus and the operator of that mechanism, but the child finds the projection room to be dull and boring and not as stimulating as the film show it produces. He feels that it is not interactive with him. So the student yogi usually fights tooth and nail with advanced teachers who come down from siddhaloka to free them.

The difference in the sequential change of ideas and images in the mind occur because of how the memory and imagination interact with the information which comes in a compressed form from the senses from the subtle and gross world. This admixture is bewildering. Advanced yogis advise us to forgo them, to just ignore them. Their policy is that instead of looking at those impressions, we should just avoid them all together. This avoidance disempowers them and weakens their grip on us.

The analogy of the boy in the movie house would help in this case. The more and more he stays out of the movie house, the more detached and disinterested he may become. The more he goes to it, the more his nature reacts in response to it and the more attached and interested he becomes. But in that case his interest is being abused, being needlessly exploited by fiction. This is why in India, there was a period of history where many leading yogis condemned human consumption of name and forms. If we become enthralled again and again with names of things and with the forms of things, it will cause us to become more and more fascinated with this world and that will push us away from liberation.

According to the sequence of the various film slides, the movie shows in particular ways which may invoke our interest, either to cause happiness, distress or indifference, and according to how the memory, imagination, reasoning and sensual intake interact, we become fascinated with the differences in the transformation within our minds and emotions. Thus the important thing is to understand how the mind operates, not what the content of it comprises.

Even though this is the solution, this is easier said than done. When one becomes determined to follow this advice, he discovers that somehow he is enthralled by the content of the mind. That itself entraps him. At least that is how a student yogin will feel. But again, he should study the operation of the entrapment mechanism.

The boy in our analogy must study how the movie building was constructed with a small door for entry on a back street and a large attractive door for entry on a main street. The very construction of the place is bewildering and causes the body to go into the theater through the front door, which leads into the gallery where the movie is showing. Once the boy understands this he can avoid that door and find his way to the small door on the back street which leads to the projection room where he will be able to study something that is of vital importance to him, which is the way the projection apparatus operates.

Sometimes a student yogi finds that he repeatedly finds himself in front of a series of images which are projected by the imagination faculty or which were released from the memory or from the sensual organs which collect information. Before he can realize it, or be objective to it, he finds himself looking, analyzing, interacting with these images. This procedure, though impulsive must be stopped by the student yogin.

Verse 16

परिणामत्रयसंयमादतीतानागतज्ञानम्॥ १६ ॥

pariṇāmatraya saṁyamāt atīta anāgatajñānam

pariṇāma – transformation change; traya – threefold; saṁyamāt – from the complete restraint of the mento-emotional energy; atīta – past; anāgata – future; jñānam – information.

From the complete restrain of the mento-emotional energy in terms of the three-fold transformations within it, the yogi gets information about the past and future.

Commentary:

This set of verses regarding the perfectional skills or siddhis gained by certain practices, have caused *Śrī Patañjali* to be criticized by those religious leaders who feel that the siddhi perfectional powers are a distraction either from liberation or from attaining love of God. However, the accusation is ungrounded, because *Śrī Patañjali* very realistically informs us about the course of our development, alerting us to what lies ahead. These perfectional skills cannot be avoided by anyone who advances in spiritual disciplines. We need training in how not to be charmed by these powers of the lower and higher subtle bodies.

Everything about the past, in microscopic and atomic impressions, is in our individual memories and in the cosmic memory pool. Any of this information can be retrieved by the Supreme Being.

śrī-bhagavān uvāca
bahūni me vyatītānijanmāni tava cārjuna
tāny aham veda sarvānina tvam vettha parantapa

The Blessed Lord said: Many of My births transpired, and yours, Arjuna. I recall them all. You do not remember, O scorcher of the enemies. (Gītā 4.5)

Everything about the future is potentially present in the existence right now. The parameters which will cause the formation of the future are present. The Supreme Being can look at it and accurately gage the probabilities.

One should not interpret this verse to mean that a yogi can know everything. A yogi can know much if he applies himself sufficiently and can enter into the cosmic memory and decipher its impressions. First of all, he must be allowed to do that. This allowance is not always granted to a yogi by the Supreme Being. However a yogi does not need the permission of the Supreme Being to enter his own limited memory bank. His ability to do that relies on his expertise in the complete restrain of his mento-emotional energy.

A great yogin, *Śrīla* Yogeshwarananda can decipher the cosmic parameters which will control what happens in the future of this universe. Therefore it is possible but only a rare yogin can do this. The complete conquest of the mento-emotional energy is a feat reserved for a select few great yogis like him. The important achievement is to get your own memory under control. When this is done one can check on the relationship between one limited memory and the cosmic reservoir of past impressions.

Some people feel that if a yogi reaches a stage of knowledge about the past and future, he would be omniscient, but that is an exaggeration. Such information will not affect the course of history nor change the probability, nor affect how the Supreme Being relates to the limited personalities. Its value is in the potency to convince the yogi to make an exit from these gross and subtle mundane histories. But that is not all, because a yogin has to acquire permission to do that. That permission must be gained from the Supreme Being, who might not grant it to a particular yogin.

Verse 17

शब्दार्थप्रत्ययानामितरेतराध्यासात्सङ्करस्तत्प्रविभागसंयमात्सर्वभूतरुतज्ञानम् ॥ १७ ॥

śabda artha pratyayānām itaretarādhyāsāt
saṅkaraḥ tatpravibhāga saṁyamāt
sarvabhūta rutajñānam

śabda – sound; artha – meaning; pratyayānām – pertaining to the mind content, convictions, idea; itaretara = itara + itara = one for the other; adhyāsāt – resulting from the super-imposition; saṅkaraḥ – intermixture; tat – their; pravibhāga – differentiation, sorting, classification, mental clarity; saṁyamāt – from the complete restraint of the mento-emotional energy; sarva – all; bhūta – creature; ruta – sound, cry, yell, language; jñānam – information, knowledge.

From the complete restraint of the mento-emotional energy in relation to mental clarity, regarding the intermixture resulting from the superimposing one for the other, of sound, its meaning and the related mentality, knowledge about the language of all creatures is gained.

Commentary:

When a student yogin simplifies his mentality by sorting out the various parts of it, and when he detaches his imagination faculty from it's involuntary connection to the memory, as well as when he consistently retracts his sensual energies from the gross and lower subtle worlds, he gains a certain mental clarity, by which his buddhi organ instantaneously sorts the sound, it's meaning and related idea which was made by any other creature.

Verse 18

संस्कारसाक्षात्करणात्पूर्वजातिज्ञानम्॥ १८॥

saṁskāra sākṣātkaraṇāt pūrvajātijñānam

saṁskāra – the subtle impressions stored in memory; sākṣātkaraṇāt – from causing to be visibly present, direct intuitive perception; pūrva – before, previous; jāti – status, life; jñānam – knowledge.

From direct intuitive perception of the subtle impressions stored in the memory, the yogi gains knowledge of previous lives.

Commentary:

A yogi may know his own or some past lives of others. He can intuit into the memory impressions and pull up from there the compressed information, which can be instantly translated by his purified buddhi organ.

Verse 19

प्रत्ययस्य परचित्तज्ञानम्॥ १९॥

pratyayasya paracittajñānam

pratyayasya – of the mind content; para – of others; citta – of the mento-emotional energy; jñānam – information.

A yogi can know the contents of the mental and emotional energy in the minds of others.

Commentary:

Even though a student yogi might experience this, he must check the purity of his buddhi organ to be sure that his intuition has interpreted accurately. He should not inform others that he has this ability. Unless he gets directions from Lord Shiva or from an advanced yogi, he should not disclose to others anything about his intuitions.

Generally, a yogi should not interfere with the lives of others, for he should be aware of the supervision of the supernatural persons like Lord Krishna and Lord Shiva.

Verse 20

न च तत्सालम्बनं तस्याविषयीभूतत्वात्॥ २०॥

na ca tat sālambanaṁ tasya aviṣayī bhūtatvāt

na – not; ca – and; tat – that; sālambanaṁ – leaning on, resting on, support; tasya – of that; aviṣayī – not an object of anything, imperceptible; bhūtatvāt – the actual object.

And he does not check a factor which is the support of that content, for it is not the actual object in question.

Commentary:

This explains the accuracy of the intuitional powers of an advanced yogin.

Verse 21

कायरूपसंयमात्तद्ग्राह्यशक्तिस्तम्भे चक्षुःप्रकाशासम्प्रयोगेऽन्तर्धानम्॥ २१ ॥

kāya rūpa saṁyamāt tadgrāhyaśakti
stambhe cakṣuḥ prakāśa asaṁprayoge 'ntardhānam

kāya – body; rūpa – form; saṁyamāt – from the complete restraint of the mento-emotional energy; tad – that; grāhya – appropriating, grasping, sensual perceptiveness; śakti – power, potency, energy; stambhe – on the suspension; cakṣuḥ – vision; prakāśa – light; asaṁprayoge – on not contacting; 'ntardhānam = antardhānam – invisibility.

From the complete restraint of the mento-emotional energy
in relation to the shape of the body,
on the suspension of the receptive energy,
there is no contact between light and vision,
which results in invisibility.

Commentary:

The mento-emotional energy emanates a psychic light, which is called an aura. Now if this aura is restrained or if it loses its expressiveness, the particular form cannot be seen by another. A yogi may also suspend this energy from operating. In that case, others who send out psychic feelers to find him, discover to their dismay that he is missing. Sometimes when this happens, the persons who are trying to find that yogi know that he is in the vicinity or that he is where they think he is, therefore they become annoyed and attribute the lack of contact to his anti-social tendency.

The lack of contact (*saṁprayoga*) between the light and vision has to do with the light coming from the yogi's form and the vision beam which emanates from the person who searches psychically or physically for him. Sometimes a yogi can sit right next to a person and that person cannot realize that the yogi is by his side. One of my gurus, a certain Rishi Singh Gherwal was hired by the British Government to find himself. Being employed as a spy to find a spy he remained in the services of the British for many years. He was a mahayogi but was unknown because of his great humility and resistance to popularity.

Verse 22

एतेन शब्दादि अन्तर्धानम् उक्तम्

etena śabdādi antardhānam uktam

etena – by this; śabdādi = śabda – sound + ādi – and the related sensual pursuits; antardhānam – invisibility, non-perceptibility; uktam – described.

By this method,
sound and the related sensual pursuits, may be restrained,
which results in the related non-perceptibility.

Commentary:

A yogi may use a mystic process to cause imperceptibility in any or all aspects of sensual energy, so that he may not be detected by others. But this might only be done for the sake of yoga practice progression, and not otherwise. If a yogi uses these mystic skills for other reasons, it will distract from yoga practice and cause a long or short lapse in progression.

Sometimes people send out thoughts to attract a yogi. They do this by thinking. These thoughts are transmitted from their psyches just like radio waves being transmitted from a radio station. These thoughts are usually disruptive to yoga practice and are usually meant to engage a yogi in cultural activities which do not accelerate, but which rather decelerate yoga. Thus a yogi has to protect his practice by causing such thoughts not to reach him. There are many ways of doing this. The yogi uses a method, which he is allowed according to the level of his practice.

Just as a yogi might sit next to someone on a bus or train and travel miles with that person, without the person recognizing him, even though he is the very same person whom that searcher seeks, so a yogi might stay out of reach of the others even though he might be right next to them or even though they might know him so well that their thoughts instantly reach his psyche.

Verse 23

सोपक्रमं निरुपक्रमं च कर्म तत्संयमादपरान्तज्ञानमरिष्टेभ्यो वा॥२३॥

sopakramaṁ nirupakramaṁ ca karma
tatsaṁyamāt aparāntajñānam ariṣṭebhyaḥ vā

sopakramaṁ – set about, undertaken, already operative; nirupakramaṁ – dormant, destined; ca – and; karma – cultural activities; tat - that; saṁyamād = saṁyamāt – from the complete restraint of the mento-emotional energy; aparānta – of the other end, of death entry into the hereafter; jñānam – knowledge; ariṣṭebhyaḥ – from portents; vā – or.

Complete restraint of the mento-emotional energy
in relation to current and destined cultural activities
results in knowledge of entry into the hereafter.
Or, the same result is gained
by the complete restraint in relation to portents.

Commentary:

Both the current and the future cultural activities are the result of destiny, which is a combination of several forces. These destined energies work now. They worked in the past. They will work in the future. By restraining the mento-emotional energy in relation to the confusing impressions, which we take in now, and the ones which are stored in our memory we may derive intuitive or direct supernatural perceptions into the subtle world to see when it would be necessary for any of us to leave a material body. By this process, a yogi can leave his body and enter other dimensions of the hereafter where civilizations are currently taking place.

Each person who is about to leave his or her body experiences portents. Most persons cannot properly interpret the indications. A yogi can accurately gage those signs and messages.

Verse 24

मैत्र्यादिषु बलानि ॥ २४ ॥

maitryādiṣu balāni

maitrī – friendliness; ādiṣu – and by related qualities; balāni – powers.

By complete restraint of the mento-emotional energy in relation to friendliness, he develops that very same power.

Commentary:

When the yogi detaches himself from the cultural prejudices, which were cultivated in this and in some past lives, he develops universal friendliness which is applied evenly without biases which come up from the subconscious memory as predispositions. However, being aware of those attitudes in his memory, he can know what sort of friendly or antagonistic relationship he had with others in past lives.

Verse 25

बलेषु हस्तिबलादीनि ॥ २५ ॥

baleṣu hasti balādīni

baleṣu – by strength; hasti – elephant; bala – strength; ādīni – and the same for other aspects.

By complete restraint of the mento-emotional energy in relation to strength, the yogin acquires strength of an elephant. The same applies to other aspects.

Commentary:

A yogi develops certain mystic perfections during practice. This cannot be avoided. A yogi must stick to his objectives as shared with him by advanced teachers. Then he is not distracted by the mystic perfections, but observes their development and notes the various powers of the subtle and supersubtle bodies.

Verse 26

प्रवृत्त्यालोकन्यासात्सूक्ष्मव्यवहितविप्रकृष्टज्ञानम् ॥ २६ ॥

pravṛitti āloka nyāsāt sūkṣma
vyavahita viprakṛṣṭajñānam

pravṛttyālokanyāsāt = pravṛtti – destined activity, the force of cultural activity + āloka – supernatural insight + nyāsāt – from placing or applying; sūkṣma – subtle; vyavahita – concealed; viprakṛṣṭa – remote; jñānam – knowledge.

**From the application of supernatural insight
to the force producing cultural activities,
a yogi gets information about what is subtle, concealed
and remote from him.**

Commentary:

Sometimes it is necessary to side-step destiny and to see what will happen if one takes one kind of action or if one stays in a particular dimension or world. Then a yogi might apply supernatural vision to peer into the future, so that he can make a decision to remain in one dimension or be transcribed into another. A yogi can only find out what he is allowed to by the Supreme Being, but that allowance is very wide. He may get special insight from Lord Shiva or from some other divine being.

Verse 27

भुवनज्ञानं सूर्ये संयमात्॥ २७॥

bhuvanajñānaṁ sūrye saṁyamāt

bhuvana – the solar system; jñāna – knowledge; sūrye – on the sun-god or the sun planet; saṁyamāt – from the complete restraint of the mento-emotional energy.

**From the complete restraint of the mento-emotional energy
in relation to the sun god or the sun planet,
knowledge of the solar system is gained.**

Commentary:

If for some reason or the other, a yogi wants to know about the jurisdictional influences of the sun-god or sun planet, he may find out if he applies his spiritual sight to the spiritual, supernatural, or gross influences of the sunlight. The sun god's influence abounds physically, supernaturally, and spiritually as well. This is why *Śrī* Krishna described the paths used by proficient yogis at the time of death.

yatra kāle tv anāvṛttim   āvṛttim caiva yoginaḥ
prayātā yānti taṁ kālaṁ   vakṣyāmi bharatarṣabha
agniḥ jyotiḥ ahaḥ śuklaḥ   ṣaṇmāsā uttarāyaṇam
tatra prayātā gacchanti   brahma brahmavido janāḥ
dhūmo rātriḥ tathā kṛṣṇaḥ   ṣaṇmāsā dakṣiṇāyanam
tatra cāndramasaṁ jyotiḥ   yogi prāpya nivartate
śuklakṛṣṇe gatī hyete   jagataḥ śāśvate mate
ekayā yāti anāvṛttim   anyayāvartate punaḥ

O bullish man of the Bharata family, I will tell you of the departure for the yogis who do or do not return.

The summer season, the bright atmosphere, the daytime, the bright moonlight, the six monthswhen the sun appears to move north; if at

that time, they depart the body, those people who know the spiritual dimension, go to the spiritual location.

The smoky, misty or hazy season, as well as in the night-time, the dark-moon time, the six months when the sun appears to move south; if the yogi departs at that time, he attains moonlight, after which he is born again. The night and the dark times are two paths which are considered to be perpetually available for the universe. It is considered so by the authorities. By one, a person goes away not to return; by the other he comes back again. (Gītā 8.23 - 26)

Verse 28

चन्द्रे ताराव्यूहज्ञानम्॥ २८॥

candre tārāvyūhajñānam

candre – on the moon or moon-god; tārā – stars; vyūha – system; jñānam – knowledge.

By complete restraint of the mento-emotional energy,
in reference to the moon or moon-god,
the yogi gets knowledge about the system of stars.

Commentary:

This is in the case of a yogi who has an interest of going beyond the jurisdiction of the solar deity. To relieve himself of reliance on this person, a yogi must get permission for transference to another zone of some other deity. All places are controlled. Thus a yogi needs permission both to leave this realm as well as to enter any other.

A yogi's desire for something is no guarantee that he will acquire it. It all depends on if he is permitted and if he qualifies by the required austerities. Yogis, who are spiritually linked to a local deity like the sun-god or moon-god, cannot relinquish their spiritual connection, even though they may get permission for a change of services or for a relocation to another zone that is controlled by the same deity.

Verse 29

ध्रुवे तद्गतिज्ञानम्॥ २९॥

dhruve tadgatijñānam

dhruve – on the Pole Star; tat – that; gati – course of heavenly planets and stars; jñānam – knowledge.

By the complete restraint of the mento-emotional energy
in relation to the Pole Star,
a yogi can know of the course of planets and stars.

Commentary:

Some yogis do develop whimsical interest and inquiries which satisfy their curiosity. But other yogis who are serious about it and who hope to migrate from this planet to other superior places do check on the other zones before leaving their bodies, to be sure that their conceptions of these places perfectly match the actual situations there. Such yogis use their higher astral bodies to move from sphere to sphere checking the various living conditions in the other places.

Verse 30

नाभिचक्रे कायव्यूहज्ञानम् ॥ ३० ॥

nābhicakre kāyavyūhajñānam

nābhi – navel; cakre – on the energy gyrating center; kāya – body; vyūha – arrangement, lay out; jñānam – knowledge.

By complete restraint of the mento-emotional energy in relation to the focusing on the navel energy-gyrating center, the yogi gets knowledge about the layout of his body.

Commentary:

It is necessary in the course of *kuṇḍalini* yoga to energize the energy gyrating centers or chakras. These are located on the spinal column in the subtle body. This corresponds to the central nervous system in the gross form. The navel chakra point extends to the front of the body, to the solar plexus region. In the case of student yogis, it may also point downward. But in advanced celibate yogis it points upwards.

A yogin may enter the navel chakra of his own body or that of others, from the front of the body, from the navel, where the umbilical cord was connected while that body was in the womb of its mother. From there a yogi can see the entire layout of the body, including its lifespan, its potential for disease and its maximum capacity for helping the soul in the quest for liberation.

In some cases, a person cannot be liberated in his present body. When a yogi sees this he does not waste time with that person. He directs that person to earn more conducive birth opportunities. In yogic terminology the navel chakra is called manipuraka. It is the third major chakra when counting these from the bottom of the spine. By completing the course of *haṭha* yoga, a yogi curbs this chakra.

Verse 31

कण्ठकूपे क्षुत्पिपासानिवृत्तिः ॥ ३१ ॥

kaṇṭhakūpe kṣutpipāsā nivṛttiḥ

kaṇṭha – throat; kūpe – on the gullet; kṣut – hunger; pipāsā – thirst; nivṛttiḥ – cessation, suppression.

By the complete restraint of the mento-emotional energy in focusing on the gullet, a yogi causes the suppression of hunger and thirst.

Commentary:

The practice of suppressing hunger and thirst is part of *haṭha* yoga. The purpose of this is to get the life force to cease its independent activities. A *haṭha* yogi endeavors to bring the life force under his control, not to stop it from functioning but to cease its independent activities which are counter productive to the aims of yoga. Thus, a yogi surcharges and subsequently purifies the energy gyrating centers (chakras) one by one, beginning at the base of the spine.

Some people feel that they can use *rāja* yoga to purify the chakras from the top downwards, from the brow or crown chakra. Actually this cannot be done, except in a person's imagination. One has to do *kuṇḍalini* yoga by a vigor practice like bhastrika *prāṇāyāma*. By charging the body with *prāṇa* and pushing it down into the passages which are filled with apana, one causes purification from the base chakra upwards. It takes a certain amount of practice according to the extent of impurities.

A yogi does cause his hunger and thirst to be suppressed initially when he sets out to control those urges, but over a time of practice, his subtle body changes and the urges for solid and liquid food go away. This is because the throat chakra become altered.

Of course a yogi can be degraded, because whatever low habits or vices he acquired in the past, he can again take up in the future if he is not careful, or if he is not transferred into a dimension where such sordid aspects are unavailable.

Verse 32

कूर्मनाड्यां स्थैर्यम्॥ ३२॥

kūrmanāḍyāṃ sthairyam

kūrma – tortoise, a particular subtle nerve; nāḍyāṁ – on the nadi or subtle nerve; sthairyam – steadiness.

By the complete restraint of the mento-emotional energy in focusing on the kurma nāḍi subtle nerve, a yogi acquires steadiness of his psyche.

Commentary:

This has to do with being ready to enter *samādhi*, which is continuous effortless linkage of one's attention to a higher concentration force, object or person. Unless one can keep his body in a steady pose, preferably the *padmāsana* lotus posture, and also have the bodily urges like hunger quelled completely, he cannot enter into *samādhi*. *Śrī Patañjali* brings this to our attention at this point.

The *kūrmanāḍi* is supposed to be located below the gullet. In other words if one has not stilled the gross and subtle nerves in this area, one will not be able to enter *samādhi*. When those nerves are stilled, the life force gives up its effort to protect and overly maintain the lower part of ūbe relieved from its creature survival duties, it does not allow the person to enter *samādhi*.

Verse 33

मूर्धज्योतिषि सिद्धदर्शनम्॥ ३३॥

mūrdhajyotiṣi siddhadarśanam

mūrdha – the head; jyotiṣi – on the shinning light; siddha – the perfected being; darśanam – the view of.

By the complete restraint of the mento-emotional energy as it is focused on the shining light in the head of the subtle body, a yogi gets views of the perfected beings.

Commentary:

Mūrdhajyotiṣi is known otherwise as *jñānadīpa* or *jñānadīptiḥ* or *jñānacakṣu*. It is a light seen in the front central area of the subtle head. This light is the energized buddhi organ. In its normal stage in a human being, it is dark and cloudy, like a filament of a light bulb which gets insufficient current. The insufficient current warms the filament but does not cause it to glow noticeable. When the yogi masters *prāṇāyāma* and perfects himself in the disciplines of *kuṇḍalini* and celibacy yoga, his buddhi organ gets sufficiently charged. It glows with shining light (*jyotiṣi*), otherwise it remains dull but is felt as the centre of the mind, as one's ability to understand, analyse, plan and draw conclusions.

When a yogi develops himself to the extent that his buddhi organ begins to glow in his lower subtle body even, then he perceives the perfected beings, the siddhas like *Śrī* Babaji Mahasya, *Śrī* Gorakshanath, and other mahayogins. Sometimes fortunately he sees Lord Shiva at Kailash in the other dimensions. Once a yogin sees the siddhas, it is understood that he is blessed. If he accelerates the practice further, he will develop a yoga siddha body. He can take advices and get rare *kriyā* yoga practices from those siddhas whom he is allowed to perceive. Such a yogin does not rely on physical contact with a yoga guru. Hence he does not have to have a guru who uses a physical form. He takes initiation either physically or subtly from these teachers.

Verse 34

प्रातिभाद्वा सर्वम्॥ ३४॥

prātibhād vā sarvam

prātibhād = prātibhāt – resulting from samyama on the shinning organ of divination; vā – or; sarvam – everything, all reality.

By complete restraint of the mento-emotional energy, while focusing on the shining organ of divination in the head of the subtle body, the yogin is able to know all reality.

Commentary:

This *prātibhā* is the brahmarandra development in the head of the subtle body of a yogi. At first a yogi develops the top part of the subtle body which is known as the brahmarandra. *Śrī Patañjali* used the terms, *prātibhā* which literally means relating to divination or genius. A yogi who has developed his brahmarandra is said to be liberated even while using a gross body. Such a yogi can select which of the dimensions he would live in after he sheds his material body, but of course again, since he is a limited being in the conditioned and liberated stages, he has to get approval from higher authorities like Lord Shiva or Lord Krishna.

Verse 35

हृदये चित्तसंवित्॥ ३५॥

hṛdaye cittasaṁvit

hṛdaye – on the samyam on the causal body; citta – mento-emotional energy; saṁvit – thorough insight.

By the complete restraint of the mento-emotional energy as it is focused on the causal body in the vicinity of the chest, the yogi gets thorough insight into the causes of the mental and emotional energy.

Commentary:

For all these practices, one should have mastered the *samyama* procedure described before by *Śrī Patañjali* as a development from *dhāraṇā*, to *dhyāna* and to *samādhi*. Once this is mastered, one can apply himself to the practices described. Stated differently on who mastered *samādhi* can use *samādhi*.

A person whose mind is jumpy, whose emotions are reactive and who is still linked to the cultural affairs of this world, cannot develop *samādhi*. It is as simple as that. In fact such a person cannot go beyond attempts at *dhāraṇā*, which is effortful linkage of the attention to a higher concentration force, object or person. This is because the mento-emotional energy will remain unstable, locking and unlocking unto various ideas and images which emerge from the memory, come in through sensual perception or are developed by the dull darkish non-glowing buddhi organ.

Until the mento-emotional energy is established by a complete *pratyāhāra* sensual withdrawal procedure, the attention will not be freed to focus on the void which occurs before a split second interval between locking and unlocking of the mento-emotional energy. All these factors must be properly mastered before one can get to the *dhyāna* effortless linkage of the attention to higher concentration force, object or person. And when that is mastered by regular practice, then one can do *samādhi* which is the continuous effortless linkage of the same.

Verse 36

सत्त्वपुरुषयोरत्यन्तासङ्कीर्णयोः प्रत्ययाविशेषो भोगः

परार्थत्वात्स्वार्थसंयमात्पुरुषज्ञानम्॥ ३६ ॥

sattva puruṣayoḥ atyantāsaṁkīrṇayoḥ
pratyayaḥ aviśeṣaḥ bhogaḥ parārthatvāt
svārthasaṁyamāt puruṣajñānam

sattva – intelligence energy of material nature; puruṣayoḥ – of the individual spirit; atyanta – excessively, extremely, very; asaṁkīrṇayoḥ – of what is distinct or separate; pratyayaḥ – mental content, awareness within the psyche; aviśeṣaḥ – not distinct, inability to distinguish; bhogaḥ – experience; parārthatvāt – what is apart from another thing; svārtha – one own, self interest; saṁyamāt – from the complete restraint of the mento-emotional energy; puruṣa – individual spirit; jñānam – knowledge.

Experience results from the inability to distinguish
between the individual spirit
and the intelligence energy of material nature,
even though they are very distinct.
By complete restraint of the mento-emotional energy
while focusing on self-interest distinct from the other interest,
a yogi gets knowledge of the individual spirit.

Commentary:

To understand this verse we must go back to Chapter 2 verses 20-25 as follows:

draṣṭā dṛśimātraḥ śuddhaḥ api pratyayānupaśyaḥ
tadarthaḥ eva dṛśyasya ātma
kṛtārthaṁ prati naṣṭam api
anaṣṭaṁ tadanya sādhāraṇatvāt
sva svāmiśaktyoḥ svarūpa *upalabdhi hetuḥ saṁyogaḥ*
tasya hetuḥ avidyā
tad abhāvāt saṁyogā abhāvaḥ
hānaṁ taddṛśeḥ kaivalyam

The perceiver is the pure extent of his consciousness but his conviction is patterned by what is perceived.

The individual spirit who is involved in what is seen exists here for that purpose only. It is not effective for one to whom its purpose is fulfilled but it has a common effect on the others. There is a reason for the conjunction of the individual self and his psychological energies. It is for obtaining the experience of his own form. The cause of the conjunction is spiritual ignorance.

The elimination of the conjunction which results from the elimination of that spiritual ignorance is the withdrawal that is the total separation of the perceiver from the mundane psychology.

This verse, which defines experience as being the inability to distinguish between the individual spirit and the intelligent energy of material nature, is the heart of the matter of self-realization. It causes us to bow down very low to the Maharishi Mahayogi *Śrī Patañjali*. In a very rare and precise declaration, he outrightly condemns our experiences (*bhogas*) in material nature.

They come to us because of our inability to distinguish between our spirits and the intelligent energy of material nature. The implication is this: If we could distinguish between our spirits and the intelligence energy of material nature, then we would not have to take the course of experience (*bhogaḥ*) through material nature, through the various species of life, in and out of the various subtle and gross dimensions, which are produced in and are formed of subtle and gross material nature.

However, there is a way out, which is the focusing on the spirit itself apart from the other interests, which is material nature. *Śrī Patañjali* earmarked, not just material nature but its *sattva* features or its highest most sensitive and intelligent energy.

Verse 37

ततः प्रातिभश्रावणवेदनादर्शास्वादवार्ता जायन्ते ॥ ३७ ॥

tataḥ prātibha śrāvaṇa vedana
ādarśa āsvāda vārtāḥ jāyante

tataḥ – thence, therefore, from that focus; prātibha – the shining organ of divination; śrāvaṇa – hearing; vedana – touching; ādarśa – sight; āsvāda – taste; vārtāḥ – smell; jāyante – is produced.

From that focus is produced smelling, tasting, seeing, touching and hearing, through the shining organ of divination.

Commentary:

Now all of a sudden, *Śrī Patañjali* continues with some promising statement about yoga development. The student will have to review *sūtra* 36 of this chapter at a later date. It is vital that he understands the implications of it, which is nirvana or the blowing out of the subtle and gross material existence.

From complete restraint of the mental and emotional energy and the focusing on the self-interest of the spirit, leaving aside completely the interests of material nature, the yogi becomes occupied applying his organ of divination, his developed *brahmarandra*, to all his sensual pursuits. Then, instead of sensing through the mento-emotional energy (*citta*), he senses directly through spiritual energy. This was recommended before:

drastrdrsyayoh samyogo heyahetuh

The cause which is to be avoided is the indiscriminate association of the observer and what is perceived. (Yoga Sūtra 2.17)

The idea that the individual spirit will merge into the absolute and will then be without senses is not given in *Patañjali*'s *sūtras*, even through many yogis and yogi philosophers seem to think so.

Verse 38

ते समाधावुपसर्गा व्युत्थाने सिद्धयः ॥ ३८ ॥

te samādhau upasargāḥ vyutthāne siddhayaḥ

te – they, those abilities; samādhau – in samādhi continues effortless linkage of the attention to a higher concentration force, object or person; upasargāḥ – impediments; vyutthāne – in expressing, going outwards, rising up; siddhayaḥ – mystic perfectional skills.

Those divination skills are obstacles
in the practice of continuous effortless linkage of the attention
to a higher concentration force, object or person.
But in expressing,
they are considered as mystic perfectional skills.

Commentary:

A yogi is stalled if he is distracted for exhibitions of the perfectional skills which are manifested as he progresses. Those student yogis who cannot resist such exhibitions are doomed. They become premature gurus of a very gullible and stupid public.

Verse 39

बन्धकारणशैथिल्यात्प्रचारसंवेदनाच्च चित्तस्य परशरीरावेशः ॥ ३९ ॥

bandhakāraṇa śaithilyāt pracāra
saṁvedanāt ca cittasya paraśarīrāveśaḥ

bandha – bondage; kāraṇa – cause; śaithilyāt – due to relaxation, collapse; pracāra – channel flow; saṁvedanāt – from knowing; ca – and; cittasya – of the mento-emotional energies; para – another; śarīra – body; āveśaḥ – entrance, penetration.

The entrance into another body is possible
by slackening the cause of bondage
and by knowing the channels of the mento-emotional energy.

Commentary:

The slackening of the cause of bondage is done by a yogi, when he reaches the causal level mentioned in verse 35. From the causal plane, he is able to slacken the cause of his having to take his current body. Then he leaves that body temporarily while it stays in hibernation in *samādhi*. He enters forms of others. A spiritual master may do this after his body dies. He enters into the forms of his disciples on earth and speaks to small or large audiences, giving instructions. This prevents him from having to take a new material form. In that way he remains in the astral world for many years, avoiding physical rebirth.

Some great yogis like *Śrī* Adi Shankaracarya and Mahayogin *Śrī* Matsyendranath entered the bodies of others, while their disciples maintained their gross bodies. They did this for special purposes. Over all, a student yogi should not endeavor for this parasarīrāveśaḥ siddhi since it is very dangerous. It is said that recently in our era, T. Lobsang Rampa who was a Tibetan mystic yogi in his past life, entered into an Englishman's body after the said occupant agreed to give over his body in exchange for some merits of Lobsang. Generally such a course is not recommended for a student yogin.

If one gets in the causal plane and stays there long enough one may develop an ability to adjust one's resultant reactions which are left in a particular dimension and which would forestall one's liberation. Thus one may do so and not have to exhibit the parasarīrāveśaḥ siddhi. It is not recommended.

If one enters the form of another, one has to go through the channels of that person's mento-emotional energy. That entails adopting part of his nature and assuming some of his responsibilities. That is dangerous since one may forget oneself, and begin to feel as if one is the other person, all because of becoming too familiar in identity to that person's psyche. *Śrī* Matsyendranath even though he was a siddha at the time, was rescued by his most advanced disciple, the mahayogin *Śrī* Goraksnatha. Matsyendranatha entered the body of another person and forgot his identity after adopting the stranger's psyche. In the case of *Śrī* Adi Shankaracarya, he did not forget himself, but the queen of the King's body whom he adopted, wanted to kill Shankara's yogi body. She wanted him to stay on as her husband and not to return to his body. There are dangers in adopting the body of another.

It is interesting that a great yogin as *Śrī* Adi Shankara had to enter the almost dead body of a king, just to experience sexual intercourse with a female, because after all a yogi can get such experiences on the astral planes which are near to this world or he may enter a parallel world and get such experiences. It is not necessary to enter any other person's physical body to get such experiences. We must conclude therefore that destiny plays hard cards against a certain yogin at specific stages of his advancement, in order to force him to do certain dangerous and risky things.

Śrī Adi Shankaracharya is rated as an incarnation of Lord Siva. From what I learned in the association of the siddhas in the higher astral world, he is Skanda Kumara, the celibate son of Lord Shiva. They claimed that due to his insubordination to Devi, Lord Shiva's wife, he had that difficulty in that incarnation. If one plans to be celibate, one should not expect much help from Goddess Durga, but all the same, She is in a position to cause disruptions in one's practice.

Verse 40

उदानजयाज्जलपङ्ककण्टकादिष्वसङ्ग उत्क्रान्तिश्च ॥ ४० ॥

udānajayāt jala paṅka kaṇṭakādiṣu asaṇgaḥ utkrāntiḥ ca

udāna – air which rises from the throat and enters the head; jayāt – from the conquest of; jala – water; paṅka – mud; kaṇṭaka – thorns; ādiṣi – and similar aspects; asaṅgaḥ – non contact; utkrāntiḥ – rising above; ca – and.

By mastery over the air which rises from the throat into the head, a yogi can rise over or not have contact with water, mud or sharp objects.

Commentary:

Udāna vayu is the air which moves up from the throat area to the top of the head. Initially a yogi controls that in *kuṇḍalini* yoga practice, when he is able to force the apana air, the lowest most polluted air in the body, up and out of the body through the spinal column. Sometimes for convenience sake, one is able to cross water or mud or sharp objects, miraculously even though one may not willfully exhibit such perfectional power, which was demonstrated by many great yogis before and by Lord Jesus Christ.

Certain animals have the natural power since their spirit use forms which are able to suppressed and regulate the *udāna vayu*. Of course, a yogi's exhibition of that siddhi is something different. The expression of miracles, even though it helps a yogi on occasion, can cause impediments under other conditions. These exhibitions are not recommended. *Śrī Patañjali* lists these not to encourage their use but to alert student yogis of the landmarks of yoga practice.

Verse 41

समानजयाज्ज्वलनम् ॥ ४१ ॥

samānajayāt jvalanam

samāna – digestive energy; jayāt – conquest; jvalanam – shining, burning, blazing, with firey glow.

By conquest of the samāna digestive force, a yogi's psyche blazes or shines with a fiery glow.

Commentary:

Conquest of the samana digestive force comes by the practice of *kuṇḍalini* yoga which entails various *āsanas* combined with *prāṇāyāma*, especially bhastrika *prāṇāyāma*. By that a yogi gets control over diet. He purifies the navel region of the body. This sets the stage for purification of the sexual functions which opens a gate for the yogi to attack the muladhar anal region. After this is achieved in the downward course, it must be achieved in the upward course, as the *prāṇa* is pushed down and forces the apana energy to move upwards through a subtle tubing called the sushumna nadi. When a yogi on the upward purification course, purifies his navel region, he experiences frontal *kuṇḍalini*. It is then that he achieves conquest over the *samāna* digestive fire. His subtle body then appears with an orangish fiery glow.

Verse 42

श्रोत्राकाशयोः सम्बन्धसंयमाद्दिव्यं श्रोत्रम् ॥ ४२ ॥

śrotra ākāśayoḥ saṁbandha saṁyamāt divyaṁ śrotram

śrotra – hearing sense; ākāśayoḥ – of space; saṁbandha – relationship; saṁyamāt – from the complete restraint of the mento-emotional energy; divyaṁ – divine, supernatural; śrotram – hearing sense.

**By the complete restraint of the mento-emotional energy,
while focusing on the hearing sense and space,
a yogin develops supernatural and divine hearing.**

Commentary:

Each yogi masters a particular mystic skill, all depending on the force of practice, on association while progressing and because of his cultural background from many previous lives. By this, particular skills attract his attention. However, if he has the superior association of Lord Shiva, and other maha-yogis, he will not invest time in using the mystic skills but will stay focused on the objective of psyche purification; something from which he could quickly gain spiritual perfection.

Verse 43

कायाकाशयोः सम्बन्धसंयमाल्लघुतूलसमापत्तेश्चाकाशगमनम् ॥ ४३ ॥

*kāya ākāśayoḥ saṁbandha saṁyamāt
laghutūlasamāpatteḥ ca ākāśagamanam*

kāya – body; ākāśayoḥ – of the sky, atmosphere; saṁbandha – relation; saṁyamāt – from the complete restraint of the mento-emotional energy; laghu – light; tūla – cotton fluff; samāpatteḥ – of meeting, of linking; ca – and; ākāśa – atmosphere; gamanam – going through, passing through.

**By the complete restraint of the mento-emotional energy,
while linking the mind
to the relationship between the body and the sky
and linking the attention to being as light as cotton fluff,
a yogi acquires the ability to pass through the atmosphere.**

Commentary:

This does not necessarily mean levitation of the physical body. It can mean that usage of the subtle body. Since every user of a physical body, already has a subtle form which can pass through the atmosphere with ease, it is not necessary to focus on making the physical body as buoyant as a cotton fluff which can float easily in the air, as if to deny the power of gravity. In addition, a yogi who can see or hear from afar, would not require that his gross body be moved from one place to another merely to perceive through it, what he can divine from a distance.

Verse 44

बहिरकल्पिता वृत्तिर्महाविदेहा ततः प्रकाशावरणक्षयः ॥ ४४ ॥

bahiḥ akalpitā vṛttiḥ mahāvidehā tataḥ
prakāśa āvaraṇakṣayaḥ

bahiḥ – outside, external; akalpitā – not manufactured, not artificial, not formed; vṛttiḥ – operation; mahā – great; videhā – bodiless state; tataḥ – thence, from that, resulting from that; prakāśa – light; āvaraṇa – covering, mental darkens; kṣayaḥ – dissipation, removal.

By the complete restraint of the mento-emotional energy which is external, which is not formed, a yogi achieves the great bodiless state. From that the great mental darkness which veils the light, is dissipated.

Commentary:

The great bodiless state, *mahāvidehā*, is a special accomplishment of great yogis, who go beyond the causal plane but who do not get an exception to leave this solar system. Because they fail to obtain the exemption for whatever reason, they remain in the unformed, untapped pure mental energy which was not parceled out to individual spirits. They remain free of involvements. Such yogins hardly interact in the cultural world which is so important to a human being. For those great yogis the mental darkness which human beings consistently experience, does not exist. They moved beyond the subtle negative influences of material nature.

Verse 45

स्थूलस्वरूपसूक्ष्मान्वयार्थवत्त्वसंयमाद्भूतजयः ॥ ४५ ॥

sthūla svarūpa sūkṣma anvaya arthavatva
saṁyamāt bhūtajayaḥ

stūla – gross form; svarūpa – real nature; sūkṣma – subtle; anvaya – following, connection, distribution; arthavatava – purpose, value; saṁyamāt – from the complete restraint of the mento-emotional energy; bhūta – states of matter; jayaḥ – conquest.

By the complete restraint of the mento-emotional energy, while linking the attention to the gross forms, real nature, subtle distribution and value of states of matter, a yogi gets conquest over them.

Commentary:

Some yogins are diverted from their progression by too much research into the material nature. However, for them that diversity is necessary, until they reach a stage of greater resistance. The main asset of a yogi is to keep in touch with more advanced yogins so that even if the student yogin becomes fascinated or stalled somewhere in the practice, his advanced teachers can guide him away from degradation.

Verse 46

ततोऽणिमादिप्रादुर्भावः कायसम्पत्तद्धर्मानभिघातश्च ॥ ४६ ॥

tataḥ aṇimādi prādurbhāvaḥ kāyasaṁpat
taddharma anabhighātaḥ ca

tataḥ – thence, from that; aṇandi = aṇima – minuteness + ādi – and the related mystic skills; prādurbhāvaḥ – coming into existence, manifesting; kāya – subtle body; saṁpat – wealth, prosperity, perfection; tad – tat = of that; dharma – attributes, functions; anabhighātaḥ – non-obstruction; ca – and.

From minuteness and other related mystic skills, come the perfection of the subtle body and the non-obstruction of its functions.

Commentary:

When the yogi develops the mystic skills, he finds that the subtle body is perfected to such a degree that the nadis, subtle tubes within it carry a subtle fluid which is as crystal clear as pure water. From certain dimensions this appears to be liquid light traveling through the subtle body of the yogi. Some of this purity filters into the gross body and the yogi is said to perform miracles.

The obstructions a common man experiences, and those a neophyte yogi are fascinated with, are removed from the perfected yogin, because his subtle form is completely purified. The way of operation of the subtle body is obstructed by impurities which arise by attachments to the material energy. When a yogi completes this *pratyāhār*, fifth stage of yoga and when he ceases interactions with the *citta* mento-emotional energy, thus resting his buddhi organ from involvements and calculations regarding cultural activities, then he reaches the required purity.

Verse 47

रूपलावण्यबलवज्रसंहननत्वानि कायसम्पत् ॥ ४७ ॥

rūpa lāvaṇya bala vajra saṁhananatvāni kāyasaṁpat

rūpa – beautiful form; lāvaṇya – charm; bala – mystic force; vajra – diamond-like, infallible; saṁhananatvāni – definiteness, hardness; kāya – subtle body; saṁpat – perfection.

Beautiful form, charm, mystic force, and diamond-like definition come from perfection of the subtle body.

Commentary:

Most commentators give *kāya* as the physical body. However, in advanced yoga practice, *kāya* is the subtle body, the temporary but long lasting body which the yogin must perfect before he can attain liberation.

When the subtle body is upgraded by the practice of *kuṇḍalini* yoga, it attains beauty of form, mystic force and diamond-like definition. It attains clarity in it. Its colors become free from cloudiness and vagueness. It moves into the higher pranic force. It is experienced as a *sattva guṇa* body, a form of the mode of pure goodness.

Verse 48

ग्रहणस्वरूपास्मितान्वयार्थवत्त्वसंयमादिन्द्रियजयः ॥ ४८ ॥

grahaṇa svarūpa asmitā anvaya arthavattva
saṁyamāt indriyajayaḥ

grahaṇa – sensual grasping; svarūpa – own form; asmitā – identification; anvaya – connection, association; arthavatva – value, worth; saṁyamāt – from the continuous effortless linkage of the attention; indriyajayaḥ – the mastery of the sensual energy by psychological control.

From the continuous effortless linkage of the attention
to sensual grasping, to the form of the sensual energy,
to its identifying powers, to its connection instinct
and to its actual worth,
a yogi acquires conquest over his relationship with it.

Commentary:

It is important to understand and to accept for oneself, that these achievements occur after prolonged practice. Those who feel they can achieve these overnight will definitely be frustrated. Yoga practice matures and remains firm only after long practice, and not just for one life but through a succession of lives, until the practice becomes an instinct.

A yogin must study his own sensual energy. He must also take hints from the way others use their sensual powers. It takes time to accomplish this. The sensual energy is subtle and moves at a rapid rate to execute its functions. It is mostly involuntary, which means that it operates on its own. This makes it difficult to track. However, after long practice, a yogin gets a foothold in these achievements described by *Śrī Patañjali*. One must study how the sensual energy appropriates or grasps subtle phenomena. This is indicated by the term *anvaya*. One must study how the energy connects with and associates with various types of subtle and gross objects. One must know the form of the sensual energy, its *svarūpa*. This is its form when it does not assume the identity of other objects. One should understand its nature for identification as well as its worth to the self. When all this is achieved, then the yogi gains mastery over his relationship to that sensual force.

Verse 49

ततो मनोजवित्वं विकरणभावः प्रधानजयश्च॥४९॥

tataḥ manojavitvaṁ vikaraṇabhāvaḥ pradhānajayaḥ ca

tataḥ – subsequently; manojavitvaṁ = manah – mind + javitvaṁ – swiftness, rapidity; vikaraṇabhāvaḥ = vi – parting away from, dispersing + karana – creating, making + bhāvaḥ – mento-emotional energy, feeling; pradhānah – subtle matter; jayaḥ – conquest; ca – and.

Subsequently, there is conquest over the influence of subtle matter and over the parting away or dispersion of the mento-emotional energy, with the required swiftness of mind.

Commentary:

These aspects are on the mystic plane. This is attained after long practice at *dhāraṇā*. At first a yogi practices *dhāraṇā*, feeling that he mastered the *pratyāhār* sensual restraint. Thereafter he discovers that he only mastered particular phases of such restraint. Under direction of higher yogis, he goes back to his restraint practice. Then he again returns to *dhāraṇā*. This occurs frequently, until at last his perception of the subtle realities develop fully. What was subtle becomes gross; what was gross fades away completely. He purifies himself even further and grasps more higher reality which used to affect him in lower stages.

Verse 50

सत्त्वपुरुषान्यताख्यातिमात्रस्य सर्वभावाधिष्ठातृत्वं सर्वज्ञातृत्वं च॥५०॥

sattva puruṣa anyatā khyātimātrasya
sarvabhāva adhiṣṭhātṛtvaṁ sarvajñātṛtvaṁ ca

sattva – clarifying perception of material nature; puruṣa – the spiritual personality; anyatā – other than distinct from; khyātimātrasya = khyāti – the discriminating faculty of the intellect + mātrasya – only; sarva – all; bhāva – states of feelings and perceptions; adhiṣṭhātṛtvaṁ – authority, complete disaffection; sarvajñātṛtvaṁ = sarva – all + jñātṛtvaṁ – knowledge, intuition; ca – and.

Only when there is distinct discrimination between the clarifying perception of material nature and the spiritual personality, does the yogi attain complete disaffection and all-applicative intuition.

Commentary:

Khyāti means the well-developed, truth-yielding discrimination of the buddhi organ. But this is attained after long practice only. When this is developed, then the yogi sees clearly at all times the distinction between his spiritual person and the clarifying influences of material nature, influences from which he took assistance all along.

In advanced yoga, or *kriyā* yoga, one has to maintain the distinction between oneself and the perceiving instruments of the subtle body, even through initially one must take help from those truth-yielding perceptions. *Adhiṣṭhātṛtvam* means complete or full disaffection from the subtle influence of material nature, even from the clarifying powers which are so helpful.

Verse 51

तद्वैराग्यादपि दोषबीजक्षये कैवल्यम्॥५१॥

tadvairāgyāt api doṣabījakṣaye kaivalyam

tadvairāgyāt = tad (tat) – that + vairāgyāt – from a lack of interest; api – also, even; doṣabījakṣaye = doṣa – fault, defect + bīja – seed, origin, source + kṣaye – on elimination; kaivalyam – the absolute isolation of the self from what is lower than itself, isolation of the self from the lower psyche of itself.

By a lack of interest, even to that (discrimination between the clarifying mundane energy and the self) when the cause of that defect is eliminated, the absolute isolation of the self from its lower psyche, is achieved.

Commentary:

Kaivalyam, which is a popular word in yoga and meditation circles, is greatly mistranslated and misinterpreted. Its meaning is not that the yogi would become one with God. For *Patañjali*, the master of yoga, never says that in these verses. *Kaivalya* is the isolation of the self from its lower psyche, such that the subtle mundane instruments of the psyche are separated from the self or atma. The atma becomes freed from it's reliance to those useful and domineering subtle tools.

Previously *Śrī Patañjali* described *kaivalyam* in this way:

tad abhāvāt saṁyogā abhāvaḥ
hānaṁ taddṛśeḥ kaivalyam

"The elimination of the conjunction which results from the elimination of that spiritual ignorance is the withdrawal that is the total separation of the perceiver from the mundane psychology." (Yoga Sūtra 2.25)

It is amazing how so many translators, following the one-ness craze completely distorted *Śrī Patañjali* by giving so many misleading and totally out-of-context meanings for the term *kaivalyam*. Vaman Shivram Apte in his practical Sanskrit-English dictionary gives the following plain meaning for these terms; perfect isolation, soleness, exclusiveness, individuality, detachment of the soul from matter, identification with the Supreme Spirit, final emancipation or beatitude.

Verse 52

स्थान्युपनिमन्त्रणे सङ्गस्मयाकरणं पुनरनिष्टप्रसङ्गात्॥ ५२॥

sthānyupanimantraṇe saṅgasmayākaraṇaṁ punaraniṣṭa prasaṅgāt

sthāni – person from the place a yogi would then attain if his material body died; upanimantraṇe – on being invited; saṅga – association; smaya – fascination, wonderment; akaraṇaṁ – non-responsiveness; punaḥ – again; aniṣṭa – unwanted features of existence; prasaṅgāt – due to association, due to endearing friendliness.

On being invited by a person from the place one would attain if the body died, a yogi should be non-responsive, not desiring their association and not being fascinated, otherwise that would cause unwanted features of existence to arise again.

Commentary:

A perfect example of a person who implemented this advice of *Śrī Patañjali*, long before *Patañjali* took his material body to write the yoga *sūtras*, is Mudgala, who in the Mahābhārata rejected proposals for transference to the Swarga angelic world. Mudgala had reached a stage of progression where he was eligible to live in a special palace of the lord of the angelic world. He was visited by Matali the lord's charioteer, but when questioned by Mudgala, Matali admitted that there were defects in the angelic world, even for great yogins who would go there. They would again (*punaḥ*) have to revert back to this world after sometime of enjoying paradisiacal enjoyments. Thus Mudgala said that he did not want to go to such a place but would continue his austerities to go somewhere which was devoid of all unwanted features of existence (*aniṣṭa*).

For others, who are not as strong and determined as Mudgala, it is easier said than done. They may not avoid the temptation of the angelic world. By developing endearing friendless (*prasaṅgāt*), they will succumb to angelic association and the fascinations of such a world. Just as governments of the developed countries skim off the intelligent people from the lesser-developed lands, so the angelic people attract the higher minds of the earthly planets.

Verse 53

क्षणतत्क्रमयोः संयमाद्विवेकजं ज्ञानम्॥ ५३॥

kṣaṇa tatkramayoḥ saṁyamāt vivekajaṁ jñānam

kṣaṇa – moment; tat – that; kramayoḥ – on the sequence; saṁyamāt – due to the continuous effortless linkage of the attention; vivekajaṁ – the distinction caused by subtle discrimination; jñānam – knowledge.

By the continuous effortless linkage of the attention to the moment and to the sequence of the moments, the yogi has knowledge caused by the subtle discrimination.

Commentary:

Every word in these texts must be understood within the context of *Patañjali* and not just for our own fancy according to our stage of development or agenda of spiritual mission. To understand *Patañjali* and to get the most benefit from his *sūtras*, we have to stay with his meanings, and then try to see where we have progressed to and where we should advance onwards.

When a yogi can observe subtle mystic moments and see how they flow on one to another, he develops a very subtle insight which gives definite knowledge of things. *Viveka* means very subtle insight and jam means what is caused or produced from the super knowledge of that yogi.

Verse 54

जातिलक्षणदेशैरन्यतानवच्छेदात्तुल्ययोस्ततः प्रतिपत्तिः ॥५४॥

jāti lakṣaṇa deśaiḥ anyatā anavacchedāt
tulyayoḥ tataḥ pratipattiḥ

jāti – type genius, genus, general category; lakṣaṇa – individual characteristics; deśaiḥ – by what location; anyatā – otherwise, in a different manner; anavacchedāt – due to or resulting from lack of definition; tulyayoḥ – of two similar types; tataḥ – hence, subsequently; pratipattiḥ – perception.

Subsequently, the yogi has perception of two similar realities which otherwise could not be sorted due to a lack of definition in terms of their general category, individual characteristics and locations.

Commentary:

Persistence in higher yoga brings on more definition. Things which before, seemed to be one or seem to be merged, appear clearly by their category, individual characteristics and locations. This begins by his sorting out his buddhi intellect organ, its various parts, as well as the sense of identity. A yogi thus develops mystic clarity.

Verse 55

तारकं सर्वविषयं सर्वथाविषयमक्रमं चेति विवेकजं ज्ञानम्॥५५॥

tārakaṁ sarvaviṣayaṁ sarvathāviṣayaṁ
akramaṁ ca iti vivekajaṁ jñānam

tārakaṁ – crossing over transcending; sarva – all; viṣayaṁ – subtle and gross mundane objects; sarvathā – in all ways; viṣayaṁ – subtle and gross mundane object; akramaṁ – without sequential perceptions; ca – and; iti – thus, subsequently; vivekajaṁ – the distinction caused by subtle discrimination; jñānam – knowledge.

The distinction caused by subtle discrimination is the crossing over or transcending of all subtle and gross mundane objects in all ways they are presented, without the yogi taking recourse to any other sequential perceptions of mind reliance.

Commentary:

Śrī Patañjali highlights the culmination of yoga, so that as a yogi we can gage ourselves to know where we are on the course of crossing over the mundane reality which keeps us so occupied when we try to transcend it.

Verse 56

सत्त्वपुरुषयोः शुद्धिसाम्ये कैवल्यमिति॥५६॥

sattva puruṣayoḥ śuddhi sāmye kaivalyam iti

sattva – intelligence energy of material nature; puruṣayoḥ – of the spirit; śuddhi – purity; sāmye – on being equal; kaivalyam – total separation from the mundane psychology; iti – thus.

When there is equal purity between the intelligence energy of material nature and the spirit, then there is total separation from the mundane psychology.

Commentary:

Readers should check verses 2:25 and 3:36 to understand *Śrī Patañjali*'s use of the terms *sattva*, *puruṣyoḥ* and *kaivalyam*. Obviously the key term in this verse is *sattva*. What is *sattva*? It is clear however that for the aspiring yogi, he must use *sattva* to become self-realized. This being established, all questions as to why he is to depend on nature are irrelevant. It is not why he has to depend, but rather how he can protect himself or cause himself to be situated in alliance with the material nature in its primal purity (*śuddhi-sāmye*). What will happen to him thereafter? Is there something higher? Where will he go after that? What will be his status? Is there a world to which he will escape if he attains that? Will that world have the same purified *sattva*-energy (intelligence energy of material nature)? Is there any place or world where he could encounter only energy like his spirit (*puruṣaḥ*). These are the questions to be considered by the yogin.

Chapter 4

Kaivalya Pāda:

Segregation Accomplishment

Verse 1

जन्मौषधिमन्त्रतपःसमाधिजाः सिद्धयः ॥ १ ॥

janma auṣadhi mantra tapaḥ samādhijāḥ siddhayaḥ

janma – birth, particular species; auṣadhi – drugs; mantra – special sound; tapaḥ – physical bodily austerities in haṭha yoga; samādhi – continuous effortless linkage of the attention to a higher concentration force, object or person; jāḥ – what is produced from; siddhayaḥ – mystic skills.

**The mystic skills are produced
by taking birth in particular species,
by taking drugs, by reciting special sounds,
by physical bodily austerities or
by the continuous effortless linkage of the attention
to a higher concentration force, object or person.**

Commentary:

The mystic skills are inherent in the subtle body of each creature but the manifestation of these depends on particular circumstances. Taking birth in a particular species either as an animal, angel, or human being, can cause one to express unusual powers. Taking narcotic drugs or stimulants may cause shifts in pranic force in the subtle body. This would activate some paranormal powers. Repeating special sounds or having these recited on one's behalf might affect the pranic arrangement in one's subtle body, resulting in paranormal powers. And of course yoga austerities in *haṭha* yoga would definitely cause the development of psychic powers. *Samādhi*, which is listed last by *Śrī Patañjali*, is definitely yielding of paranormal perceptions.

Verse 2

जात्यन्तरपरिणामः प्रकृत्यापूरात्॥ २ ॥

jātyantara pariṇāmaḥ prakṛtyāpūrāt

jātyantara = jāti – category + antara – other, another; pariṇāmaḥ – transformation; prakṛiti – subtle material nature; āpūrāt – due to filling up or saturation.

**The transformation from one category to another
is by the saturation of the subtle material nature.**

Commentary:

Modern authorities like Timothy Leary and Aldous Huxley, preferred the use of drugs for the development of higher perception. But *Śrī* Gorakshanath wanted us to use the *haṭha yoga* austerities. *Śrī* Babaji Mahasaya recommended the *samādhi* continuous effortless linkage of the attention to a higher concentration force, object or person. However modern spiritual masters from India usually hawk the mantra special sounds as the means of perfection. And some psychics say that a person should be gifted from birth with mystic abilities.

When a living entity develops a higher quality and when that expression becomes saturated in his nature, he is automatically transferred into a higher species of life, either as an elevated human being, an angelic personality or a divine being.

Śrī Babaji Mahasaya gave me a notation for verse one:

> *"Each of the methods for developing or manifesting the mystic skills are listed in orderof the particularefforts made by the yogi. The first is janma or birth opportunity. That is based on efforts in the past lives. Thus in the current life, no effort is required. Some might take the janma or appearance in higher realms like in siddhaloka. There, taking a siddha yoga body, one experiences the result of his previous austerities. Others take an earthly body again and by the force of their past penance, experience mystic skills even in another gross body."*

....Auṣadhi means herbs, drugs or chemical means of adjusting the gross and subtle body. This used to be a method in the Vedic period. This is why one might read about the soma plant. This does not require much endeavor, only the acquirement of the particular plant species. By ingesting that plant in its concentrated form, pranic energy in one's subtle body is affected and certain abilities of the subtle body become manifested. Herbs were used by shamans, the religious leaders of primitive people.

The herbal method is a risky one, since the dosage may be wrong. It might be too high or too low, too concentrated or too diluted. It might kill or disable the body.

Mantra, special sounds is the general method preferred by most human beings. This operates the confidence energy of the person, but he may or may not succeed in experiencing something about the subtle body. This is an easy method requiring only the working of the vocal chords or silent mental sounding. This method remained popular for thousands of years due to human tendency for relying on hope for calling on superior authority for assistance.

Tapaḥ means the *haṭha* yoga austerities which purify both the gross and subtle bodies. This includes *kuṇḍalini* yoga for displacing bad subtle energy. This is the classic method for attaining purity of the intelligence energy of material nature; an energy mentioned in verse 56 of the last chapter:

sattva puruṣyoḥ śuddhi sāmye kaivalyam iti

When there is equal purity between the intelligence energy of material nature and the spirit, then there is total separation from the mundane psychology. (Yoga Sūtra 3.56)

If that energy is not purified, then the progress will be erratic causing the yogi to fall to a lower level sooner or later. The *haṭha* yoga austerities are the definite way for such purity. Study what Krishna said in the chapter 6 verse 12 of His *Bhagavad-gītā* discourse.

The last method which is the best is *samādhi*, the continuous effortless linkage of the attention to a higher reality. This is the choice method. However this is merely an advancement of the *tapaḥ* or *haṭha* yoga austerity method. It does not stand alone. One cannot attain *samādhi* without doing the *haṭha* yoga austerities proficiently.

In summary, *janma* means efforts in a past life. *Auṣadhi* means eating, drinking, smelling or otherwise ingesting chemicals which affects the subtle body. Mantra means using one's faith or confident energy. *Tapaḥ* means physical austerities which eradicate impurities in the subtle form. *Samādhi* means using one's psychic force to reach higher realities.

Verse 3

निमित्तमप्रयोजकं प्रकृतीनां वरणभेदस्तु ततः क्षेत्रिकवत्॥ ३ ॥

nimittaṁ aprayojakaṁ prakṛtīnāṁ
varaṇabhedaḥ tu tataḥ kṣetrikavat

nimittaṁ – cause, motive, apparent cause; aprayojakaṁ – not used, not employed, not causing; prakṛtīnāṁ – of the subtle material energy; varaṇa – impediments, obstacles; bhedaḥ – splitting, removing, disintegrating; tu – but, except; tataḥ – hence; kṣetrikavat – like a farmer.

The motivating force of the subtle material energy is not used except for the disintegration of impediments, hence it is compared to a farmer.

Commentary:

Even though a yogin is assisted by material nature, which exhibits powerful motivating forces from time to time, still his spiritual progress is not really caused by nature. It is just that sometimes nature removes its own forces which acted as impediments to the efforts of the yogi. Even though a farmer does so many things to facilitate the growing of seeds, still that does not mean that any of his actions are the real causes of plant growth. The development from seeds to plant has more to do with the potential within the seed that it does with the farmer's efforts. Similarly material nature does not cause a yogi's development, even though nature may facilitate that progression.

Verse 4

निर्माणचित्तान्यस्मितामात्रात्॥ ४॥

nirmāṇacittāni asmitāmātrāt

nirmāṇa – producing, creating, measuring, fabricating; cittāni – regions within the mento-emotional energy; asmitā – sense of identity which is developed in relation to material nature; mātrāt – from that only.

The formation of regions within the mento-emotional energy, arises only from the sense of identity which is developed in relation to material nature.

Commentary:

Even though the spirit's attention is one only, still because of the mento-emotional energy, there appears to be various regions within the mind and feelings of a personality. A yogi by mystic research in *kriyā* yoga, within his psyche, traces all these mental regions and emotional moods to the sense of identity which he experiences anytime his attention goes in the direction of the gross or subtle material nature. Thus eventually he develops a disgust (*nirvedaḥ*), and becomes very serious about spiritual progression. He no longer wants to be entertained by the various imaginings within the mind.

Verse 5

प्रवृत्तिभेदे प्रयोजकं चित्तमेकमनेकेषाम्॥ ५॥

pravṛtti bhede prayojakaṁ cittam ekam anekeṣām

pravṛtti – frantic activity, disperal of energy; bhede – in the difference; prayojakaṁ – very, much used or employed; cittam – the mento-emotional energy; ekam – one; anekeṣām – of what is numberless.

The one mento-emotional energy is that which is very much used in numberless different dispersals of energy.

Commentary:

With this in mind, a yogi takes steps to stop the innumerable impulsive operations of the mind.

Verse 6

तत्र ध्यानजमनाशयम्॥ ६॥

tatra dhyānajam anāśayam

tatra – there, in that case; dhyānajam – produced by the effortless linkage of the attention to a higher reality; anāśayam – without harmful emotions.

In that case, only subtle activities which are produced from the effortless linkage of the attention to a higher reality are without harmful emotions.

Commentary:

Āśayam is the seat of feelings, the place in the mento-emotional energy from which is derived endearing but harmful emotions. This location is difficult to track since it is in a mystic domain. Until a yogi gets clarity of consciousness he cannot transcend his feelings. He is continually fooled by them. When he masters the effortless linkage of the mind to higher realities, then he gains objectively and can sort out the endearing but harmful feelings, even the memory which is a storehouse of these.

Verse 7

कर्माशुक्लाकृष्णं योगिनस्त्रिविधमितरेषाम्॥ ७॥

karma aśukla akṛṣnaṁ yoginaḥ trividham itareṣām

karma – cultural activity; aśukla – not white, not rewarding; akṛṣnaṁ – not black, not penalizing; yoginaḥ – of the yogis; trividham – three-fold; irtareṣām – for others.

The cultural activity of the yogis is neither rewarding nor penalizing, but others have three types of such action.

Commentary:

An advanced yogi, who has mastered the *dhyāna* effortless linkage of the mind to a higher reality, may perform cultural activities just as others do, but for him, these do not result in rewarding, penalizing nor fruitless results.

What then does the yogi gain from cultural activities? He gains absolutely nothing, because his detachment allows the reactions to fall back into material nature without a claimant.

Verse 8

ततस्तद्विपाकानुगुणानामेवाभिव्यक्तिर्वासनानाम्॥ ८॥

tataḥ tadvipāka anuguṇānām
eva abhivyaktiḥ vāsanānām

tataḥ – subsequently; tad – that, those; vipāka – development, fruition; anuguṇānām – of the corresponding features; eva – only, alone; abhivyaktiḥ – manifestation; vāsanānām – of tendencies within the mento-emotional energy.

Subsequently from those cultural activities there is development according to corresponding features only, bringing about the manifestation of the tendencies within the mento-emotional energy.

Commentary:

Everything in the material creation works according to innate tendency, manifesting according to time and place. Sometimes it takes thousands of years before something can manifest or be given any type of satisfaction.

In terms of the time of the earth, modern civilization is very recent. Still we see that the majority of people feel comfortable within the modern world. This is due to latent desires, which are being fulfilled under the present circumstances.

Because a yogi has mystic insight, he understands how numberless different dispersals of energy arise in the mento-emotional force by its proximity to the spirit's sense of identity. Thus he withdraws that sense and deactivates the mundane consciousness, freeing himself from being a slave to desires which arise in the seat of feelings. Others however must comply with the urges

Verse 9

जातिदेशकालव्यवहितानामप्यानन्तर्यं स्मृतिसंस्कारयोरेकरूपत्वात्॥ ९॥

jāti deśa kāla vyavahitānām api ānantaryaṁ smṛti saṁskārayoḥ ekarūpatvāt

jāti – status; deśa – location; kāla – time; vyavahitānām – of what is placed apart or separated; api – even, also; ānantaryaṁ – timeful sequence; smṛti – memory; saṁskārayoḥ – of the impressions formed of cultural activities; ekarūpatvāt – due to one form.

Even though circumstances are separated by status, location and time, still the impressions which form cultural activities and the resulting memories, are of one form and operate on a timely sequence.

Commentary:

This has to do with why past lives affect the present one, even though the individual may or may not recall his past. A different status, a different place and a different time, though separated from a cultural activity of the past, is in fact timeful and in sequence according to how it was laid into the memory within the mento-emotional energy of the individual concerned. Something that makes sense subjectively may seem totally inappropriate to the conscious mind which takes into account only what it can grasp about the present. Irrespective of the present circumstances, the memory and the urges from past lives, operate in timeful sequence.

Verse 10

तासामनादित्वं चाशिषो नित्यत्वात्॥ १०॥

tāsām anāditvaṁ ca āśiṣaḥ nityatvāt

tāsām – those; anāditvaṁ – what is without beginning, primeval; ca – and; āśiṣaḥ – hope and desire energies; nityatvāt – what is eternal.

**Those memories and impressions are primeval,
without a beginning.
Energies of hope and desire are eternal as well.**

Commentary:

When a yogi sees that the hope and desire energy is eternal, he makes a decision to let it be and to detach himself from the urges. He must, by all means, get himself separated from the mento-emotional force or remain a victim of it. The memories and the circumstance-forming impressions will be there for all eternity. A yogin has no choice but to extract his existence from the realm of it.

Verse 11

हेतुफलाश्रयालम्बनैः सङ्गृहीतत्वादेषामभावे तदभावः ॥ ११ ॥

*hetu phala āśraya ālambanaiḥ saṅgṛhītatvāt
eṣām abhāve tad abhāvaḥ*

hetu – cause; phala – effect; āśraya – storage place, causal plane, supportive base; ālambanaiḥ – by what supports or lifts; saṅgṛhītatvāt – what holds together; eṣām – of those, these; abhāve – in what is not there; tad – them; abhāvaḥ – not existing.

**They exist by what holds them together
in terms of cause and effect, supportive base and lifting influence.
Otherwise if their causes are not there,
they have no existence.**

Commentary:

For a yogi, his involvement is the supportive element, which makes the subtle material nature exist for him and engage him or use his consciousness. Thus if he detaches himself the supportive element being removed, material nature no longer affects him.

Verse 12

अतीतानागतं स्वरूपतोऽस्त्यध्वभेदाद्धर्माणाम् ॥ १२ ॥

*atīta anāgataṁ svarūpataḥ
asti adhvabhedāt dharmāṇām*

atīta – the past; anāgataṁ – the future; svarūpataḥ – true form; asti – there is, it exists; adhvabhedāt – due to different courses or events; dharmāṇām – of the characteristics.

**There is a true form of the past and future,
which is denoted by the different courses of their characteristics.**

Commentary:

Śrī Patañjali establishes that the past and future are real existences, having contents, which cause the present. Time is not an illusion. It is real in that sense. Because of definite characteristics, there is a certain course which time takes from the past into the present and into the yet-emerging future. The inherent characteristics (*dharmāṇām*) from the past mold the future. The changes which come about in the present are stockpiled by time as the basis for slight or major differences which are to come.

Verse 13

ते व्यक्तसूक्ष्मा गुणात्मानः ॥ १३ ॥

te vyakta sūkṣmāḥ guṇātmānaḥ

te – they; vyakta – gross; sūkṣmāḥ – subtle; guṇātmānaḥ = guṇā – subtle material nature + ātmānaḥ – of itself.

They are gross or subtle, all depending on their inherent nature.

Commentary:

The three phases of time, the past, present and future, are perpetual, having a relationship one with the other. They are reliant on their inherent energies which comprise the subtle and gross material nature. A limited being cannot permanently affect these, even though he may take part in their operations according to how he is positioned in time and place.

Verse 14

परिणामैकत्वाद्वस्तुतत्त्वम् ॥ १४ ॥

pariṇāma ekatvāt vastutattvam

pariṇāma – transformation, change; ekatvāt – singleness, uniqueness; vastu – object; tattvam – essence, actual composition.

The actual composition of an object is based on the uniqueness of the transformation.

Commentary:

Each object, no mater how similar, has certain unique qualities which are based on the particular transformations which caused its production. The varieties in material nature are researched by a yogi. Underlying all this, he finds the manifesting force of time along with the inherent qualities of material nature, mixed in various ways.

Verse 15

वस्तुसाम्ये चित्तभेदात्तयोर्विभक्तः पन्थाः ॥ १५ ॥

vastusāmye cittabhedāt tayoḥ vibhaktaḥ panthāḥ

vastu – object; sāmye – in the same; citta – mento-emotional energy; bhedāt – from the difference; tayoḥ – of these two; vibhaktaḥ – separated, divided; panthāḥ – ways of viewing, prejudices.

Because of a difference in the mento-emotional energy of two persons, separate prejudices manifest in their viewing of the very same object.

Commentary:

Separate prejudices lie dormant in the mento-emotional energy of each living entity. When viewing the same object which has the same composition, persons react differently. These prejudices are sponsored in material nature by time which, with the power of the past, regulates the present and future.

Verse 16

न चैकचित्ततन्त्रं वस्तु तदप्रमाणकं तदा किं स्यात्॥ १६॥

na ca ekacitta tantraṁ ced vastu
tat apramāṇakaṁ tadā kiṁ syāt

na – not, nor; ca – and; eka – one; citta – mento-emotional perception; tantraṁ – dependent; ced = cet – if, otherwise; vastu – object; tat – that; apramāṇakaṁ – not being observed; tadā – then; kiṁ – what; syāt – would occur.

An object is not dependent
on one person's mento-emotional perception.
Otherwise, what would happen
if it were not being perceived by that person?

Commentary:

Śrī Patañjali refutes the idea that the world is dependent on a limited mind or on a group of such minds. Otherwise if that or those limited minders were to lose perception of an object, the item would no longer exist.

Verse 17

तदुपरागापेक्षित्वाच्चित्तस्य वस्तु ज्ञाताज्ञातम्॥ १७॥

taduparāga apekṣitvāt cittasya vastu jñāta ajñātam

tad = tat – that; uparāga – color, mood; apekṣitvāt – from the expectation; cittasya – of the mento-emotional energy; vastu – object; jñāta – known; ajñātam – unknown.

An object is known or unknown,
all depending on the mood and expectation
of the particular mento-emotional energy of the person
in reference to it.

Commentary:

The application or non-application of consciousness is what brings objects into purview.

Verse 18

सदा ज्ञाताश्चित्तवृत्तयस्तत्प्रभोः पुरुषस्यापरिणामित्वात्॥ १८॥

sadā jñātāḥ cittavṛttayaḥ tatprabhoḥ
puruṣasya apariṇāmitvāt

sadā – always; jñātāḥ – known; citta – mento-emotional energy; vṛttayaḥ – the operations; tat – that; prabhoḥ – of the governor; puruṣasya – of the spirit; apariṇāmitvāt – due to changelessness.

**The operations of the mento-emotional energy
are always known to that governor
because of the changelessness of that spirit.**

Commentary:

Here an explanation is given, as to why the spirit appears to be affected by the operations of the mento-emotional energy of the psyche. It is due to the changelessness of the spirit, which serves as a background for the movements of consciousness.

Verse 19

न तत्स्वाभासं दृश्यत्वात्॥ १९॥

na tat svābhāsaṁ dṛśyatvāt

na – not; tat – that; svābhāsaṁ – self-illuminative; dṛśyatvāt – for it is due to being something to be perceived.

**That mento-emotional energy is not self-illuminative
for it is rather only capable of being perceived.**

Commentary:

The mento-emotional energy has for its nature the capability of being perceived but is not self-illuminative. This has to be studied objectively in meditation by the particular yogin.

Verse 20

एकसमये चोभयानवधारणम्॥ २०॥

ekasamaye ca ubhaya anavadhāraṇam

ekasamaye – at the same time; ca – and; ubhaya – both; anavadhāraṇam – of what cannot focus.

It cannot execute the focus of both at the same time.

Commentary:

This means that the mento-emotional energy cannot both focus on itself and the seer at the same time. This has to be verified in deep meditation.

Verse 21

चित्तान्तरदृश्ये बुद्धिबुद्धेरतिप्रसङ्गः स्मृतिसङ्करश्च ॥ २१ ॥

cittāntaradṛśye buddhibuddheḥ
atiprasaṅgaḥ smṛtisaṅkaraḥ ca

cittāntara – dṛśye = citta – mento-emotional energy + antara – another person + dṛśye – in the perception of; buddhi-buddher = buddhi – the intellect organ + buddheḥ – of the intellect organ; atiprasaṅgaḥ – absurd argument, unwarranted stretching of a rule or argument; smṛti – memory; saṅkaraḥ – confusion; ca – and.

In the perception of mento-emotional energy by another such energy, there would be an intellect perceiving another intellect independently. That would cause absurdity and confusion of memory.

Commentary:

Śrī Patañjali states here that it is absurd to think that without a spirit one's mind could perceive another mind. It would be absurd. Unless there is a spirit behind a mind, there would be no perception in that energy.

Verse 22

चितेरप्रतिसङ्क्रमायास्तदाकारापत्तौ स्वबुद्धिसंवेदनम् ॥ २२ ॥

citeḥ apratisaṁkramāyāḥ tadākārāpattau svabuddhisaṁvedanam

citeḥ – of the spirit; apratisaṁkramāyāḥ – not moving from one position to another; tad – tat – that; ākāra – form, aspect; āpattau – turning into, changing, assuming; sva – itself, oneself; buddhi – intellect organ; saṁvedanam – perception.

The perception of its own intellect occurs when it assumes that form in which there is no movement from one operation to another.

Commentary:

Until the mind is still and the mento-emotional energy ceases to fluctuate, one cannot perceive one's intellect objectively. Otherwise, one feels as though one's self and one's intellect were part of an homogeneous consciousness.

Verse 23

द्रष्टृदृश्योपरक्तं चित्तं सर्वार्थम् ॥ २३ ॥

draṣṭṛ dṛśya uparaktaṁ cittaṁ sarvārtham

draṣṭṛ - the perceiver; dṛśya – the perceived; uparaktaṁ – prejudiced; cittaṁ – mento-emotional energy; sarvārtham - what is all-evaluating.

The mento-emotional energy which is prejudiced by the perceiver and the perceived, is all-evaluating.

Commentary:

When the mento-emotional force absorbs energy from the spirit, as well as from an object, it seems to be all-evaluating. Thus the spirit becomes absorbed by its operations of analysis, conclusion and action.

Verse 24

तदसङ्ख्येयवासनाभिश्चित्रमपि परार्थं संहत्यकारित्वात्॥ २४॥

tat asaṅkhyeya vāsanābhiḥ citram
api parārthaṁ saṁhatyakāritvāt

tat – that; asaṅkhyeya – innumerable; vāsanābhiḥ – subtle impressions; citram – diversified; api – even, although; parārthaṁ – for another's sake; saṁhatya – because of it; kāritvāt – activity, force, factor.

Although the mento-emotional energy is diversified
by innumerable subtle impressions,
it acts for the sake of another power
because of its proximity to that other factor.

Commentary:

Everything done by the mento-emotional energy, even those subtle actions which seem to imperil the spirit are done for the sake of the spirit itself, even though the spirit may not deliberately motivate the psyche.

The proximity (*saṁhatya*) of the spirit is itself, the cause of the innumerable moods and urges.

Verse 25

विशेषदर्शिन आत्मभावभावनाविनिवृत्तिः॥ २५॥

viśeṣadarśinaḥ ātmabhāva bhāvanānivṛttiḥ

viśeṣa – distinction, specific perception; darśina – of the one who sees; ātma – the spirit; bhāva – feeling; bhāvanā – absorption in feelings; nivṛttiḥ – total stopping of the operations of the mento-emotional energy.

There is total stopping
of the operations of mento-emotional energy
for the person who perceives the distinction
between feelings and the spirit itself.

Commentary:

This is repeated again and again in different verses. A yogin has to sort out between his spirit and his mento-emotional energy. He has to transcend the proximity of the two.

Verse 26

तदा हि विवेकनिम्नङ्कैवल्यप्राग्भारञ्चित्तम्॥ २६॥

tadā hi vivekanimnaṁ kaivalya prāgbhāraṁ cittam

tadā – then; hi – indeed; viveka – discrimination; nimnaṁ – leaning towards, inclined to; kaivalya – total separation from the mundane psychology; prāg – towards; bhāraṁ – gravitating; cittam – mento-emotional force.

Then, indeed,
the mento-emotional force is inclined towards discrimination
and gravitates towards the total separation
from the mundane psychology.

Commentary:

The yogi has to achieve this. It does not come by wishful thinking. Only through higher yoga can this be achieved consistently.

Verse 27

तच्छिद्रेषु प्रत्ययान्तराणि संस्कारेभ्यः॥ २७॥

tat cchidreṣu pratyayāntarāṇi saṁskārebhyaḥ

tat – that; chidreṣu – in the relaxation of the focus; pratyayaḥ – conviction or belief as mind content, inlaid impression in the mento-emotional energy; antarāṇi – in between, interval; saṁskārebhaḥ – from the subtle impressions.

Besides that, in the relaxation of focus,
other mind contents arise in the intervals.
These are based on subtle impressions.

Commentary:

The yogi has to work through this without being disappointed or frustrated. He should not give up the higher yoga practice. He faces failures at every step but he must forge ahead. He must work for emancipation from his helpless alliance with the mento-emotional force. His main energy is the mind's content, which is deeply inlaid, in the mento-emotional force as urge-producing impressions from the past. Some of these surface as memory and others surface as pictures, sound formation, and then are expanded into meaningful or meaningless picturizations and sounds which distract the yogi by keeping him occupied in the picture-sound show of the mind. A yogi has to fight this to gain self-conquest.

Verse 28

हानमेषां क्लेशवदुक्तम्॥ २८॥

hānam eṣāṁ kleśavat uktam

hānam – killing off, complete removal; eṣāṁ – of these; kleśavad = kleśavat – like the mento-emotional afflictions; uktam – authoritatively said.

As authoritatively stated, the complete removal of these is like the elimination of the mento-emotional afflictions.

Commentary:

It is a personal struggle. The God is there but each yogi has to master this himself. As a beginning yogi becomes preoccupied removing all causes for the mental and emotional troubles, so the advanced yogi has to remove the mind content which poses a botheration and which the mind clings to automatically when it relaxed from the proper focus.

Great yogis went on before. They can help us with this inner struggle. They encourage us to practice. They have shown the way by their personal lives on earth, or by their current austerities in higher dimensions. Besides that, each yogi has to endure this inner conflict alone.

Verse 29

प्रसङ्ख्यानेऽप्यकुसीदस्य सर्वथा विवेकख्यातेर्धर्ममेघः समाधिः॥ २९॥

prasaṁkhyāne api akusīdasya sarvathā
vivekakhyāteḥ dharmameghaḥ samādhiḥ

prasaṁkhyāna – in the abstract meditation; api – even so; akusīdasya – of one who has no interest or sees no gain in material nature; sarvathā – in all ways; vivekakhyāteḥ – with super discrimination; dharmameghaḥ = dharma – nature's way of acting for beneficial results + meghaḥ – mento-emotional clouds of energy; samādhi – continuous effortless linkage of the attention to higher reality.

For one who sees no gains in material nature,
even while perceiving it in abstract meditation,
one has the super discrimination.
One attains the continuous effortless linkage of the attention
to higher reality which is described
as knowing the mento-emotional clouds of energy
which compel a person to perform
according to nature's way of acting for beneficial results.

Commentary:

Dharmameghaḥ is usually translated as cloud (*meghaḥ*) of virtue (*dharma*). However we took hints from I. K. Taimni, where he stated that *dharma-meghaḥ samādhi*, means the final *samādhi* in which the yogi shakes himself free from the world of *dharmas* which obscure reality like a cloud.

He is perhaps, the first commentator who understood this particular verse of *Śrī Patañjali*. That is to be regretted. The key to the meaning of this verse lies in the terms *akusīdasya*. This is because *kusīda* means a moneylender, or any money lent at a rate exceeding 5%. When "a" is added as a prefix, it means not having any desire to gain anything.

Śrīla Yogeshwarananda asked us to develop *paravairāgya*, which is complete disinterest in this world. *Śrī Patañjali* was specific in stating that one has to lose interest even in the very subtle aspect of material nature, aspects which we encounter in deep meditation on other levels of this reality. This is indicated by the term *prasaṁkhyāne* which means that one may see something of value in deep meditation, in which case one cannot develop the *paravairāgya* and one will not lose interest in the *dharmas* or ways of righteous living which are legated by material nature for different beings on different gross and subtle levels.

If we want to benefit in any way (*sarvathā*) from material nature, on any level, we will be attracted proportionally, and we will fall under the cloud (*meghaḥ*) of values (*dharmas*) which dictate how we should act to gain in the particular realm of our interest. This will keep us in the material world.

All yogis are forewarned by *Śrīla* Yogeshwaranada, who warned this writer in the same way, that the main obstacle is the desire for fame as a spiritual master. From that comes the idea that one should develop a territory where one can have his own kingdom with loyal disciples. Material nature will then show one a layout of values which one must adapt for success as a territorial spiritual master or god. This will cause a fall down.

Even though *Śrīla* Yogeswarananda had left behind many books, as well as ashrams and spiritual missions, still when I see him come down from the causal level where he is completing more austerities and researched into our complication, I never see him with disciples. He is not interested in any of the rules and regulations or *dharmas* which are laid out for spiritual masters who want to be worshipped as exalted saviors or gurus.

Everything in the material world, in the subtle, supersubtle or gross parts of it, is dangerous. We should know this. There were many people who came to me to be disciples and who suggested that they become elevated so that they can help others. All of them are conceited.

Verse 30

ततः क्लेशकर्मनिवृत्तिः ॥ ३० ॥

tataḥ kleśa karma nivṛttiḥ

tataḥ – subsequently; kleśa – afflictions; karma – cultural activities; nivṛttiḥ – stoppage of the operation of the mento-emotional energy.

Subsequently there is stoppage of the operation of the mento-emotional energy in terms of generation of cultural activities and their resulting afflictions.

Commentary:

The meaning of *dharma-meghaḥ* in the preceding verse is now explained by the subsequently result of the stoppage of generation of cultural activities which are themselves dictated by various types of *dharma* righteous lifestyle for particular results in the gross or subtle mundane world. None of these karmas or cultural activities are completely free from afflictions. Thus when the yogi reaches the causal level and sees the various clouds of energy (*meghaḥ*) in which the *dharmas* or laws for righteous life, are created and maintained, he gets an ease in his higher yoga practice. He smiles for he will never again fall into the trap of making spiritual missions to help or to save others. Such things are a complete farce, and are very disgusting to one who has seen the reality as it is.

An example of a yogin who left aside such things is Swami Satyananda of Bihar, who though he complete all duties given to him by his spiritual master, the great Swami Shivananda, did not himself continue to be a guru in this world, but carefully and efficiently left all that aside to proceed honestly with his advancement. Such a high class person is neither selfish nor conceited. If anything, he is realistic.

Verse 31

तदा सर्वावरणमलापेतस्य ज्ञानस्यानन्त्याज्ज्ञेयमल्पम्॥ ३१॥

tadā sarva āvaraṇa malāpetasya
jñānasya ānantyāt jñeyam alpam

tadā – then; sarva – all; āvaraṇa – mental darkness; mala – impurities; āpetasya – of what is removed; jñānasaya – of knowledge; ānantyāt – due to being unlimited; jñeyam – what is known; alpam – small trivial.

Then, because of the removal of all mental darkness and psychological impurities, that which can be known through the mento-emotional energy, seems trivial in comparison to the unlimited knowledge available when separated from it.

Commentary:

For this world, the mento-emotion energy is the linking agent. It is the means of prying into various things. It shows us how to be interested in and how to invest in this world for a benefit. But once we become freed from that energy, and we experience the self by itself, we no longer consider this world as being essential.

Verse 32

ततः कृतार्थानां परिणामक्रमसमाप्तिर्गुणानाम्॥ ३२॥

tataḥ kṛtārthānāṁ pariṇāmakrama samāptir guṇānām

tataḥ – thus; kṛtārthānāṁ – having done their purpose; pariṇāma – changes, alteration; krama – a step, succession, progression, process of development; samāptir = samāptiḥ – end conclusions; guṇānām – of the influence of the subtle material nature.

Thus, the subtle material nature, having fulfilled its purpose, its progressive alterations end.

Commentary:

This is only for the yogin who achieved isolation from his mento-emotional energies and their impulsive operations. For him, the natural power transfer from his spirit to the mento-emotional force ceases. For others it continues just as before.

Verse 33

क्षणप्रतियोगी परिणामापरान्तनिर्ग्राह्यः क्रमः ॥ ३३ ॥

kṣaṇa pratiyogī pariṇāma
aparānta nirgrāhyaḥ kramaḥ

kṣaṇa – moment; pratiyogī – corresponding, being a counter-part; pariṇāma – change, alteration; aparānta – the end; nirgrāhyaḥ – clearly perceived; kramaḥ – process.

The process, of which moments are a counterpart, and which causes the alterations, comes to an end and is clearly perceived.

Commentary:

The advanced yogi alone achieves this. This is an individual accomplishment, where the yogi sees the moments, which in sequence make up time which is itself the changing mundane energy (*guṇānām*). The yogi clearly perceives this from afar. What hypnotizes other and keeps them under its control subjectively and objectively, is looked upon by the yogin, just as the God would normally see it.

sa esah purvesam api guruh kalena anavacchedat

He, this particular person, being unconditioned by time is the guru evenof the ancient teachers, the authorities from before. (Yoga Sūtra 1.26)

Verse 34

पुरुषार्थशून्यानां गुणानां प्रतिप्रसवः कैवल्यं स्वरूपप्रतिष्ठा वा चितिशक्तिरिति ॥ ३४ ॥

puruṣārtha śūnyānāṁ guṇānāṁ
pratiprasavaḥ kaivalyaṁ
svarūpapratiṣṭhā vā citiśaktiḥ iti

puruṣārtha – the aims of a human being; śūnyānāṁ – devoid of; guṇānāṁ – of the influences of material nature; pratiprasavaḥ – reabsorption, retrogression, neutralization; kaivalyam – separation of the spirit from psychology; svarūpa – own form; pratiṣṭhā – established; vā – thus, at last; citiśaktiḥ – the power of pure consciousness; iti – that is all.

Separation of the spirit
from the mento-emotional energy (*kaivalyam*)
occurs when there is neutrality i
n respect to the influence of material nature,
when the yogi's psyche becomes devoid
of the general aims of a human being.
Thus at last, the spirit is established in its own form
as the force empowering the mento-emotional energy.

Commentary:

This ends the description of higher yoga practice, given to us by *Śrī Patañjali* Muni, that authority for all times. Undoubtedly, *Śrī Patañjali* Mahamuni covered everything in the mystic practice of yoga. All glories unto him.

END

Glossary
Word-for-Word Meanings

A

abhāva – absence of awareness
abhāvaḥ – disappearance, elimination, not existing
abhāvāt – resulting from the elimination
abhāve – in what is not there
abhibhava – disappearance
abhijātasya – of what is produced, all around or transparent
ābhimata – what is dearly desired
abhiniveśaḥ – strong focus on mundane existence which is due to instinctive fear of death
abhivyaktiḥ – manifestation
ābhyantara – internal
abhyāsa – effective yoga practice
ādarśa – sight
ādayaḥ – and related matters
adhigamaḥ – accomplishment
adhimātraḥ – substantial
adhimātratvāt – from intense
adhiṣṭhātṛtvaṁ – authority, complete disaffection
adhvabhedāt – due to different courses or events
adhyāsāt – resulting from the super-imposition
adhyātma – relationship between the supreme soul and the limited one
ādi – and the related mystic skills
ādīni – and the same for other aspects
ādiṣi – and similar aspects
ādiṣu – and by related qualities
adṛṣṭa – not perceived, not realized
āgamāḥ – correct reference
ahiṁsā – non-violence
ajñāna – spiritual ignorance
ajñātam – unknown
akalpitā – not manufactured, not artificial, not formed
ākāra – form, aspect
akaraṇaṁ – non-responsiveness
ākāśa – atmosphere
ākāśayoḥ – of the sky, atmosphere
akliṣṭāḥ – non-troublesome
akramaṁ – without sequential perceptions
akṛṣnaṁ – not black, not penalizing
ākṣepī – transcending
akusīdasya – of one who has no interest or sees no gain in material nature
alabdhabhūmikatva – not being able to maintain the progress made
ālambanā – support, prop, means of conversion
ālambanaiḥ – by what supports or lifts
ālambanaṁ – taking recourse
ālasya – lack of energy
aliṅga – without characteristics
aliṅgāni – that which has no indication
āloka – supernatural insight
ālokaḥ – illuminating
alpam – small trivial
anabhighātaḥ – non-obstruction, no shrinking, no attacking, no botheration
anāditvaṁ – what is without beginning, primeval
anāgata – future

anāgataṁ – the future, what has not manifested
ānanda – introspective happiness
ananta – endless, infinite
ānantaryaṁ – timely sequence
ānantyāt – due to being unlimited
anāśayam – without harmful emotions
anaṣṭaṁ – not finished, still existing, effective
anātmasu – in what is not the spirit
anavacchedāt – due to or resulting from lack of definition, unconditioned
anavacchinnāḥ – not restricted by, not adjusted by
anavadhāraṇam – of what cannot focus
anavasthitatvāni – unsteadiness in the progression
anekeṣām– of what is numberless
aṅga – limbs, part
aṅgamejayatva – nervousness of the body
aṅgāni – parts of a thing
aṇima – minuteness
aniṣṭa – unwanted features of existence
anitya – not eternal, temporary
añj – to smear with, to mix with
añjanatā – assuming the nature of or characterization of
āntaḥ – ending, extending to
antar – internal, psychological, concerning the thinking and feeling organs
aṅgaṁ – part
antara – another person, other
antarāṇi – in between, interval
antarāya – obstacle
antardhānam – invisibility, non-perceptibility
anu – following along, patterning after
anubhūta – the experience
anugamāt – by accompaniment, occurring with
anuguṇānām – of the corresponding features
anukāraḥ – imitation, patterning, assuming
anumāna – correct analysis
anumāna – what is surmised or seasoned out
anumoditāḥ – endorsed, approved
anupātī – reach full retrogression, followed by
ānuśāsanam – explanation
anuśayi – connected to, devotedly attached to
ānuśravika – what is conjectured on the basis of scripture, valid
anuṣṭhānāt – from consistent practice
anuttamaḥ – supreme, the very best
anvaya – following, connection, distribution, association
anya – others
anyatā – other than distinct from
anyatā – otherwise, in a different manner
anyatvaṁ – otherness, difference
anyatve – in difference
aparāmṛṣṭaḥ – unaffected
aparānta – of the other end, of death entry into the hereafter, the end
aparigraha – non-possessiveness
apariṇāmitvāt – due to changelessness
āpattau – turning into, changing, assuming
apavarga – liberation
apekṣitvāt – from the expectation
āpetasya – of what is removed
api – also, even, although, but

apramāṇakaṁ – not being observed
apratisaṁkramāyāḥ – not moving from one position to another
aprayojakaṁ – not used, not employed, not causing
apuṇya – demerits, vice
āpūrāt – due to filling up or saturation
ariṣṭebhyo – from portents
artha – purpose, objective, meaning
ārtham – for the sake of, value or purpose
arthaś – for the value of purpose
arthavāt – because of an object
arthavatava – purpose, value
arthavatva – value, worth
asaṁkīrṇayoḥ – of what is distinct or separate
asaṁpramoṣaḥ – retention
asaṁprayoge – in not contacting, on not contacting
asaṁsargaḥ – non-association, lack of desire to associate
āsana – body postures
āsanan – bodily posture
asaṅgaḥ – non-contact
asaṅkhyeya – innumerable
āsannaḥ – whatever is very near, what will occur soon
āśayaḥ – storage, reservoir
āśayaiḥ – by subconscious motivations
āsevitaḥ – sustained practice, aggressive interest
āśiṣaḥ – hope and desire energies
asmitā – identification, misplaced identity
asmitā – sense of identity which is developed in relation to material nature
asmitārūpa – I-ness, self-consciousness
āśraya – storage place, causal plane, supportive base
āśryatvam – what serves as a support for something else
aṣṭau – eight
asteya – non-stealing
asti – there is, it exists
aśuci – not clean, not pure
aśuddhi – impurity
aśukla – not white, not rewarding
āsvāda – taste
asya – of his, him
atadrūpa – not this form
atha – now
atiprasaṅgaḥ – absurd argument, unwarranted stretching of a rule
atīta – the past
ātma – spirit
ātmakaṁ – self, nature
ātmānaḥ – of itself
atyanta – excessively, extremely, very
auṣadhi – drugs
āvaraṇam – covering, mental darkness
avasthā – condition
avasthānam – is situated
āveśaḥ – entrance, penetration
avidyā – spiritual ignorance
aviplavā – unbroken, continuous
avirati – proneness to sensuality
aviṣayī – not an object of anything, imperceptible
aviśeṣa – what is regular
aviśeṣaḥ – not distinct, inability to distinguish
avyapadeśya – what is not to be defined, what is latent
āyuḥ – duration of life

B

bādhane – in annoyance or disturbance
bahiḥ – outside, external

bahiraṅga – external part
bāhya – external
bala – mystic force, strength
balāni – powers
baleṣu – by strength
bandha – bondage
bandhaḥ – confinement, restriction
bhāraṁ – gravitating
bhāva – states of feelings and perceptions, inherent nature, psychology
bhāvaḥ – mento-emotional energy, feeling
bhāvanā – absorption in feelings, producing
bhāvanam – manifesting, imagining, conceiving, considering
bhāvanātaḥ – abstract meditation
bhedaḥ – splitting, removing, disintegrating
bhedāt – from the difference
bhede – in the difference
bhoga – experience
bhogāḥ – type of experience
bhrāntidarśana – mistaken views
bhūmiḥ – ground, foundation, basis, territory, range
bhūmiṣu – in stages
bhūta – the various states of matter, mundane elements, creature
bhūtatvāt – the actual object
bhuvana – the solar system
bīja – seed, origin, source
bījam – origin
brahmacarya – sexual non-expressiveness which results in the perception of spirituality
buddheḥ – of the intellect organ
buddhi – the intellect organ

C

ca – and
cakre – on the energy gyrating center
cakṣuḥ – vision
candre – on the moon or moon-god
caturthaḥ – the fourth
ced (cet) – if, otherwise
cetana – sense
consciousnesschidreṣu – in the relaxation of the focus
citeḥ – of the spirit
citiśaktiḥ – the power of pure consciousness
citram – diversified
citta – mento-emotional energy
cittam – mento-emotional force
cittāni – regions within the mento-emotional energy
cittasya – of the mento-emotional energy
cittavikṣepaḥ – scattered mental and emotional energy

D

darśana – sight, vision, what is seen
darśanam – the view of
darśina – of the one who sees
daurmanasya – of mental depression
deśa – location, place
deśaiḥ – by what location
dhāraṇā – linking of the attention to a concentration force or person
dharma – attributes, functions, quality, law, sustaining force, nature's way of acting for beneficial results
dharmāṇām - of the characteristics
dharmī – most basic condition

dhruve – on the Pole Star
dhyāna – effortless linkage of the attention to higher concentration forces
dhyānajam – produced by the effortless linkage of the attention to a higher reality
dhyānam – effortless linking of the attention to a higher concentration force or person
dhyānāt – from effortless linkage of the mind to a higher concentration force
dīrgha – long, prolonged
divyaṁ – divine, supernatural
doṣa – fault, defect
draṣṭā – the perceiver
draṣṭṛ – the observer
dṛḍha – firm
drg (drk) – supernatural vision
dṛśeḥ – of the perceiver
dṛśi – perception, consciousness
dṛṣṭa – what is seen or perceived directly
dṛśya – the perceived
dṛśyam – what is perceived
dṛśyasya – of what is seen
dṛśyatvāt – for it is due to being something to be perceived
dṛśyayoḥ – of what is perceived
dṛśye – in the perception of
duḥka – distress
duḥkhaiḥ – with distress
duḥkham – distress
dvandvāḥ – the dualities of happiness and distress, heat and cold
dveṣa – impulsive emotional disaffection

E, F

eka – one
ekāgra – ability to link the attention to one concentration force or person
ekāgratā – of what is in front of one aspect before the attention
ekāgratayoḥ – of the one aspect before the attention
ekam – one
ekarūpatvāt – due to one form
ekasamaye – at the same time
ekātmatā – having one nature, identical
ekatra – in one place, all taken together as one practice
ekatānatā – one continuous threadlike flow of attention
ekatvāt – singleness, uniqueness
eṣaḥ – this particular person
eṣām – of those, these
etaya – by this
etena – by this
eva – only, alone, indeed

G

gamanam – going through, passing through
gati – course of heavenly planets and stars, the flow
grahaṇa – flow perception, sensual grasping
grahītṛ – perceiver
grāhya – appropriating, grasping, sensual perceptiveness
grāhyeṣu – in what is perceived
guṇa – influences of material nature
guṇānām – of the influence of the subtle material nature
guruḥ – the spiritual teacher

H

hana – avoidance
hānam – killing off, complete removal, withdrawal, escape
hasti – elephant
hetuḥ – cause, reason
hetutvāt – that which causes
heya – that which is to be avoided
heyāḥ – what is fit to be abandoned or left aside
heyaṁ – that which is to be avoided
hi – indeed
hiṁsa – violence
hlāda – happiness
hṛdaye – on the samyam, on the causal body

I

indriya – sense organs, sensual energy
indriyajayaḥ – the mastery of the sensual energy by psychological control
indriyāṇām – of the senses
indriyeṣu – by the sensual energy
irtareṣām – for others
iṣṭadevatā - cherished divine being
īśvara – Supreme Lord
itaratra – at other times
itareṣām – for others
itaretara – one for the other
iti – that is all, thus, subsequently
iva – as if, as it were, seems to be, like

J

jāḥ – what is produced from
jala – water
janma – birth, particular species
japaḥ – murmuring
jāti – species, status of life, category
jaya – conquest
jāyante – is produced
jayāt – from the conquest of, from the mastery
jñāna – knowledge
jñānadīptiḥ – radiant organ of perception
jñānam – information, knowledge
jñānasaya – of knowledge
jñāta – known
jñeyam – what is known
jugupsā – aversion, disgust
jvalanam – shining, burning, blazing, with fiery glow
jyotiṣi – on the shinning light
jyotiṣmatī – spiritually luminous

K

kaivalya – total separation from the mundane psychology
kaivalyam – separation of the spirit from psychology
kāla – time
kālena – by time
kaṇṭaka – thorns
kaṇṭha – throat
karaṇa – cause, causing, creating, making
kārita – cause to be done
kāritvāt – activity, force
karma – cultural activities, action
karuṇā – compassion
kathaṁtā – how, the reason for
kāya – body, subtle body
khyāteḥ – insight
khyāteḥ–of a thorough awareness
khyāti– the discriminating faculty of the intellect
khyātiḥ – what is known or identified, insight
kiṁ – what
kleśa – mento-emotional afflictions, troubles

kleśavad – like the mento-emotional afflictions
kliṣṭā – agonizing
krama – a step, succession, progression, process of development
kramaḥ – process
kramayoḥ – on the sequence
kriyā – action
kriyāyogaḥ – dynamic yoga practice
krodha – anger
kṛt – fulfilled, done
kṛta – done
kṛtārthānāṁ – having done their purpose
kṣaṇa – moment
kṣaya – decrease
kṣayaḥ – dissipation, removal
kṣayāt – from the elimination
kṣaye – on elimination
kṣetram – field, existential environment
kṣetrikavat – like a farmer
kṣīṇa – great reduction
kṣīyate – is dissipated
kṣut – hunger
kūpe – on the gullet
kūrma – tortoise, a particular subtle nerve

L

lābhaḥ – what is gained, obtained
laghu – light
lakṣaṇa – individual characteristics, shape
lāvaṇya – charm
liṅgamātra – a mark, that which is indicated
lobha – greed

M

madhya – mediocre
mahā – great
mahatva – largeness, cosmic proportions
mahāvratam – great commitment
maitrī – friendliness
mala – impurities
manasaḥ – of the mind
maṇeḥ – of a gem
manojavitvaṁ – swiftness of mind, rapidity
mantra – special sound
mātra – only, merely
mātraḥ – measure or extent
mātrasya – only
mātrāt – from that only
meghaḥ – mento-emotional clouds of energy
mithyājñānam – false information
moha – delusion
mṛdu – minor, slight
muditā – joyfulness, cheerfulness
mūlaḥ – root, cause
mūle – in the cause
mūrdha – the head

N

na – not, nor
nābhi – navel
nāḍyāṁ – on the nadi or subtle nerve
nairantarya – uninterrupted, continuous
naṣṭam – destroyed, non-existent, non-effective
nibandhanī – bond, fusion
nidrā – sleep

nimittaṁ – cause, motive, apparent cause
nimnaṁ – leaning towards, inclined to

niratiśayaṁ – unsurpassed
nirbhāsā – shining
nirbhāsaṁ – illuminating
nirbījaḥ – not motivated by the mento-emotional energy
nirbījasya – not motivated by the mento-emotional energy
nirgrāhyaḥ – clearly perceived
nirmāṇa – producing, creating, measuring, fabricating
nirodha – restraint, cessation, suppression, non-operation
nirodhāt – resulting from that non-operation
nirodhe – on the non-operation
nirupakramaṁ – dormant, destined
nirvicāra – non-investigative linkage
nirvitarka – fusion or linkage without deliberation or analysis
nitya – eternal
nityatvāt – what is eternal
nivṛttiḥ – cessation, suppression
niyama – recommended behaviors
nyāsāt – from placing or applying

O, P

pañcatayyaḥ – fivefold
paṅka – mud
panthāḥ – ways of viewing, prejudices
para – another, of others
parair – with others
paraṁ – highest (non-interest)
paramā – highest, greatest
parārthaṁ – for another's sake
parārthatvāt – what is apart from another thing
paridṛṣṭah – measured, regulated
pariṇāma – transformation, change, alteration
pariśuddhau – on complete purification
paritāpa – distress
parvāṇi – phases, stages, parts
paryavasānam – termination
paśyaḥ – what is perceived
phala – effect
phalāḥ – results
pipāsā – thirst
prabhoḥ – of the governor
pracāra – channel flow
pracchardana – exhalation
pradhānah – subtle matter
prādurbhāvaḥ – coming into existence, manifesting
prāg – towards
prajñā – insight
prajñābhyām – from the two methods of insight
prakāśa – clear perception, light
prakṛiti – subtle material nature
prakṛtilayānām – of those who are diffused into subtle material nature
prakṛtīnāṁ – of the subtle material energy
pramāda – inattentiveness
pramāṇa – correct perception
pramāṇāni – true perception, correct perception
prāṇasya – of the vital energy
praṇavaḥ – the sacred syllable *āuṁ* (*Oṁ*)
prāṇāyāma – breath enrichment of the subtle body
praṇidhānāni – profound religious meditation
praṇidhānāt – derived from profound religious meditation
prānta – boundary or edge
prāntabhūmiḥ – stage
prasādaḥ – clarity and serenity
prasādanam – serenity
prasaṁkhyāna – in the abstract meditation

prasaṅgāt – due to association, due to endearing friendliness
praśānta – spiritual peace
prasava – expressing, going outwards
prasupta – dormant
praśvāsayoḥ – of the exhalation
prati – opposing, reverting back, toward
pratibandhī – the preventer, that which effectively suppresses something
prātibha – the shining organ of divination
prātibhāt – resulting from samyama on the shinning organ of divination
pratipakṣa – what is opposite or contrary
pratipattiḥ – perception
pratiprasavaḥ – re-absorption, retrogression, neutralization
pratiṣedha – removal
pratiṣṭhā – established
pratiṣṭham – positioned, based
pratiṣṭhāyāṁ – on being firmly established
pratiyogī – corresponding, being a counter-part
pratyāhar – sensual energy withdrawal
pratyāhāraḥ – withdrawal of sensual energy and its focus on the mind
pratyak – backwards, inwards, in the opposite direction
pratyakṣa – direct but correct perception *pratyayaḥ* – conviction or belief as mental content, instinctive interest
pratyayaḥ – mental content, objective awareness within the psyche
pratyayānām – pertaining to the mind content, convictions, idea
pratyayasya – of the mind content
pravibhāga – differentiation, sorting, classification, mental clarity
pravṛtti – destined activity, the force of cultural activity
pravṛtti – frantic activity, dispersal of energy
pravṛttiḥ – the operation
prayatna – effort
prayaya – objective awareness, opinions and motives of mind content
prayojakaṁ – very, much used or employed
punaḥ – again
puṇya – merits, virtue
puruṣa – of the spiritual person, individual spirit
puruṣārtha – the aims of a human being
puruṣasya – of the spirit
pūrva – before, previous
pūrvakaḥ – caused by, proceeded by, previously practiced
pūrveṣām – of those before, the ancient teachers

Q, R

rāga – a tendency of emotional attachment, craving
rasa – essence
ratna – gems, precious things
ṛtaṁbharā – reality-perceptive, truth discerning
rūḍho – developed, produced
rūpa – form
ruta – sound, cry, yell, language

S

śabda – sound
śabdādi – sound and the related sensual pursuits
śabdajñāna – written or spoken information
sabījaḥ – with motivation from the mento-emotional energy
sadā – always
sādhāraṇatvāt – common, normal, universal
sah – he, that
sahabhuvaḥ – occurring with the symptoms
śaithilyāt – due to relaxation, collapse
sākṣātkaraṇāt – from causing to be visibly present, direct, intuitive
śakti – power, potency, energy
śaktyoḥ – of the two potencies
sālambanaṁ – leaning on, resting on, support
samādhi – continuous effortless linkage of the attention to a higher concentration force or person
samāna – digestive energy
samāpatteḥ – of meeting, of linking
samāpattibhyām – meeting, encounter
samāpattiḥ – linkage fusion
samāptir – end conclusions
samaya – condition
saṁbandha – relationship
saṁbodhaḥ – full or correct perception
saṁhananatvāni – definiteness, hardness
saṁhatya – because of it
saṁjñā – consciousness, demeanor, mind-set
saṁkāra – impression
saṁkhyābhiḥ – with numbering, accounting
saṁpat – wealth, prosperity, perfection
saṁprajñātaḥ – the observational linkage of the attention to a higher concentration force
saṁprayogaḥ – intimate contact
saṁśaya – doubt
saṁskāra – impression in the mento-emotional energy
saṁskārāt – from the impressions derived
saṁskārayoḥ – of the impressions formed of cultural activities
saṁskārebhaḥ – from the subtle impressions
saṁvedanam – perception
saṁvedanāt – from knowing
saṁvegānām – regarding those who practice forcibly
saṁvit – thorough insight
saṁyamād – from the complete restraint of the mento-emotional energy
saṁyamah – complete restraint
saṁyamāt – from the complete restraint of the mento-emotional energy
sāmye – on being equal, in the same
saṁyoga – conjunction
saṁyogo – the indiscriminate association
saṅga – association
saṅgṛhītatvāt – what holds together
saṅkaraḥ – confusion, intermixture
saṅkīrṇā – blending together, mixed
sannidhau – presence, vicinity
śānta – tranquilized, settled, subsided, collapsed
saṅtoṣa – contentment

saṅtoṣāt – from contentment
saptadhā – seven fold
śarīra – body
sārūpyam – with the same format, conformity
sarva – all
sārvabhaumāḥ – relating to all standard stages, being standard
sarvajña – all knowing
sarvajñātṛtvaṁ – all knowledge, intuition
sarvam – everything, all reality
sarvārtham - what is all evaluating
sarvārthatā – varying objective
sarvathā – in all ways
sati – being accomplished, there is existing
satkāra – reverence, care attention
sattva – clarifying perception of material nature, intelligence energy of material nature
satya – realism
śauca – purification
śaucāt – from purification
saumanasya – concerning benevolence
savicāra – investigative linkage of one's attention to a higher concetration force
savitarkā – thoughtfulness, reasoning, deliberation
śeṣaḥ – what is remaining
siddha – the perfected being
siddhayaḥ – mystic perfectional skills
siddhiḥ – perfection, skill
śīlaṁ – form, disposition
smaya – fascination, wonderment
smṛtayaḥ – memory
smṛti – memory
sopakramaṁ – set about, undertaken, already operative
śraddhā – confidence
śrāvaṇa – hearing
śrotra – hearing sense
śrotram – hearing sense
śruta – what is heard
stambha – restrained, suppressed, restrictive
stambhe – on the suspension
sthairyam – steadiness
sthairye – in the consistent
sthāni – the place a yogi would attain if his material body dies
sthira – steady
sthitau – regarding steadiness or persistence
sthiti – stability, steadiness
stūla – gross form
styāna – idleness
śuci – pure
śuddaḥ – purity
śuddhi – purification
sukha – happiness
sukham – comfortable
sūkṣma – subtle
sūkṣmaḥ – subtle energies, hardly noticeable
śunya – devoid of
śūnyam – empty, void, lacking
śūnyānāṁ – devoid of
sūrye – on the sun-god or the sun planet
sva – own nature, own psyche, itself, oneself
svābhāsaṁ – self-illuminative
svādhyāya – study of the psyche
svādhyāyāt – from study of the psyche
svāmi – the master, the individual self
svapna – dream

svarasavāhī – it's own flow of energy of self preservation
svārtha – one's own, self interest
svarūpa – own form
svarūpataḥ – true form
svarūpe – in his own form
śvāsa – inhalation
śvāsapraśvāsāḥ – labored breathing
syāt –would occur

T

tā – they
tad – that
tadā – then
tadarthabhābanam – that value with deep feelings
tadeva – that only, alone
tānatā – thread of fiber
tantraṁ – dependent
tanū – thinking reducing
tāpa – strenuous endeavor
tapaḥ – austerity
tārā – stars
tārakaṁ – crossing over, transcending
tāsām – those
tasmin – on this
tasya – of it, of this, of him, of his
tat – that
tataḥ – hence, subsequently
tatha – just as, so it is
tatra – there, in that location
tatstha – basis foundation
tattva – standard method in pursuit of reality
tattvam – essence, actual composition
tayoḥ – of these two
te – these, they
tīvra – very intense
traya – threefold
trayam – three
trividham – three-fold
tu – but, except
tūla – cotton fluff
tulya – similar
tulyayoḥ – of two similar types
tyāgaḥ – abandonment

U

ubhaya – both
udāna – air which rises from the throat and enters the head
udārāṇām – expanded
udayau – and increase
udita – emergent
uditau – and agitated, emerging
uktam – authoritively said, described
upalabdhi – obtaining experience
upanimantraṇe – on being invited
uparāga – color, mood
uparaktaṁ – prejudiced
upasargāḥ – impediments
upasthānam – approaching, waiting upon
upāyaḥ – means, method
upekṣaṇam – indifference, neutrality, non-responsiveness
utkrāntiḥ – rising above
utpannā – produced, brought about
uttareṣāṁ – of the other afflictions

V

vā – thus, at last, or
vācakaḥ – what is denoted or named
vāhī – flow current, instinct for self-preservation
vāhita – flow
vaira – hostility
vairāgyābhyāṁ – non-interest, a total lack of concern, non-interference

vairāgyam – non-interest
vairāgyāt – from a lack of interest
vaiśāradye – on gaining competence
vaitṛṣṇyam – freedom from desire
vajra – diamond-like, infallible
varaṇa – impediments, obstacles
vārtāḥ – smell
vāsanābhiḥ – subtle impressions
vāsanānām – of tendencies within the mento-emotional energy
vaśīkāra – through control
vaśīkāraḥ – mastery of the psyche
vastu – object
vastuśūnyaḥ – devoid of reality, without reality
vaśyatā – subdued, subjugation, control
vedana – touching
vedanīyaḥ – what is experienced or realized
vi – parting away from, dispersing
vibhaktaḥ – separated, divided
vicāra – deliberation, reflection
vicchedaḥ – the separation
vicchina – alternating, periodic
videhā – bodiless state
vidhāraṇābhyāṁ – by inhalation
viduṣaḥ – the wise man
vikalpa – imagination
vikalpaiḥ – with option, alternative, doubt, uncertainty
vikṣepa – distraction
viniyogaḥ – application, employment, practice
vipāka – development, fruition
vipākaḥ – what is resulting
viparyaya – incorrect perception
viprakṛṣṭa – remote
virāma – losing track of, dropping
virodhāt – resulting from confrontation or clashing aspects
vīrya – vigor, stamina
viṣayā – object
viṣayaṁ – an object or person
viṣayaṁ – subtle and gross mundane objects
viṣayāṇāṁ – relating to attractive objects
viṣayatvaṁ – what is concerning the nature of gross objects
viṣayavatī – like normal sensuality, something different but similar to a normal object
viśeṣa – distinction, specific perception
viśeṣaḥ – rating
viśokāh – sorrowless
vīta – without
vitarka – doubt, argument, analysis
vitṛṣṇasya – of one who does not crave
viveka – discrimination
vivekajaṁ – the distinction caused by subtle discrimination
vivekakhyāteḥ – with super discrimination
vivekinaḥ – the discriminating person
vṛttayaḥ – vibrational modes of the mento-emotional energies
vṛtteḥ – concerning the mento-emotional operations
vṛtti – vibrational mode of the mento-emotional energy
vṛttiḥ – activity, movement, operation
vyādhi – disease
vyākhyātā – explained
vyākhyātāḥ – is described
vyakta – gross
vyavahita – concealed
vyavahitānām – of what is placed apart or separated

vyūha – arrangement, layout, system
vyutthāna – expression
vyutthāne – in expressing, going outwards, rising up

W, X, Y, Z

yama – moral restraints
yatha – as, according
yatnaḥ – endeavor
yoga – yoga process
yogaḥ – the skill of yoga
yogānuśāsanam – yoga and its practice
yoginaḥ – of the yogis
yogyatā – being conducive for abstract meditation
yogyatvāni – being fit for yoga or abstract meditation

Index to Verses: Selected Sanskrit Words

Q, R

S

T, U

V

W, X, Y, Z

Index to Verses: Selected English Words

Q, R

S

T

U, V

W, X

Y, Z

Index to Commentary of Part 3

N

O

P

Q

R

S

XYZ

Scheme of pronounciation

Gutturals:	क	ख	ग	घ	ङ
	ka	kha	ga	gha	ṅa
Palatals:	च	छ	ज	झ	ञ
	ca	cha	ja	jha	ña
Cerebrals:	ट	ठ	ड	ढ	ण
	ṭa	ṭha	ḍa	ḍha	ṇa
Dentals:	त	थ	द	घ	न
	ta	tha	da	dha	na
Labials:	प	फ	ब	भ	म
	pa	pha	ba	bha	ma

Semi

य र	ल	व		० १ २ ३ ४ ५ ६ ७ ८ ९
ya ra	la	va		0 1 2 3 4 5 6 7 8 9

Sibilants:	श	ष	स	**Aspirate:**	ह
	śa	ṣa	sa		ha

Vowels:

अ आ	इ	ई	उ	ऊ	ऋ	ऋ
a ā	i	ī	u	ū	ṛ	ṝ
ए औ	ओ	औ	ऌ	ॡ	ं	:
e ai	o	au	lṛ	lṝ	ṁ	ḥ

Apostrophe ऽ

About the Author

Michael Beloved (Yogi Madhvāchārya) took his current body in 1951 in Guyana. In 1965, while living in Trinidad, he instinctively began doing yoga postures and tried to make sense of the supernatural side of life.

Later in 1970, in the Philippines, he approached a Martial Arts Master named Mr. Arthur Beverford. He explained to the teacher that he was seeking a yoga instructor. Mr. Beverford identified himself as an advanced disciple of *Śrī* Rishi Singh Gherwal, an astanga yoga master.

Beverford taught the traditional astanga yoga with stress on postures, attentive breathing and brow chakra centering meditation. In 1972, Michael entered the Denver Colorado Ashram of kuṇḍalinī yoga Master *Śrī* Harbhajan Singh. There he took instruction in bhastrika *prāṇāyāma* and its application to yoga postures. He was supervised mostly by Yogi Bhajan's disciple named Prem Kaur.

In 1979 Michael formally entered the disciplic succession of the Brahma-Madhava-Gaudiya Sampradaya through Swāmī Kirtanananda, who was a prominent sannyasi disciple of the Great Vaishnava Authority *Śrī* Swāmī Bhaktivedanta Prabhupāda, the exponent of devotion to *Śrī* Krishna.

However, yoga has a mystic side to it, thus Michael took training and teaching empowerment from several spiritual masters of different aspects of spiritual development. This is consistent with *Śrī* Krishna's advice to Arjuna in the *Bhagavad Gītā*:

tad viddhi praṇipātena paripraśnena sevayā

upadekṣyanti te jñānaṁ jñāninas tattva darśinaḥ

This you ought to know. By submitting yourself as a student, by asking questions, by serving as requested, the perceptive, reality-conversant teachers will teach you the knowledge. (Bhagavad Gītā 4.34)

Most of the instructions Michael received were given in the astral world. On that side of existence, his most prominent teachers were *Śrī* Swāmī Shivananda of Rishikesh, Yogiraj Swāmī Vishnudevananda, *Śrī* Bābāji Mahasaya - the master of the masters of kriyā yoga, *Śrīla* Yogeshwarananda of Gangotri - the master of the masters of rāj yoga (spiritual clarity), and Siddha Swāmī Nityananda the brahma yoga authority.

If you have some interest in yoga, nurture and develop it. *Śrī* Krishna, the Supreme Being offers all encouragement to those who are attracted to yoga. This is what the God said:

tatra taṁ buddhi saṁyogaṁ labhate paurva dehikam

yatate ca tato bhūyaḥ saṁsiddhau kuru nandana

In that environment (in the new birth), he (the yogi) is inspired with the cumulative intellectual interest from a previous birth. And from

that time, he strives again for yoga perfection, O dear son of the Kurus. (Bhagavad Gītā 6.43)

Publications

English Series

Bhagavad Gita English

Anu Gita English

Markandeya Samasya English

Yoga Sutras English

Uddhava Gita English

These are in 21st Century English, very precise and exacting. Many Sanskrit words which were considered untranslatable into a Western language are rendered in precise, expressive and modern English, due to the English language becoming the world's universal means of concept conveyance.

Three of these books are instructions from Krishna. **In Bhagavad Gita English** and **Anu Gita English**, the instructions were for Arjuna. In the **Uddhava Gita**

English, it was for Uddhava. Bhagavad Gita and Anu Gita are extracted from the Mahabharata. Uddhava Gita was extracted from the 11th Canto of the Srimad Bhagavatam (Bhagavata Purana). One of these books, the **Markandeya Samasya English** is about Krishna, as described by Yogi Markandeya, who survived the cosmic collapse and reached a divine child in whose transcendental body, the collapsed world was existing. Another of these books, the **Yoga Sutras English,** is the detailed syllabus about yoga practice.

My suggestion is that you read **Bhagavad Gita English**, the **Anu Gita English, the Markandeya Samasya English,** the **Yoga Sutras English** and lastly the **Uddhava Gita English**, which is much more complicated and detailed.

For each of these books we have at least one commentary, which is published separately. Thus your particular interest can be researched further in the commentaries.

The smallest of these commentaries and perhaps the simplest is the one for the Anu Gita. We published its commentary as the Anu Gita Explained. The Bhagavad Gita explanations were published in three distinct targeted commentaries. The first is Bhagavad Gita Explained, which sheds lights on how people in the time of Krishna and Arjuna regarded the information and applied it. Bhagavad Gita is an exposition of the application of yoga practice to cultural activities, which is known in the Sanskrit language as karma yoga.

Interestingly, Bhagavad Gita was spoken on a battlefield just before one of the greatest battles in the ancient world. A warrior, Arjuna, lost his wits and had no idea that he could apply his training in yoga to political dealings. Krishna, his charioteer, lectured on the spur of the moment to give Arjuna the skill of using yoga proficiency in cultural dealings including how to deal with corrupt officials on a battlefield.

The second commentary is the Kriya Yoga Bhagavad Gita. This clears the air about Krishna's information on the science of kriya yoga, showing that its techniques are clearly described free of charge to anyone who takes the time to read Bhagavad Gita. Kriya yoga concerns the battlefield which is the psyche of the living being. The internal war and the mental and emotional forces which are hostile to self-realization are dealt with in the kriya yoga practice.

The third commentary is the Brahma Yoga Bhagavad Gita. This shows what Krishna had to say outright and what he hinted about which concerns the brahma yoga practice, a mystic process for those who mastered kriya yoga.

There is one commentary for the **Markandeya Samasya English**. The title of that publication is Krishna Cosmic Body.

There are two commentaries to the Yoga Sutras. One is the Yoga Sutras of Patanjali and the other is the Meditation Expertise. These give detailed explanations of the process of Yoga.

For the Uddhava Gita, we published the Uddhava Gita Explained. This is a large book and requires concentration and study for integration of the information. Of the books which deal with transcendental topics, my opinion is that the discourse between Krishna and Uddhava has the complete information about the realities in existence. This book is the one which removes massive existential ignorance.

Meditation Series

Meditation Pictorial

Meditation Expertise

Core-Self Discovery

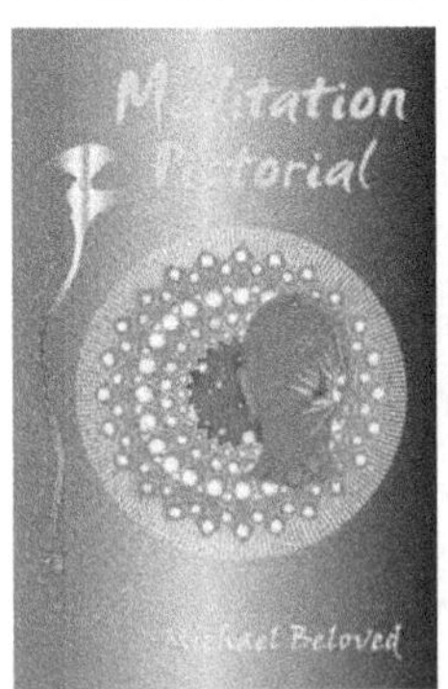

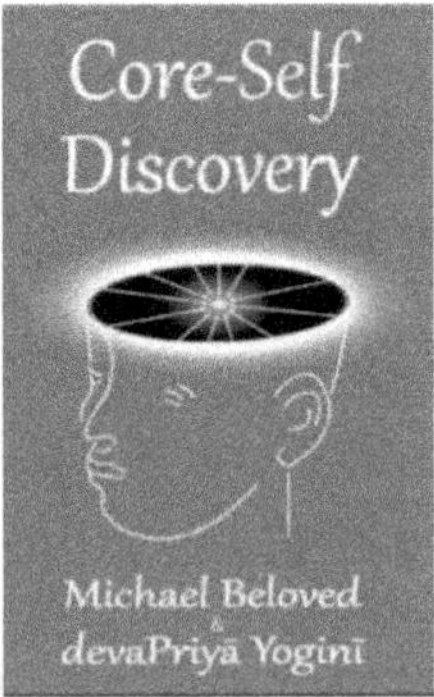

The specialty of these books is the mind diagrams which profusely illustrate what is written. This shows exactly what one has to do mentally to develop and then sustain a meditation practice.

In the **Meditation Pictorial**, one is shown how to develop psychic insight, a feature without which meditation is imagination and visualization, without any mystic experience per se.

In the **Meditation Expertise**, one is shown how to corral one's practice to bring it in line with the classic syllabus of yoga which Patanjali lays out as the ashtanga yoga eight-staged practice.

In **Core-Self Discovery**, one is taken though the course of pratyahar sensual energy withdrawal which is the 5th stage of yoga in the Patanjali ashtanga eight-process complete system of yoga practice. These events lead to the discovery of a core-self which is surrounded by psychic organs in the head of the subtle body. This product has a DVD component for teachers and self-teaching students.

These books are profusely illustrated with mind diagrams showing the components of psychic consciousness and the inner design of the subtle body.

Explained Series

Bhagavad Gita Explained

Uddhava Gita Explained

Anu Gita Explained

The specialty of these books is that they are free of missionary intentions, cult tactics and philosophical distortion. Instead of using these books to add credence to a philosophy, meditation process, belief or plea for followers, I spread the information out so that a reader can look through this literature and freely take or leave anything as desired.

When Krishna stressed himself as God, I stated that. When Krishna laid no claims for supremacy, I showed that. The reader is left to form an independent opinion about the validity of the information and the credibility of Krishna.

There is a difference in the discourse with Arjuna in the Bhagavad Gita and the one with Uddhava in the Uddhava Gita. In fact these two books may appear to contradict each other. In the Bhagavad Gita, Krishna pressured Arjuna to complete social duties. In the Uddhava Gita, Krishna insisted that Uddhava should abandon the same.

The Anu Gita is not as popular as the Bhagavad Gita but it is the conclusion of that text. Anu means what is to follow, what proceeds. In this discourse, an anxious Arjuna request that Krishna should repeat the Bhagavad Gita and again show His supernatural and divine forms.

However Krishna refuses to do so and chastises Arjuna for being a disappointment in forgetting what was revealed. Krishna then cites a celestial yogi, a near-perfected being, who explained the process of transmigration in vivid detail.

Commentaries

Yoga Sutras of Patanjali

Meditation Expertise

Krishna Cosmic Body

Anu Gita Explained

Bhagavad Gita Explained

Kriya Yoga Bhagavad Gita

Brahma Yoga Bhagavad Gita

Uddhava Gita Explained

Yoga Sutras of Patanjali is the globally acclaimed text book of yoga. This has detailed expositions of yoga techniques. Many kriya techniques are vividly described in the commentary.

Meditation Expertise is an analysis and application of the Yoga Sutras. This book is loaded with illustrations and has detailed explanations of secretive advanced meditation techniques which are called kriyas in the Sanskrit language.

Krishna Cosmic Body is a narrative commentary on the Markandeya Samasya portion of the Aranyaka Parva of the Mahabharata. This is the detailed description of the dissolution of the world, as experienced by the great yogin Markandeya who transcended the cosmic deity, Brahma, and reached Brahma's source who is the divine infant, Krishna.

Anu Gita Explained is a detailed explanation of how we endure many material bodies in the course of transmigrating through various life-forms. This is a discourse between Krishna and Arjuna. Arjuna requested of Krishna a display of the Universal Form and a repeat narration of the Bhagavad Gita but Krishna declined and explained what a siddha perfected being told the Yadu family about the sequence of existences one endures and the systematic flow of those lives at the convenience of material nature.

Bhagavad Gita Explained shows what was said in the Gita without religious overtones and sectarian biases.

Kriya Yoga Bhagavad Gita shows the instructions for those who are doing kriya yoga.

Brahma Yoga Bhagavad Gita shows the instructions for those who are doing brahma yoga.

Uddhava Gita Explained shows the instructions to Uddhava which are more advanced than the ones given to Arjuna.

Bhagavad Gita is an instruction for applying the expertise of yoga in the cultural field. This is why the process taught to Arjuna is called karma yoga which means karma + yoga or cultural activities done with a yogic demeanor.

Uddhava Gita is an instruction for apply the expertise of yoga to attaining spiritual status. This is why it is explains jnana yoga and bhakti yoga in detail. Jnana yoga is using mystic skill for knowing the spiritual part of existence. Bhakti yoga is for developing affectionate relationships with divine beings.

Karma yoga is for negotiating the social concerns in the material world and therefore it is inferior to bhakti yoga which concerns negotiating the social concerns in the spiritual world.

This world has a social environment and the spiritual world has one too.

Right now Uddhava Gita is the most advanced informative spiritual book on the planet. There is nothing anywhere which is superior to it or which goes into so much detail as it. It verified that historically Krishna is the most advanced human being to ever have left literary instructions on this planet. Even Patanjali Yoga Sutras which I translated and gave an application for in my book, **Meditation Expertise**, does not go as far as the Uddhava Gita.

Some of the information of these two books is identical but while the Yoga Sutras are concerned with the personal spiritual emancipation (kaivalyam) of the individual spirits, the Uddhava Gita explains that and also explains the situations in the spiritual universes.

Bhagavad Gita is from the Mahabharata which is the history of the Pandavas. Arjuna, the student of the Gita, is one of the Pandavas brothers. He was in a social hassle and did not know how to apply yoga expertise to solve it. Krishna gave him a crash-course on the battlefield about that.

Uddhava Gita is from the Srimad Bhagavatam (Bhagavata Purana), which is a history of the incarnations of Krishna. Uddhava was a relative of Krishna. He was concerned about the situation of the deaths of many of his relatives but Krishna diverted Uddhava's attention to the practice of yoga for the purpose of successfully migrating to the spiritual environment.

Specialty

These books are based on the author's experiences in meditation, yoga practice and participation in spiritual groups:

Spiritual Master

sex you!

Sleep **Paralysis**

Astral Projection

Masturbation Psychic Details

In **Spiritual Master**, Michael draws from experience with gurus or with their senior students. His contact with astral gurus is rated. He walks you through the avenue of gurus showing what you should do and what you should not do, so as to gain proficiency in whatever area of spirituality the guru has proficiency.

sex you! is a masterpiece about the adventures of an individual spirit's passage through the parents' psyches. The conversion of a departed soul into a sexual urge is described. The transit from the afterlife to residency in the emotions of the parents is detailed. This is about sex and you; learn about how much of you comprises the romantic energy of your would-be parents!

Sleep Paralysis clears misconceptions so that one can see what sleep paralysis is and what frightening astral experience occurs while the paralysis is being experienced. This disempowerment has great value in giving you confidence that you can and do exist even if you are unable to operate the physical body. The implication is that one can exist apart from and will survive the loss of the material body.

Astral Projection details experiences Michael had even in childhood, where he assumed incorrectly that everyone was astrally conversant. He discusses the life force psychic mechanism which operates the sleep-wake cycle of the physical form, and which budgets energy into the separated astral form which determines if the individual will have dream recall or no objective awareness during the projections. Astral travel happens on every occasion when the physical body sleeps. What is missing in awareness is the observer status while the astral body is separated.

Masturbation Psychic Details is a surprise presentation which relates what happens on the psychic plane during a masturbation event. This does not tackle moral issues or even addictions but shows the involvement of memory and the sure but hidden subconscious mind which operates many features of the psyche irrespective of the desire or approval of the self-conscious personality.

Online Resources

Visit The Website And Forum

Email:	michaelbelovedbooks@gmail.com axisnexus@gmail.com
Website:	michaelbeloved.com
Forum:	inselfyoga.com

www.ingramcontent.com/pod-product-compliance
Lightning Source LLC
LaVergne TN
LVHW010611100826
845148LV00014B/2913

* 9 7 8 0 9 7 9 3 9 1 6 1 3 *